AF271402

The Republic v. Obama and Progressives

the prosecution's case

Caroline Reynolds

ISBN 978-0-7414-9880-9 Paperback
ISBN 978-0-7414-9881-6 eBook
Library of Congress Control Number: 2013917057

Printed in the United States of America

Published October 2013

INFINITY PUBLISHING
1094 New DeHaven Street, Suite 100
West Conshohocken, PA 19428-2713
Toll-free (877) BUY BOOK
Local Phone (610) 941-9999
Fax (610) 941-9959
Info@buybooksontheweb.com
www.buybooksontheweb.com

Contents

Opening Statement

I was sure President Obama would lose the 2012 election and I wanted to get it all down on paper before I forgot how bad the situation really had been and how close we had come to losing our republic. I had barely begun to write when I became amazed, not just over the substance of my complaints against the Obama administration, but over the sheer number of those complaints. I quickly had a rough sketch of a president who really did want to "transform America"—and not in a good way.

I began to think that the electorate needed to realize the same thing. My thinking, somewhat naively, was that maybe writing this could help prevent the public from being deceived again as it had been in 2008. We had come so close to disaster. So I decided to turn my observations into a book—not long before the November 6, 2012 election.

Of course, President Obama won reelection. But, I became even more resolved to report the facts as I saw them. For me it was urgent to do so. The republic was in crisis. That is why the flag is upside-down on the cover.

This book is not written for scholars. The information it contains is basic, easily searchable and publically available. You are encouraged to dig for more detail on the topics if they interest you or if you think I haven't provided enough information to make the case.

1

The case to which I refer is the case against Obama, and by extension against all progressives. What I have written is in the rough format of a legal brief: Opening statement, Evidence, Issues, Decisions, Rationales for each Decision, and Analysis.

Most of this book is an alphabetical listing of incidents, associations, decisions, actions, quotes, policies, and philosophies of Barack Obama. This is what I call Evidence and I present it as thumbnail sketches so anyone may easily get an overview of what can happen when the electorate is not well enough informed to make decisions based on fact rather than emotion.

I then proceed to Issues. The preponderance of evidence itself suggested six major issues. These issues are presented along with the supporting evidence for each and a Decision based on the evidence for each issue is given.

The next section provides the Rationale for the decision made for each issue.

Finally there is an Analysis which ties it all together.

This book is not fair and balanced. I have purposefully highlighted all I see as wrong with the Obama administration and its policies in the same way that a prosecuting attorney might set about getting a guilty verdict against the perpetrator of a crime. Obama fans and other progressives should probably not even consider reading this book.

The opinions are my own although I know I am not alone in them. The incidents and actions highlighted are factual as near as I can tell. However, attorneys for the defense would present different evidence. I have tried to stick to facts before making judgments. However, this book is judgmental. Some material is subject to interpretation, and mine tends to be negative. But there is good evidence for that negativity. I hope you can get something out of it.

Evidence

A123: a company in Waltham, Massachusetts, that made batteries for Fisker Automotive and BMW. In 2009, it received[1] $249 million in federal grant money from the Obama administration after receiving tax credits during Romney's time as governor of Massachusetts and $100,000 in 2006 under the Bush administration. It declared bankruptcy in October 2012[668] after posting fourteen straight quarters of loss. Throwing good money after bad is not a good idea especially with taxpayers' money. A123 is now 80% owned by a Chinese company and its name has been changed to B456.

See also Fisker.

Abbas, Mahmoud: Two days after President Obama's 2009 inauguration, among his first phone calls[2] to a foreign leader was to Palestinian Authority President Mahmoud Abbas. Abbas has been a steadfast enemy of Israel.

Abedin, Huma Mahmood[3]: an American-born deputy chief of staff and top aide to Hillary Clinton during her time as secretary of state. Abedin's father, born in India, was a professor; her mother, born in Pakistan, is a professor in Saudi Arabia. Abedin grew up in Saudi Arabia and returned to the United States to attend George Washington University. She is a practicing Muslim and speaks fluent Arabic.

Abedin worked for the Institute for Muslim Minority Affairs, an organization founded by her family as part of a Saudi Arabian plan to mobilize American Muslim minorities to transform America into a strict, Wahhabi-style Islamic state. Abedin was also on the executive board of the Muslim Student

Association, which has been identified as a Muslim Brotherhood front group and for which Anwar al-Awlaki became a spiritual advisor shortly after she left. The document[4] revealing a connection between the student group and the Muslim Brotherhood stated that Muslim Brotherhood members, "must understand that their work in America is a kind of grand jihad in eliminating and destroying the Western civilization from within and 'sabotaging' its miserable house by their hands and by the hands of the believers so that it is eliminated and Allah's religion is made victorious over all other religions."

Abedin, from a prominent Muslim family, married a Jew, Anthony Weiner, and yet was apparently not castigated or even criticized by her family or the Brotherhood. Why?

Guilt by association is not sufficient reason to condemn Huma Abedin. There is no indication she has acted inappropriately. However, one should not ignore such associations for fear of being called an Islamophobe or racist or sexist. Close associations, and possibly old allegiances, such as those which Abedin may have can make one susceptible to decisions or actions or the providing of advice not always in the best interest of the United States and should be questioned.

She served as Secretary of State Hillary Clinton's Deputy Chief of Staff.

See also Muslim Brotherhood.

ACA: See Obamacare.

ACORN: The acronym stands for Association of Community Organizations for Reform Now. This radical group, operating primarily in urban areas opposed capitalism, welfare reform, and what it called predatory lending. It often used the in-your-face protest tactics touted by Saul Alinsky in his book *Rules for Radicals.* In the '90s, Barack Obama was an ACORN leadership trainer[5]. He also defended the group in a court case. As a community organizer on Chicago's South Side, Obama organized demonstrations modeled after those of the radical ACORN. He developed an association with the group and a hard-line member, activist Madeline Talbot.

While in the Illinois Senate, Obama introduced ACORN-friendly legislation[6] on living wages and banking practices. While ACORN had a political arm—501(c) 4—and a nonpartisan arm,—501(c) 3—used to register voters and get out the vote, the distinction between the two sections seemed blurred although they were supposed to be distinct entities for tax purposes.

Obama served on the boards of two charitable foundations—the Woods Fund and the Joyce Foundation. Millions of dollars in grant money were funneled through these foundations to ACORN in Chicago.

Obama was endorsed by ACORN in his local campaigns and for the presidency, and many of his ACORN associates helped personally in these races. When Obama was a presidential candidate, it was claimed[7] that he was never an ACORN organizer, that ACORN never hired him as a trainer, and that Project Vote was not part of ACORN—at least on paper.

8

After widely publicized scandals, ACORN was officially disbanded. But the New York Communities for Change was reportedly[8] a player in the Occupy Wall Street protests. Patrick Gaspard, political adviser to Obama (Karl Rove's position under Bush), was director for the New York City chapter of ACORN and has worked closely with the largest local within the Service Employees International Union (SEIU).

The executive director of the Washington-based Center for Community Change (CCC) is Deepak Bhargava a former chief lobbyist for ACORN. He has been enlisted[661] by Obama to run a video contest to encourage young people to sign up for Obamacare. The CCC will also provide some of the navigators for the Obamacare program. Cecilia Munoz, the former chair of the CCC board of directors was appointed Obama's top domestic policy advisor.

ACORN appears to be alive and well operating under different names.

See also Alinsky, Saul.

Agenda 21: The terms *sustainable development* and *smart growth* have crept into local governments' vocabulary and thus into our thinking. At first, these terms sound not only harmless, but even good. That is not the case. The terms are code for the plans of the United Nations' Agenda 21.

Agenda 21 is a political agenda[9] to subjugate the rights of individuals to the rights of the collective for the supposed greater good of all. Underlying this agenda is the premise that those who are relatively well off are living better lives at the expense of the poor and that redistribution of wealth is therefore required. This idea is called social equity. The ultimate goal is a centrally managed global society in which our living space (how much is allocated to us and where it is), how we commute, and even what we eat is prescribed by the government.

Agenda 21 is being accomplished not from the top down, but from the bottom up, starting with infiltration of town councils, county commissions, and the like. Various conferences and training sessions have schooled the local officials in manipulative processes such as the Delphi technique and *visioning* that give their constituents a feeling that they are stakeholders and are helping to devise community or county plans that in fact, officialdom had already predetermined. The process is often a sham complete with trained facilitators who guide work and study groups to the conclusions that local liberal politicians wanted in the first place.

The health of the environment (global warming/climate change, wildlife) is used as justification to promote the goals of Agenda 21. The plan puts nature above man and relegates humans to the status of just another biological resource. It applies to every area in which man impacts the environment. Thus anything that reduces man's carbon footprint or enhances the wildlife experience is a desirable Agenda 21 target: mass transit systems instead of cars, clustered, stacked housing in city centers (so that bicycling to work is the norm) instead of suburban and rural dwelling, bicycle and walking/hiking paths, and wildlife and view corridors. The ultimate goal is the abolition of private property and the elimination of human presence on "at least 50 percent of the American landscape."

President Obama is doing all he can to end run Congress and implement Agenda 21 policies. So far, he is doing it very quietly. In 2010, he signed Executive Order 13547[10] (See Ocean Control by UN). In 2011, he signed Executive Order 13575[11], creating the White House Rural Council, which has a very high-powered membership and will implement Agenda 21 in the nation's heartland. In 2012, he signed executive orders establishing the White House Council on Strong Cities, Strong Communities (EO # 13602)[12] and policies on "national defense resources preparedness[13]," both tied to Agenda 21.

In June 2012, Alabama became the first state to adopt a tough law[14] protecting property and due process by prohibiting Agenda 21 involvement or participation in these matters. The legislation passed both state houses unanimously. A similar bill passed the Oklahoma House and is pending in the Senate.

On June 25, 2013, the Supreme Court ruled[15] that the fifth amendment of the Constitution protects landowners from local, state and federal government extortion of money or any other form of property. In Koontz v. St. Johns River Water Management District, the court issued an opinion in favor of the Koontz family who were trying to develop their land. They had been required to spend up to one hundred and fifty thousand dollars to improve property distant from their own – property the government owned. The principal attorney, Paul J. Beard II said, "The ruling underscores that homeowners and other property owners who seek permits to make reasonable use of their property cannot be forced to surrender their rights. Regulators can't hold permit applicants hostage with unjustified demands for land or other concessions including, as in this case, unjustified demands for money."

UN.
See also Climate change, Green agenda, Ocean control by

Al Arabiya interview: On January 26, 2009, Obama's first TV interview[16] as president was with Al Arabiya, a Saudi-owned pan-Arabic TV news channel. He wasted no time courting the Arab world.

Alaska National Wildlife Refuge: See ANWR.

Al-Awlaki, Anwar: An American-born citizen of the United States, al-Awlaki was described as a moderate cleric at one time, but he became more and more radical. His links to al-Qaeda are not disputed. He was suspected[17] of influencing Major Nidal Hassan and was linked to the failed Times Square bombing. Awlaki is reported[18] to have personally directed the plot to bring down an American commercial plane on Christmas Day, 2009 (the underwear bomber incident). He emigrated from the United States to the United Kingdom and then to Yemen and reportedly renounced his US citizenship.

Anwar al-Awlaki was killed by an American drone attack on September 30, 2011. Two weeks later, his sixteen-year-old son, still a US citizen, was killed by a CIA drone attack. Al-Awlaki had not been indicted of any crime and may not have committed any although he was clearly not America's friend.

What happened to the Fifth Amendment, which bars the depriving of life without due process? If al-Awlaki's assassination can be justified because he was considered an imminent threat (though this was unlikely), what about his son's assassination?

The Obama administration attempted to justify the death of Anwar al-Awlaki in a 16-page unsigned, undated Justice Department white paper[19] revealed in February, 2013. According to the document if an informed, high level official decides there is an imminent threat of violent attack against the United States, a kill is warranted. This has apparently been interpreted to include senior operational leaders of al Qaeda or an associated force. The words imminent threat have been watered-down to include those who are generally engaged in terrorist activities aimed at the US and they apparently need not be engaged in an active plot.

The administration has not attempted to justify the boy's death—not even as collateral damage. In fact, it has said nothing about this at all.

See also Fort Hood; Times Square bomber; Underwear bomber.

Alikhan, Arif[20]: described as a devout Sunni Muslim, whose parents emigrated from Pakistan and India, he was born in Canada and is a graduate of Loyola Law School. Alikhan was appointed by President Obama and Homeland Security Secretary Janet Napolitano to the position of Assistant Secretary for Policy Development at the US Department of Homeland

Security (DHS). He reportedly[21] once called Hezbollah a "liberation movement" and is considered strongly anti-Israel. He also opposed President George W. Bush's war on Islamist terrorism.

Alinsky, Saul[22]: an American writer and community organizer. He was educated as an archaeologist but gained recognition as a skilled organizer working to improve the living conditions of people in poor communities.

Alinsky's major work, *Rules for Radicals*, has become a classic handbook for radical activist demonstrators. Alinsky wrote, *"The Prince* was written by Machiavelli for the haves on how to hold power. *Rules for Radicals* is written for the have-nots on how to take it away."* He also wrote[23] that in order to weaken and take over the American economy and people, it was necessary to "destroy the middle class" and that "wealth redistribution" was the catalyst to bring down the U.S. economy and free-market capitalism. He wrote that "an organizer must stir up dissatisfaction and discontent ..." According to John Fund, *The Washington Post* described[24] Alinsky's approach to social justice as relying on "generating conflict to mobilize the dispossessed." Alinsky's thirteenth rule in *Rules for Radicals* is "Pick the target, freeze it, personalize it, and polarize it." The strategy works.

Alinsky is said to have influenced Wade Rathke, founder of ACORN and SEIU Local 100, and Barack Obama, among others. Barack Obama wrote[25] a chapter for the book *After Alinsky: Community Organizing in Illinois*. He attended[26] eight days of training at an Alinsky foundation and in turn trained other community organizers in Alinsky agitation tactics and taught Alinsky's "power analysis" methods at the University of Chicago.

See also ACORN; Unions.

All Dulles Area Muslim Society: Also referred to as ADAMS, it is considered[27] a front for the Muslim Brotherhood and was founded by the two most senior Muslim Brothers in the United States. It is associated with the Islamic Society of North America.

Al-Mansour, Dr. Khalid Abdullah Tariq[28]**:** Born Donald Warden, he is described as an Israeli-hating Islamist supporter and top adviser to radical Saudi Prince al-Waleed bin Talal.

In 2008, in an interview[29] on a New York cable television channel, Percy Sutton revealed a possible al-Mansour/Obama connection. Sutton, a former lawyer for Malcolm X, a former New York City mayoral candidate, and a business partner of al-Mansour, said in the interview that he was introduced to a young Barack Obama by al-Mansour and that al-Mansour was raising money for Obama's graduate school education. He asked Sutton to write a letter of recommendation to Harvard for Obama, which Sutton did. However, as Sutton was in his eighties when interviewed, and possibly suffering from a failing memory, and because there was no hard evidence that Obama received such funds, this connection was discounted by the press.

But more recently, another interesting connection has surfaced. Vernon Jarrett—a friend of Frank Marshall Davis, who mentored the young Barack Obama in Hawaii—explained[30] in a 1979 newspaper column how al-Mansour had proposed to OPEC an expenditure of $20 million a year for ten years to aid minority students in the United States.

There is still no proof of anything untoward here, but enough coincidence exists to raise serious questions.

See also Davis, Frank Marshall.

American Clean Energy and Security Act of 2008: See Cap-and--Trade Bill.

ANWR: an acronym for Arctic National Wildlife Refuge[31] which consists of 19 million acres in northeast Alaska. At issue is a two thousand-acre parcel known as the "1002 area" in the coastal plain—not the wilderness area. The 1002 area amounts to 0.01 percent of ANWR's land area – that is one-one hundredth of one percent. The small parcel is the subject of controversy because of the vast oil and gas reserves it contains.

The coastal plain is a relatively barren wasteland and was set aside by Congress in 1981 for further study to determine the extent of its oil and gas production potential. In 1987, development was recommended[32] by the Department of the Interior.

Prudhoe Bay, sixty miles to the west of the proposed ANWR drilling site, has produced more than 10 billion barrels of oil over the past twenty years with arguably no environmental damage although the operation has been extensively studied. In fact, the caribou herd[644] at Prudhoe Bay increased from three

16

thousand to as high as 23,400 during those twenty years of production.

Drilling has been permitted in other wildlife preserves: the National Audubon Society's Rainey Wildlife Sanctuary and in the Galveston Bay Prairie Preserve of the Nature Conservancy of Texas. Both the Audubon Society and the Nature Conservancy benefited from generous royalties. In fact, a study[33] in 2001 determined that there were oil and gas activities in seventy-seven of the 567 wildlife refuges in twenty-two states in the federal system. Why not ANWR?

President Obama opposes drilling in ANWR and has said[34] so. In August 2011, the Obama administration moved[35] one step closer to getting the 1002 area set aside as wilderness. The wilderness designation rests ultimately with Congress. It has now been nominated. So far President Obama is winning his agenda to block oil and gas drilling in ANWR.

See also Coal industry; EPA's CO2 regulations; Drilling moratorium; Fracking; Green agenda.

AP leak investigation: In May 2012 the Associated Press (AP) learned[36] through an information leak of a terrorist threat to one of our airplanes. The threat was considered to be of national security concern and the Obama administration rightly asked the AP to hold back the story. The AP complied and withheld the story for five days until the White House said the threat had passed.

But the White House wanted one more day so they could make the announcement of the foiled threat themselves. The AP published the story anyway.

The White House was not pleased about the leak or the AP's publishing of the story ahead of them. The FBI which is the enforcement arm of the Department of Justice, launched[37] an investigation to determine the source of the leak. They did this by searching the phone records of twenty phone lines involving more than one hundred AP reporters during a sixty day period. AP was not notified in advance.

It appears that the Obama administration may have retaliated against the AP for scooping the story and that there was not sufficient probable cause to intrude on the privacy of reporters. Would there not have been more justification for commandeering the phone records of the potential leakers than of the potential receivers of the information? This is considered by many to be unreasonable search and seizure and a violation of the Fourth Amendment.

Attorney General Eric Holder testified[38] under oath before an investigative hearing in the House of Representatives that the leak was one of the top two or three leaks he had ever seen. If this is the case, is it not reasonable to assume that he informed President Obama about it? Yet, the President said[39] through his press secretary, Jay Carney that the White House had no knowledge of the DOJ's efforts to obtain Associated Press phone records.

Holder also testified[40] that he did not authorize the phone record seizure nor know anything about it. This is not plausible as he signed off on the seizure of the phone records. The House GOP Judiciary committee found[635] that he was misleading in his congressional testimony and has requested that Obama fire him.

Holder said he had recused himself from the FBI investigation into the leaks because he himself had been interviewed by the FBI. There is no written record of his recusal.

Even Senate majority leader, Harry Reid denounced[602] the seizure of the AP phone records.

President Obama directed[609] Eric Holder to investigate the incident. Really? Is this not the fox watching the chicken coop?

Freedom of the press and our privacy rights are at stake.

See also Atkisson, Sharyl; FOX News Channel, attack on.

Apology Tour: After President Obama's overseas tour in April 2009, Karl Rove wrote an op-ed piece[41] for *The Wall Street Journal* titled "The President's Apology Tour." Obama visited Saudi Arabia, Egypt, Turkey and Iraq, but not Israel. During these visits, he, on several occasions, seemed to be apologetic for America's past dealings with foreign powers, especially those of the Muslim world. Although Obama never used the word *apologize*, Karl Rove's description stuck.

See also Apology Tour #2; Apology Tour #3; Bow to Saudi king; Derisive quote; Exceptionalism quote.

Apology Tour #2: In May of 2013 President Obama in a speech[42] during a visit to Mexico admitted that most of the guns used to commit crimes in Mexico come from the US. He also planted the idea that the US imposes itself on Mexican sovereignty and that America disrespects Mexico.

See also Apology Tour; Apology Tour #3; Bow to Saudi king; Derisive quote; Exceptionalism quote.

Apology Tour #3: President Obama on his trip in Africa Sunday, June 30, 2013 warned[43] Africans against assuming that "folks come here and they're automatically benefiting Africans. And that includes the United States. Ask questions in terms of what we do."

See also Apology Tour; Apology Tour #2; Bow to Saudi king; Derisive quote; Exceptionalism quote.

Arab-American Action Network[44]**:** This organization is described[45] as virulently anti-Israel and strongly supportive of the Palestinian Arab terrorist movement. It considers creation of the state of Israel a "catastrophe." The cofounders of this organization are Rashid and Mona Khalidi. Earlier, Rashid was the director of the PLO's press agency during a time when numerous Israelis were killed by PLO terrorists.

Barack Obama and Rashid became friends when they were teaching at the University of Chicago (1992–2003). When Rashid was leaving to take a position elsewhere, Obama gave a glowing testimonial[45] at a farewell banquet for him and mentioned that he and Michelle had been frequent dinner guests of the Khalidis and that the Khalidis were frequent babysitters for the Obamas' daughters.

In both 2001 and 2002, Barack Obama, as a board member of the Woods Fund, voted[46] to give the Arab-American Action Network seventy-five-thousand-dollars in grants. In 2000, the Khalidis held a fund-raiser at their home for Obama's congressional run.

See also Shora, Kareem.

Arctic National Wildlife Refuge: See ANWR

Arizona: S.B. 1070[47] was passed by the Arizona State Legislature to help deal with a severe illegal immigration problem along its border with Mexico. Arizona's governor, Jan Brewer, had asked the federal government for enforcement help through Immigration and Customs Enforcement (ICE) but was denied. S.B. 1070 was modeled precisely after federal law so there would be no conflict between it and the federal Immigration Act.

In May 2010, Mexican President Felipe Calderon visited President Obama. The day after the visit, President Calderon criticized[48] Arizona's law in a speech to a joint session of the US Congress. For the Mexican president to criticize state law before US lawmakers was inappropriate. But Calderon would probably not have made such comments unless he was quite sure he would not offend Obama by making them.

In July 2010, the Obama administration sued the State of Arizona, contending the federal government had sole authority over immigration. The Supreme Court struck down three minor provisions of S.B. 1070, but unanimously upheld the centerpiece provision. Arizona police are now required under this provision to verify the legal status of those whom they reasonably suspect to be in this country illegally.

Immediately after the Supreme Court decision, the Obama administration rescinded[49] section 287(g) of the Immigration Act for Arizona only. In so doing, the administration prevented Arizona police from accessing the federal database to determine the immigration status of suspected illegal immigrants. This appears to be strictly a retaliatory act by a vindictive Obama and may not even be within a president's legal authority.

If that were not enough, the Obama administration included a statement[50] in its August 2010 report to the UN Human Rights Council disparaging Arizona's new law as an example of a human rights violation.

See also Immigration.

Arpaio, Joe: the sheriff of Maricopa County, Arizona. In response[51] to a request from 250 private citizens, Arpaio organized an investigation into the validity of Barack Obama's long-form birth certificate, which he had finally provided in April 2011. After six months of investigation, the volunteer cold-case posse, headed by former New Jersey detective Mike Zullo, found reasonable evidence to suspect fraud but made no presumptions about who had committed it. They also questioned[645] the validity of Obama's selective service card and his social security number.

About three months later, the posse revised[52] its conclusion to "definitely fraudulent." Apparently the supposed birth certificate had been patched together in electronic layers, giving it characteristics that a copy of a real birth certificate would not have. This conclusion was all but ignored by the mainstream media although Sheriff Arpaio called[53] for a congressional investigation.

Arrogance: See "Derisive" quote.

Assault on unions quote: In February 2011 in an interview with Milwaukee radio station WTMJ, President Obama said[54] about Wisconsin Governor Scott Walker's fight to achieve budget solvency over the power of public worker unions, it seemed like an "assault" on unions. Of course it was not that per se, but rather a fight against the unopposed power of public sector unions.

See also Unions.

Atkisson, Sharyl: as investigative reporter for CBS, she doggedly pursued the facts in Fast & Furious, green energy stimulus spending and Benghazi. She was criticized by the political left for doing so. In June 2013 she revealed[55] that her two computers at home –one for business, the other for personal work had been hacked. She hired a technical expert who confirmed this. Her private bank accounts were not compromised.

See also AP leak investigation; National Counterterrorism Center; NSA

Ayers, Bill[56]: A political activist who opposed America's involvement in the Vietnam War, Ayers cofounded the Weather Underground—a communist revolutionary group— bombed police stations, the US Capitol building, and the Pentagon. After the bombings, he lived underground for several years. Because the FBI used illegal tactics to target the Weather Underground, all weapons- and bomb-related charges were eventually dropped against him and he never served time.

In a *New York Times* interview[57] in 2001, Ayers is quoted as saying, "I don't regret setting bombs" and "I feel we didn't do enough." During the 2008 presidential campaign, it was learned[58] that Ayers lived in the same Chicago neighborhood as Barack Obama, was friends with him, served with him on the board of a foundation, and hosted an initial fund-raiser for Obama at his house. The mainstream media did not highlight the story.

Bailout: see TARP

Balance of power: In March 2008, then-Senator Barack Obama said[68], "The biggest problems that we're facing right now have to do with George Bush trying to bring more and more power into the executive branch and not go through Congress at all. And that's what I intend to reverse when I'm president of the United States." A promise that was broken.

By October 2011, President Obama had changed his tune and said[69], "We can't wait for an increasingly dysfunctional

Congress to do its job. Where they won't act, I will." He was proud enough of this anti-constitutional statement to publish[70] it at the top of the page on the whitehouse.gov website. Following this same theme, he said[71] in his 2013 State of the Union Address, "But if Congress won't act to protect future generations, I will."

See also al-Awlaki, Anwar; Arizona, Bondholders, secured; BP escrow; BP oil spill; Cap & Trade Bill; Coal Industry; Czars; Dodd-Frank; Drilling moratorium; Immigration; Kill list; Libya's Arab spring; New Black Panthers; NLRB; War Powers Act.

Bankrupt: See Gross debt as percentage of GDP.

Bankrupt quote: In January 2008, then presidential candidate Barack Obama said[72], "So if somebody wants to build a coal-powered plant, they can; it's just that it will bankrupt them because they're going to be charged a huge sum for all that greenhouse gas that's being emitted."

See also Coal industry; EPA's CO2 regulations; EPA's crucifixion example.

Becker, Craig: See Unions.

Beer summit: Dr. Henry Louis Gates, a black Harvard University professor, was arrested on July 16, 2009, while trying to enter his house. The door to his house was jammed and the professor enlisted the help of his driver to force it open. He was arrested after a 911 call reported the incident; he was charged but later released. President Obama inserted himself into the incident, publically criticizing the white policeman's actions by saying[73] the police had acted "stupidly," thus implying the arrest was racially motivated. When it became clear the policeman had behaved exactly as he should have, Obama asked Professor Gates and the officer to join him at the White House for what became known as the beer summit in an effort to smooth things over. Who acted stupidly?

See also Treyvon Martin.

Benghazi: Real-time e-mails on September 11, 2012, document[74] that the attacks on the US consulate and the CIA annex in Benghazi, Libya, were organized, terrorist attacks later determined to be by Islamist, jihad groups associated with al-Qaeda, primarily Ansar al-Sharia.

President Obama, Secretary of State Hillary Clinton, United Nations ambassador Susan Rice, and White House spokesman Jay Carney asserted for close to two weeks that the attacks were attributable to spontaneous Muslim outrage over a very amateurish video trailer released months earlier in July 2012 on YouTube that disparaged the Prophet Muhammad. This erroneous assertion was perpetuated by the president in his speech[75] to the UN on September 25 – a full two weeks after the attack.

The administration's lie and cover-up were exposed when e-mails[76,77] received during the attacks were released and when it was reported that a video taken by a drone[78] of the attack was watched in real time, concurrently in the Pentagon and the CIA and in the White House situation room. Then in December, three months after the attack, it was reported that the live video was viewed somewhere at the Pentagon, but not at the White House. The way the investigation is progressing (or not progressing), the truth may never be known. The official December, 2012 investigative report[79] on the disaster faulted no one.

Ambassador J. Christopher Stevens had requested[80] additional protection at least twice before the attacks. Not only was extra protection denied, but some of the existing protective support was retired[81]. During the attacks, military backup was requested[82,83] but denied. We don't know who denied it. Two former SEALs on site, Tyrone Woods and Glen Doherty, requested permission to fight back. They were told to stand down. They disobeyed orders, fought for more than six hours, and saved the lives of at least twenty people (estimated numbers vary), but were killed in the process. Ambassador Stevens and information management officer Sean Smith were also murdered.

It is not clear why air support of some sort—at a minimum, strafing—was not rushed to their aid. Hopefully, it was not because of hesitation to break our own new rules of engagement or possibly even worse, as has been rumored. Our jets from Aviano, Italy could have been there in two to three hours[598], in plenty of time to possibly have saved lives. Retired Colonel Phil Handley provides[669] a hypothetical time line that shows help could have been there twenty minutes after Woods and Doherty arrived.

Some, including a four-star general, have proposed[84] that the original plan was pre-staged to abduct Ambassador Stevens and negotiate for his release in exchange for our release of the blind sheik, Omar Abdel-Rahman. Supposedly this would be done to boost President Obama's ratings just before the election—the October surprise.

More conventional wisdom sees this incident as merely the result of the president's failure to institute foreign policy that recognizes Islamic extremist terrorists are still a dangerous threat to homeland security and to our citizens and installations abroad. Ansar al-Sharia, the group blamed for the Benghazi attacks, is a sister organization of al-Qaeda. The hypothesis is that heavy weapons Obama illegally supplied to help depose Moammar Gadhafi may have been used to kill our ambassador and three other Americans.

It is further hypothesized[85,86] that the guns supplied by Obama to Libya and/or other arms in Gadhafi's stores were being collected and recycled at the time of the attack for delivery to Syrian rebels through Turkey. Turkish Prime Minister Tayyip Erdogan is a good friend[87] of Obama's. Stevens met the Turkish consul general in Benghazi on September 11 just hours before the attacks.

The week before September 11, a heavily laden ship, sailing from Benghazi with a Libyan captain, docked in Turkey with a shipment of weapons.

Later (August, 2013) it was learned[664] from whistleblower attorney Joe DiGenova that 400 surface-to-air missiles had been stolen from Libya. These weapons had apparently been supplied by the US to the rebels (one could argue illegally – see Libya's

Arab spring) to fight against Gadhafi. The fear was that they could be used against our embassies or our passenger planes. That is reportedly at least part of the reason so many CIA personnel were in Benghazi the night of the attack. The information comes through DiGenova from his client, Mark Thompson, deputy coordinator for operations in the Bureau of Counterterrorism at the US State Department.

It is not clear if Stevens was merely trying to recoup weapons the United States had illegally supplied to Libyan rebels, collect them, and recycle them to Syria or to run other arms from Libya to Syria through Turkey. Why were up to 35 CIA agents[613] in Benghazi? Why have we not heard from any of them a year later? Something smells.

Any yet another story has surfaced.[674] This one apparently has multiple foreign sources that corroborate information. This scenario has President Obama colluding with the Muslim Brotherhood and specifically then-President Morsi of Egypt. The report is that Obama illegally provided $8 billion to Morsi as a "bribe" to put control of the Sinai Peninsula in the hands of Hamas and that some of that money was shared with Ansar al-Sharia to bankroll the Benghazi attack.

The video cover up story hatched and perpetuated by the Obama administration likely resulted from fear that the incident's real cause—either merely the failure to recognize and protect against the real strength of al-Qaeda's threat; or the possibility that our own illegally supplied US weapons were used to kill Americans; or that these and possibly other weapons were being clandestinely supplied to Syrian rebels through Turkey; or that the Muslim Brotherhood was involved and Obama may have funded them under the table; or a horribly cynical plot to increase Obama's ratings—would reflect badly on the president during his re-election campaign. No matter the cause, it does not reflect well on Obama and he was correct to have feared the truth.

The Senate confirmation of John Brennan as director of the CIA was held up until some answers[88] were provided. Under pressure, the administration finally released ninety-four e-mails[77] regarding Benghazi for review by members of Congress with monitors looking over their shoulders. This is less than 0.4% of the total number of e-mails and none was from the first sixty-seven hours of the incident and its aftermath.

The Accountability Review Board, appointed by Secretary Clinton to investigate the Benghazi incident interviewed neither Secretary Clinton nor some who were involved at the time of the incident and wanted to be interviewed. There are no official transcripts of the Board's interviews as they did not use a stenographer. As a result of investigations, four State Department employees were put on administrative leave with pay. Secretary of State John Kerry re-assigned[660] them to different positions on August 20, 2013. So, they got much extended paid vacations similar to what Lois Lerner got as "punishment" in the IRS scandal. Demoted Greg Hicks has not as of mid-August 2013 been re-assigned[665] to a position more befitting his excellent career history (See Corporate culture).

If guilty of negligence or misconduct, government employees should be fired. If not guilty, they should remain on the job. Obama's concern for getting to the bottom of these incidents/scandals appears to be for show only.

The Accountability Review Board's report[89] did, however, reveal that the talking points used by Ambassador Rice repeatedly in six talk show interviews the following Sunday, September 16, 2012, had been altered. White House and senior State Department officials altered the original, accurate version first provided by the CIA to remove all suggestions that the State Department had been fore-warned of danger, had knowledge of previous attacks, or knew that extremists linked to al-Qaeda may have participated.

ABC News, Jonathan Karl obtained and revealed[90] twelve versions of the talking points before Ambassador Rice used them in her interviews the following Sunday. Stephen Hayes of the Weekly Standard produced[91] a talking points timeline that revealed Victoria Newland played a key role in objecting to talking points wording that shed a bad light on the State Department. She was rewarded (see Corporate culture).

As late as eight months after the Benghazi attack, White House spokesman, Jay Carney, was still maintaining[599] that changes in the talking points were just "stylistic."

According to the AP[92] , the US military knows the identity of five of the terrorists involved in the Benghazi attacks but won't arrest them because there is not enough evidence to convict them in a civilian court and President Obama does not want them to be tried in a military court in Guantanamo even though there is enough evidence to try them as enemy combatants.

Finally, August 6, 2013, almost a year after the attack, comes word[600] from the DOJ that charges have been made against several suspects – no apprehension, just charges.

See also General Carter Ham; Libya; Rules of engagement; Syria's Arab spring; UN speech.

Bilderberg group[93]: a secretive society that first met at a hotel in Holland in 1954. Its members are proponents of a world government and are suspected of pulling the strings in some countries. The Bilderberg group hosts an annual, invitation-only meeting of about 120 internationally influential people, including politicians, financial, military, industrial, academic, and media leaders. These annual meetings are closed to the press, and the Bilderbergers do not issue policy statements or resolutions and reportedly do not ever take votes on issues. They also do not answer questions about or discuss their activities. The group has no official partisan affiliation.

The Bilderbergers supposedly interact with a global network of groups including the New York-based Council on Foreign Relations, the Trilateral Commission and the American Enterprise Institute—all considered having globalist agendas.

Attendees at the Bilderberg meeting in June 2009 reportedly[94] included presidential candidates Hillary Clinton and Barack Obama. Two days later, Clinton dropped out of the race. Bilderbergers also include Timothy Geithner, Larry Summers, Paul Volcker and Kathleen Sebelius.

Many critics ascribe the worst of motives to this group, and its highly secretive modus operandi reinforces this impression and justifiably gives rise to speculation and conspiracy theories. Without more information, it is impossible to know for sure.

Birth Certificate: See Arpaio, Joe.

Black liberation theology[95]: An ideology promoted by some Christian churches and the Nation of Islam to help African-Americans overcome oppression. It was established in 1966 by fifty-one black pastors demanding, in a *New York Times* ad, a nonaggressive approach to eradicating racism.

This theology's focus is on liberation in the here and now rather than in the afterlife. Its adherents contend that dominant (white) cultures have corrupted Christianity to the point where it serves its own interests, not God's. Black liberation theology asks whether God is on the side of the oppressed or the oppressors and often portrays Jesus as a brown- or black-skinned revolutionary. The true God of this branch of Christianity desires the empowerment of the oppressed through self-definition, self-affirmation, and self-determination. This theology is part politics, part social activism, and part religion.

James H. Cone, credited with originating the black liberation theology movement, said[96], "The Christian faith has been interpreted largely by those who enslaved black people and by the people who segregated them."

This philosophy—even its name—encourages an attitude of victimization: the idea that if one is black, one is oppressed and needs liberation from the white oppressor. It is racist and divisive.

See also Wright, Reverend Jeremiah; Collective salvation quotes.

Black Panthers: See New Black Panthers.

Boeing: See NLRB.

Bondholders, secured: When paying off debt, secured creditors, such as secured bondholders, are paid off first under the "absolute priority" rule.[97] Holders of common stock are paid off last.

When Chrysler was bailed out by the US government and reorganized, the company's creditors who held secured bonds were bullied into accepting twenty-nine cents on the dollar on their loans, while UAW members, who were not secured creditors, received more than forty cents on the dollar.

In addition, if a secured creditor is not paid in full, he is entitled to a deficiency claim[97] that would hold the bankrupt Chrysler liable for the debt. No such claim was awarded to the wronged creditors. Our government also pushed the reorganization of Chrysler, using an illegal sales mechanism that excluded[97] creditors from voting on the sale. This too was a denial of their rights. It appears that bankruptcy law, franchise law, and the Fifth and Fourteenth Amendments (concerning takings and due process) to the Constitution were violated in order to bail out the UAW. Good job.

See also Delphi pensions; GM's CEO fired; TARP.

Boston marathon bombing: The liberal mainstream media immediately characterized[98] the bombing of April 15, 2013 as a result of Patriot Days (celebrated on the same date), similar to right wing group attack of the Martin Luther King parade in Oregon in 2010, people of the far right ..... just extremists, and opposition to tax day. Initially, all possible was done by the liberal mainstream media to avoid a supposition that this was a terrorist attack.

President Obama in a press conference on April 30, 2013, after the perpetrators had been identified, focused[99] on the possibility the bombers were "self-radicalized." Never was the possibility of jihad mentioned.

Brothers Tamerlan and Dzhokhar Tsarnaev were responsible for the bombing. Tamerlan had been in Russia recently and the Russian intelligence service had alerted[99] us about him. The US apparently took no action. Tamerlan was killed before he could be questioned. The younger brother, Dzhokhar wrote[100] on the inside of the dry-docked boat in which he was hiding when caught that the bombings were retaliation for American action against Muslims.

Bow to Saudi king[101]: During his apology tour in April 2009, President Obama bowed to Saudi Arabia's King Abdullah in a reception line. This is not traditional protocol for a president of the United States. Some kindly called it "stooping." By any name, it was an indication of submission whether intended or not.

35

See also Apology tour.

Bowles-Simpson: shorthand for the National Commission on Fiscal Responsibility and Reform.[102] The commission was created by President Obama in 2010 to identify "policies to improve the fiscal situation in the medium term and to achieve fiscal sustainability over the long run." It was co-chaired by Erskine Bowles, a Democrat, and Alan Simpson, a Republican, and consisted of eighteen members, called the "super committee."

The debt-reduction plan to be produced by the commission needed a supermajority affirmative vote of fourteen in order to be adopted. It failed when only eleven members supported it. The plan was generally seen as even-handed, since it proposed both cutting spending and increasing taxes. Over the coming decade, 2013-2022, budget deficits would have been cut by $6.3 trillion, accomplished by nearly equal amounts of program cuts and increased taxes. Marginal tax rates would actually have decreased; the Social Security retirement age would have been gradually raised; defense procurements would have been cut 15 percent; tax revenues would have been increased by $100 billion; and some entitlements would have been reduced.

After creating the commission, Obama never apparently even considered[103] the Bowles-Simpson plan. Many thought he should have even though it failed to get a supermajority vote. It was within his power to do so. He didn't.

See also Budget, Budget Control Act; Credit rating; Fiscal cliff.

BP escrow: Although it was widely assumed that BP was, for the most part, responsible for the oil spill disaster of April 2010 in the Gulf of Mexico, many questioned the administration's very early and unilateral action to require BP to commit to a $20 billion escrow fund[104] for victim compensation. This move was seen as overstepping bounds, since the company had not yet been found guilty; the extent of its responsibility had not been determined; there was no constitutional authority or judicial foundation for the action; and the money was to be disbursed without any congressional guidelines or legal supervision. The recipients of compensation were merely those whom the administration judged to be worthy.

See also BP oil spill; DOI '30-day Safety Report; Drilling moratorium.

BP oil spill: On April 20, 2010, the oil platform Deepwater Horizon, located off the coast of Louisiana in the Gulf of Mexico, exploded, killing eleven men and starting an oil gusher that was not capped until 3 months later on July 15. The environmental and financial damages were expected to be enormous.

BP was blamed[105] for cost-cutting measures and insufficient safety systems. The Department of the Interior's Mineral Management Service was faulted[105] for accepting favors from the oil companies and falsifying inspection reports, and accused of a general dereliction of duties.

After much environmental sampling and study, it is still not possible to confidently quantify effects of the spill, partially because there was insufficient site-specific baseline data on the marine ecosystem on which to base cause-and-effect conclusions. One thing is clear and that is that recovery has been faster and better[106-108] than first expected. Seafood has been tested[109] extensively and found to be safe to eat.

Even before the damage assessment phases began and before the causes of the explosion were known, President Obama and Interior Secretary Ken Salazar required BP to set up a $20 billion fund in escrow to compensate victims and they imposed a moratorium[110] on drilling in the gulf. This seemed excessive to many. By comparison, when there is an airline disaster, all airplanes are not grounded.

See also BP escrow; DOI '30 Day Safety Report; Drilling moratorium.

Brennan, John: When President Obama nominated him for director of the CIA in February, 2013, it was known that he had converted[111] to Islam while working in a US official capacity in Saudi Arabia. This conversion was supposedly the culmination of a counter-intelligence investigation to recruit him.

White House emails regarding Benghazi released on May 15, 2013 make it clear[112] that Brennan was key in editing the talking points on the 9/11 terrorist attack.

Budget: According to federal law (the Congressional Budget Act), the president must submit a budget to Congress each year. The House and Senate budget committees consider the president's proposals and submit a budget resolution that is expected to pass in both chambers by April 15 each year. That is what is supposed to happen.

President Obama has submitted five budgets, for fiscal years 2010 through 2014. The Senate passed a budget in April 2009 for FY 2010 but the next three budgets for FY 2011, 2012, and 2013 did not receive one positive vote in the Senate—not one among Democrats or Republicans.

The exorbitant spending of our government is known to be a sore point among the electorate. Hence senators on both sides of the aisle were reluctant to be seen as complicit in President Obama's excessive, record spending. The government has been funded through continuing resolutions. Then Congress has simply raised the debt ceiling, and neither Obama nor Congress has done anything about restructuring Social Security and Medicare to save them from insolvency or made cuts in income-based entitlements such as Medicaid, food stamps, and subsidized housing.

In March, 2013 the Senate adopted[113] its first budget in four years. Although it cuts the rate of increase in spending ($1.85 trillion deficit reduction) it includes tax increases and leaves the US deep in debt a decade down the road. No Republican voted for it and four Democrats voted against it. Representative Paul Ryan's (R. Wis.) budget[114], the plan passed by the House, would balance the budget in ten years and cut the deficit by $4.6 trillion over ten years.

Since both the House and Senate passed their versions of the budget before President Obama submitted his (a reverse of the expected process), it is unlikely that Obama's will have much, if any, impact. A reconciliation budget agreed upon between the House and Senate versions should occur, but the budgets are so far apart that it is doubted that will happen.

It is clear that either government spending must decrease or taxes must increase or a combination of the two in order to balance the budget. If taxes go up too much, the private sector will become less productive which would be a drag on the economy and GDP. If government spending goes down it will temporarily, reduce GDP. But many displaced government workers would find their way back into the private sector where they actually produce something of value thus increasing GDP in a way that does not require increased taxation for support as does government spending.

In 2008, then presidential candidate Obama promised[115] a "net spending cut." Another broken promise.

See also Continuing resolution; Debt ceiling.

Budget Control Act: This law was passed in 2011 after the Bowles-Simpson commission plan of 2010 was rejected by President Obama and intense partisan bickering resulted in a stalemate on how to reduce the deficit. In the spirit of 'kicking the can down the road,' the Act was passed. It mandated across-the-board spending cuts (sequestration) amounting to $1.2 trillion (more than 5 times less than Bowles-Simpson would have saved) over ten years if the super committee could not arrive at selective cuts. It did not.

See also Bowles-Simpson; Credit rating; Fiscal cliff; Sequestration.

Business quote: In Roanoke, Virginia, on July 13, 2012, President Obama, trying to emphasize the role that government plays in everyone's life, overshot the mark when he said[116], "If you've got a business, you didn't build that. Somebody else made that happen." This statement sparked a lot of pushback by the business community. Many were clearly offended.

Cap & Trade Bill: Shorthand for the Waxman-Markey Cap-and-Trade Bill[117], or the American Clean Energy and Security Act of 2009. This bill set up a system of selling the right to emit greenhouse gases, primarily $CO2$. Companies would buy a federal permit (also called an allowance) for each ton of carbon emitted. The federal government then would distribute the money received to those groups mentioned in the act, including the poor. If enacted, the bill would have greatly reduced the gross domestic product (GDP), caused millions of jobs to be lost, increased individual's utility costs, and significantly raised the price of gasoline—a net drain on GDP and employment. The bill narrowly passed the House in June 2009 but died in the Senate.

President Obama apparently expected a defeat of the bill, because just two days after his election he said[118], "Cap-and-Trade is just one way of skinning the cat." So he turned to his Environmental Protection Agency (EPA) to use the Clean Air Act to enact regulations limiting CO_2 emissions, thus doing an end run around Congress.

With this action he may have violated the separation of powers as structured in the first three articles of the Constitution.

See also ANWR; Cash for clunkers; Coal industry; EPA's CO_2 regulations; EPA's crucifixion example; Drilling moratorium; Keystone, mpg; Ocean control by UN.

Capitalism: See Rugged individualism quote.

Car Allowance Rebate System: See Cash for Clunkers.

Card Check: the common name for a bill officially titled the Employee Free Choice Act. The legislation if it were passed would in essence unionize every company in the U.S. with three or more employees – essentially forced-unionization. It would confer union bargaining power merely with the signatures of a majority of a worker group on cards (hence "card check") and eliminate a secret ballot. There would be no privacy in deciding whether to sign the cards, which would lead to coercion and perceived coercion by union organizers. Indeed, the Employee Free Choice Act would not promote free choice. Then Senator Barack Obama co-sponsored it in 2007. It was rejected.

In April 2008, presidential candidate Obama said[120], "Let's stand up to the business lobby that's been getting their friends in Washington to block card check. I've fought to pass the Employee Free Choice Act in the Senate. And I will make it the law of the land when I'm president of the United States of America."

It was not a surprise that very soon after President Obama's 2009 inauguration, the bill was resurrected.[121] It died due to bipartisan opposition even in a Democrat-controlled Congress.

In June 2011, the National Labor Relations Board (NLRB) circumvented Congress and implemented[122] a watered-down version of part of the legislation. In this new legislation, the period between the proposal to form a union and a formal union ballot was reduced from forty-five to sixty days to only fourteen to twenty-five days. This shorter period leaves less time for workers to gather information and understand the ramifications, and less time for business managers to present the downside of unionization.

The new NLRB rule did not go all the way toward forced unionization but took one more step toward it. Death by a thousand cuts. The intent of this administration is clear regarding unionization. The card check legislation is reportedly on the president's agenda for his second term. Look for another resurrection of the bill.

See also NLRB; Unions.

Cash for Clunkers: the popular description for the 2009 Car Allowance Rebate System, President Obama's program to promote the green agenda and stimulate purchases by paying people $3,500 to $4,500 to trade in their old, fuel-inefficient cars for new, more fuel-efficient cars. The old cars could not be resold and had to be destroyed.

Toyota benefited the most of all car manufacturers from the program. Along with sales of new Hondas and Nissans this led to a gain[123] in market share for Japanese and Korean manufacturers at the expense of all American carmakers except Ford. One study[124] concluded that the costs of the program outweighed benefits by $1.4 billion. Another study[124] found the overall average fuel economy of all vehicles purchased during the program increased by only 0.6 mpg in July 2009 and by only 0.7 mpg in August 2009. Although 677,081 used cars were permanently removed from the US inventory, many were good cars. This resulted in an increase in cost of used cars still on the market including the cheaper ones and thus hurt the poor more than any other group.

Churchill bust: Columnist Charles Krauthammer alleged[125] in 2009 that President Obama had returned to Britain a bust of Churchill that had been loaned after the 9/11 attacks and had resided in the White House during the presidency of George W. Bush. The White House denied[125] returning it and even produced a photo of President Obama and British Prime Minister David Cameron inspecting "the" bust in the White House. But it was not the bust in question. Obama indeed returned the original Jacob Epstein casting of the Churchill bust, and the White House was touting a copy given to President Lyndon Johnson instead.

Obama's return of the bust had highly symbolic importance. He should have politely asked if the loan could be extended, thus acknowledging and enhancing our alliance with Britain. Instead, he insulted the British people and spurned their gesture of good will and solidarity by returning the bust.

See also Thatcher, Margaret.

Civilian security force: See TSA.

Climate change: an inappropriately used term for what leftists believe to be man-caused, or anthropogenic, global warming.

At the 2009 UN Climate Change Conference in Copenhagen, the United States signed an accord[126] agreeing to reduce by 2020 our greenhouse gas emissions by 17 percent over what they were in 2005 and to contribute to a $100 billion-a-year fund to help impoverished countries adapt to climate change and lower their emissions.

The United States was criticized for not pledging to reduce its emissions further. Perhaps because President Obama's Cap & Trade bill had passed the House but had not yet been voted on in the Senate, he did not want to jeopardize its chances of passing by being more aggressive. Obama reportedly[127] said that no matter what did or did not happen in Copenhagen "America has plotted its course and will continue to take measures to curtail carbon emissions domestically."

Nothing very substantive happened on this front at the UN's 2010, 2011, and 2012 conferences in Cancun, Durban, and Doha, respectively. However, at the UN Earth Summit in Rio de Janeiro in June 2012, climate change was reportedly[128] dropped from the agenda and replaced with *sustainable development* because this was considered an easier sell to the public than climate change. Sustainable development is code for Agenda 21, and its goal is the same: a global government that controls every aspect of daily living and redistributes wealth.

President Obama may follow this model and push his green agenda disguised as sustainable development. It is a soft approach and does not require congressional approval. The climate change issue seemed dead during the 2012 election campaign. But since then, Obama has identified[129] climate change as one of his top three priorities for his second term.

On June 25, 2013, President Obama said in a speech[130] at Georgetown University that "97 percent of scientists .... acknowledged the planet is warming and human activity is contributing to it."

The 2009 University of Illinois polling study[131] from which this 97 percent statement was first derived, asked 2 poorly worded questions of 10,257 scientists in an on-line poll. Of that number only 3,146 responded. Of that number, 157 were climate scientists. Of that number, 79 had published climate-related articles in scientific journals. Of that number 77 (97.4% of 79) said they thought humans were a significant contribution in changing global temperature.

Therefore, the sweeping consensus statements regarding 97 per cent of scientists are based on results from one inadequate questionnaire, containing only 2 questions – 1 ambiguous and the other disingenuous - asked of a subset group that purposefully excluded scientists such as physicists and meteorologists who were more likely to reject the man-caused hypothesis. Then that self-selected group was further winnowed down leaving a very small and very biased sub-sample size of 79 to produce the reported results. Furthermore the respondents are anonymous. Clearly a poll based on such faulty methodology is insufficient to indicate a consensus among scientists about the cause of anything, let alone global warming. But using the 97 percent figure from this flawed study, President Obama implied global warming was caused by man's burning of fossil fuels.

Unfortunately the mainstream press has not done its job to question this assertion and has instead perpetuated it. The general public has heard it so often, they believe it.

In the meantime the arctic ice mass has increased[705] 60 percent in the year from 2012 to 2013. Although one year does not a trend make, that is a whopping increase.

See also Agenda 21; Cap & Trade bill; EPA's CO2 regulations; Keystone XL pipeline; Skyrocket quote.

Coal-fired power plants: On August 21, 2012, plaintiffs battling the EPA won a 2-1 decision[132] before a panel of the US Court of Appeals for the District of Columbia. In trying to further limit oxides of nitrogen and sulfur from emissions of coal-fired power plants, the EPA used a regulation it was developing, the Cross-State Air Pollution Rule, also called the Transport Rule, which relies on a radical interpretation of the Clean Air Act as its justification and is applicable to twenty-nine states mostly eastern states (including Indiana and Kentucky) plus Texas, and the District of Columbia.

The court sent the rule back for revision and directed the EPA to continue using the Clean Air Interstate Rule, an established regulation. The court's rationale was that the transport rule usurped too much of the authority of individual states and required them to make deeper cuts than called for under current federal law. The transport rule would also have implemented a cap-and-trade system. EPA appealed to the full eight-member D.C. court and was defeated again. The court decision was interpreted as a clear statement that the EPA had again overstepped its legal authority.

When his Cap-and-Trade bill failed, President Obama said[118], "Cap-and-Trade is just one way of skinning the cat." The EPA will try again. On June 24, 2013, the Supreme Court agreed[133] to hear, in its next session which begins October 1, 2013, an EPA appeal of the ruling in the D.C. circuit court of appeals which invalidated use of the Cross-state air pollution rule.

See also Bankrupt quote; Cap & Trade Bill; Climate change; Coal Industry, EPA's CO2 regulations; Skyrocket quote.

Coal Industry: President Obama's persecution of the coal industry—which in 2011 provided 42 percent[134] of America's electricity—had closed or threatened the closure of 175 coal-fired power plants according to summer 2012 estimates. Estimates[135] a year later are at 280 slated for shut-down.

Another source[136] estimates this to be 10 per cent of the coal-fired power generation in the US.

Existing coal-fired plants can't meet the EPA's new air toxics standards, which take effect in 2015, without exorbitant cost, and so older plants that need expensive upgrades are closing. Many thousands of coal-fired power plant units are expected[137] to be retired within the next decade.

The EPA's new rule regulating CO_2 will effectively ban new coal-fired power plants, because the cost of new carbon-capture and storage technology unrealistically required of them is exorbitant.

Our economy will suffer higher energy costs and fewer jobs as a result of the regulations, which stem from the EPA's shoddy review[138,139] of the science of anthropogenic global warming.

The EPA has acknowledged[140] that even if the new CO_2 standards were met, the rules would not reduce carbon dioxide in the atmosphere. In part, this is because our coal would then be sold to Asian markets, providing no net global reduction in the amount of coal burned. So the only reasonable explanation for the promulgation of this rule is to put the regulatory framework in place so it can be used later for control of carbon fuel industries. Furthermore, the EPA had claimed[140] that since no new coal-fired plants would be built, there is no cost associated with the rule!

Coal mining is also under assault by the EPA. In one case, the agency revoked[141] a permit it had approved and issued four years earlier. The action was upheld in appeals court three years after that.

EPA has also attempted to use guidance as if it were de facto law. This is illegal under the Administrative Procedures Act, and the EPA lost this case in the US District Court for the District of Columbia twice—in October 2011[142] and again in August 2012.[143]

See also Bankrupt quote; Cap & Trade bill; Coal-fired power plants; EPA's CO2 regulations; Skyrocket quote.

Collective Salvation quotes: In a 1995 interview about his book *Dreams from My Father*, which had just been published, and more specifically about his work in the poor neighborhoods of Chicago as a community organizer, Barack Obama said[144] ".... my fate remained tied up with their fates, that ... my individual salvation ... is not going to come about without a collective salvation for the country. Unfortunately I think that recognition requires that we make sacrifices and this country has not always been willing to make the sacrifices that are necessary to bring about a new day and a new age."

In June 2005, in a commencement address at Knox College in Galesburg, Illinois, Obama said[145], "You need to take on the challenge because you have an obligation to yourself -- because our individual salvation depends on collective salvation."

This is clearly consistent with President Obama's focus on an unprecedented increase in entitlements for the poor, increasing taxes on the wealthy, tightening regulation of private businesses, and supporting poor nations around the world. Although seemingly altruistic, his agenda is eroding individual rights, including property rights, in the US.

See also Agenda 21; Black liberation theology; Redistribution quotes.

Constitution: In a 2001 radio interview, then-Illinois state senator Barack Obama said[146], "We still suffer from not having a Constitution that guarantees its citizens economic rights." He characterized the Constitution as a "charter of negative liberties" that "says what the states can't do to you [and] what the federal government can't do to you, but doesn't say what the federal government or state government must do on your behalf."

See also al-Awlaki, Anwar; Arizona; Bondholders, secure; BP escrow; BP oil spill; Cap & Trade bill; Consumer Financial Protection Bureau; Contraceptive mandate; Czars; Dodd-Frank; Immigration; IPAB; Kill list; Libya's Arab spring; New Black Panthers; Small Arms Treaty; TARP.

Consumer Financial Protection Bureau: Established by the Dodd-Frank Act, the Consumer Financial Protection Bureau regulates financial products and services to protect consumers. It began operation in July 2011, one year after passage.

President Obama wanted Richard Cordray, a former Ohio attorney general, to be the director. Republicans objected because they first wanted assurance that there would be a five-member commission that would oversee the bureau. So, instead of negotiating, Obama did another end run around

Congress and made a recess appointment[147] of Cordray although the Senate was technically not in recess precisely to prevent such appointments.

Although there is a provision in the Constitution providing for presidential appointments when the Senate is in recess (Article II, Section 2), Obama's so-called recess appointment circumvented the constitutional intent as explained in Federalist Paper 67 and denied the Senate its constitutional authority.

As of July 17, 2013 the D.C. circuit court, the 3rd district appeals court and the 4th district appeals court have ruled[148] Obama's recess appointments invalid. The supreme court of the United States has agreed[149] to review the lower court's decision.

However, on July 16, 2013, the Senate GOP came to agreement with Reid and the Democrats that some of Obama's recess appointments including Richard Cordray would be approved and that others would be denied. In exchange, Reid would not institute the nuclear option. It appears that whatever the supreme court's decision on the matter, it is a moot point regarding Cordray.

See also NLRB.

Continuing Resolution: Although both the House and Senate produced and passed budgets for 2014, they are not likely to be reconciled in committee. So, we are facing another continuing resolution – the proverbial kicking of the can down the road.

See also Budget.

Contraceptive mandate: In 2012, the secretary of health and human services (HHS), under authority of Obamacare, issued a ruling that requires all health plans to cover the cost of contraceptives including abortifacients and sterilizations. Religious organizations were given until August 1, 2013, to implement the mandate.

Although there was an exemption for churches that oppose contraception and sterilization on doctrinal grounds, the exemption did not extend to their religiously affiliated nonprofit institutions such as hospitals, charities, and schools. The regulations are being challenged in court on the basis of violation of First Amendment rights and of the Religious Freedom Restoration Act.[150,151] Among those suing are the United States Conference of Catholic Bishops, the Union of Orthodox Jewish Congregations of America, Baptist and Evangelical colleges and universities, a Mennonite business, and religiously affiliated hospitals. By July, 2013 there were sixty-three lawsuits[152] against the contraceptive mandate in various stages of litigation.

Some of these plaintiffs have won injunctions until the matter is settled in a higher court. There has been at least one judgment in favor of the Department of Health and Human Services.

See also Obamacare exemptions; Lawsuits against Obamacare.

Cordray, Richard: See Consumer Financial Protection Bureau.

Cornhusker kickback: Passage of Obamacare was being blocked in the Senate by a filibuster until the Obama administration offered a deal to Nebraska Senator Ben Nelson, a Democrat who was siding with the Republicans. The deal was a trade of Nelson's support of Obamacare in exchange for a higher rate of Medicaid reimbursement for Nebraskans. This became known as the "Cornhusker kickback" and was later repealed.

Corporate culture: President Obama does not have to give orders for his staff and appointees to do questionable things on behalf of his policies and he is probably too smart to engage in such activity. He merely rewards those who take chances for him and punishes those who cross him making it a matter of the culture of the corporation, or in this case the culture of his administration.

Those rewarded include Chuck Hagel who has often taken an anti-Israel stance, promoted from co-chair of Obama's Intelligence Advisory Board to Secretary of Defense; Jack Lew who was reportedly responsible for the sequestration idea, promoted from chief of staff to Secretary of the Treasury; John Brennan who converted to Islam while working in an official capacity in Saudi Arabia and was implicated in changing of the Benghazi talking points, promoted to director of the CIA; Sara Hall Ingram who was in charge of the IRS division that delayed Tea Party and other conservative groups' application for tax-free status, promoted to the administrator of the Affordable Care Act mandates; Lois Lerner who was the most recent administrator of the IRS division that delayed those applica-tions, allowed to keep her six digit salary while on administra-tive leave during the summer of 2013; Susan Rice who perpetuated a false story about the cause of the Benghazi disaster, promoted to National Security Advisor to Obama; Victoria Nuland who was spokesperson for the State Department during the Benghazi controversy, nominated for Assistant Secretary of State; voter intimidating New Black Panthers, against whom the case was dropped by the DOJ; and Thomas Perez, assistant attorney general who was involved in the New Black Panthers case and the St. Paul, MN case, subsequently nominated for Secretary of Labor.

Those who have been punished include Christian groups through the Affordable Care Act for opposing abortion; Tea Party and other conservative groups and individuals through the IRS for their political activism; the fossil fuel industry through the EPA for being profitable and contributing greenhouse gas to the atmosphere; State Department employee Gregory Hicks through a demotion for his calling attention to the inconsistencies and inaccuracies in the administration's explanations and lack thereof for Benghazi; Gibson guitars through the Fish and Wildlife Service, for supporting Republican candidates; and possibly General Petraeus who "resigned" his position as CIA director (supposedly over an extramarital affair) for opposing changes to the Benghazi talking points.

See also Bankrupt quote; Benghazi; Brennan, John; Coal industry; EPA's crucifixion example; Gibson Guitars; Hagel, Chuck; IRS scandal; Kick-ass quote; New Black Panthers; Perez, Thomas; Petraeus, David; Punish our enemies quote.

Credit rating: On July 31, 2011, after a bitter battle between Republicans and Democrats over whether to raise the debt limit (also called the debt ceiling), for how long, and for how much, an agreement[153] was reached. The debt ceiling would be raised by $1.2 trillion and spending reduced by $1.2 trillion. The spending cuts (called sequestration) would come out of all discretionary programs and the military by the same percentage unless a better solution was devised by January 1, 2013.

This procrastination in dealing with the long-term problem—specifically Social Security and Medicare—triggered a credit downgrade[153] of our country from AAA to AA-plus by credit rating agency Standard & Poors just a few days later on August 5. The United States had had a AAA rating since 1917. The risk associated with a reduced credit rating is that foreign countries could raise the interest rates they charge us on the money we borrow from them through sale of our bonds. Higher rates on mortgages and other lending instruments would be expected to follow.

In April 2012, our credit rating slipped from AA-plus to AA. In September 2012, a third credit rating downgrade from AA to AA-minus was announced. These later two downgrades[154] were announced by credit-rating agency Eagen-Jones and the last downgrade was in reaction to the Federal Reserve's decision to print more money (quantitative easing three, or QE3) with which it will purchase mortgage-backed securities. This excess of money in the system is expected to eventually reduce the dollar's value and increase the cost of commodities such as oil and gold.

See also Budget Control Act; Debt; Leadership failure quote; Quantitative easing; Sequestration.

Cross-State Air Pollution Rule: See Coal-fired power plants.

Czars: This word is media shorthand for special advisers or assistants to the president. President Obama does not call them czars. However, in the Obama administration there are from twenty-eight to forty-five of them, depending on who[155] is doing the counting. Many of these czars are controversial. All modern presidents have had them, and the numbers have ranged from one under Presidents Dwight Eisenhower and Ronald Reagan to as many as forty-five under Obama. President George W. Bush had[155] thirty-three.

A few of the Obama administration czars were confirmed by the Senate; one post was created by legislation; most officials were simply appointed. Those that are merely appointed are not accountable to Congress, and their activities are not accessible[156] through the Freedom of Information Act. Obama's use of czars is seen by much of the informed public and a large bipartisan group in the House as an effort to work in secrecy and circumvent Congress. The czars who are dealing with policy issues and who have not gone through the confirmation process are probably holding office in violation[156] of the appointments clause of the Constitution (article II, Section 2). A comprehensive report on this subject titled *President Obama's Czars*[157], put out by Judicial Watch, of Washington, DC, is elucidating.

See also Jones, Van.

Czech Republic: See Missile defense shield.

Davis, Frank Marshall[158]: Described as an American journalist, poet, pornographer, and political and labor movement activist, he was a card-carrying Communist (card # 47544), blatantly pro-Communist, anti-capitalist and hated Churchill and Truman. He wrote columns for pro-Communist Party newspapers in Chicago routinely espousing Soviet propaganda. Davis attracted enough attention to be called to testify before the Senate Judiciary Committee in 1956 where he pleaded the Fifth Amendment regarding whether he was a Communist. The FBI listed him on its Security Index and he had a six hundred-page FBI file.

Regarding "Anglo-imperialist domination," he said[159], "Big business, of course, would like to see it. You know, big business such as Standard Oil."

He is suspected[160] of being Barack Obama's biological father. Joel Gilbert develops this hypothesis in his documentary film *Dreams of My Real Father*. The evidence presented is circumstantial but nonetheless compelling.

Young Barack was sent back to Hawaii from Indonesia to be raised and schooled by his grandparents. While there this adolescent in his formative years (about ages ten to eighteen) was mentored[161] by Davis, who had relocated there. It is estimated that there were upward of fifteen meetings between the two that were substantive and lengthy. While the content of those meetings is unknown, it is clear that Davis had an impact on young Obama. Davis is mentioned twenty-two times in Obama's autobiography, *Dreams from My Father*, but never by his full name—just as Frank.

Also noteworthy is Davis's association[162] during his Chicago days with Vernon Jarrett who, as a young person, was a member of a Communist Party USA youth wing group and later wrote for the left-wing *Chicago Defender*. Vernon Jarrett's son married Valerie Bowman, now known as Valerie Jarrett, top adviser to President Obama.

See also al-Mansour, Dr. Khalid Abdullah Tariq.

Day of prayer: President Obama has discontinued George W. Bush's tradition of hosting a White House event observing the National Day of Prayer and instead has but issued a written proclamation. This is perfectly lawful, since there is no statutory requirement for his doing anything more. However, he has routinely hosted[163] celebratory Iftar dinners at the White House in honor of the end of the Ramadan fast—a Muslim holy day. He held his fifth[633] in July 2013. He has also held dinners in honor of Seder – why not the National Day of Prayer?

Death Panel: See IPAB.

Debt: The national debt is the sum of all federal budget deficits (the annual amount by which government spending exceeds government receipts) over the years. National debt is also called public debt and sometimes the federal debt or government debt. Debt is financed by borrowing. This category of national debt does not include the government bailout of Fannie and Freddie that amounted[164] to $188 billion. Although Fannie and Freddie had paid back about $46 billion in dividends to the treasury by August, 2012 they had not made payments on the principal. Also not included in this category are government's unfunded obligations such as Social Security, Medicare, and Medicaid.

President Obama has contributed more to the debt than any other president in history.[165] As of July 22, 2013 our debt was $16.738 trillion.[166] In his first term, Obama added more to the debt than George W. Bush did in two terms of office. Obama is projected to add more to the debt by the end of his second term than all other presidents combined[167].

Gross debt or total US debt is all US debt (the sum of federal, state, and local government debts, international and private debts, and federal debt to trust funds such as Social Security and Medicare).

Sovereign debt is the aggregate of primarily bonds issued in foreign countries. The accumulation of such debt has a negative impact on economic freedom and growth of the debtor nation. And, if this debt gets so high that countries holding our debt (bonds) begin to lose confidence in our ability or willingness to pay up when the bonds mature, then interest rates may rise on future debt purchases or these countries may just refrain from buying any more of our debt.

Some of the countries[168] that hold our sovereign debt are friends, some not. The debt we owed to foreign countries increased by 125 percent[169] from 2003 to 2010. The United Kingdom and Japan are the world's two most indebted countries[170].

See GDP; Gross debt as % of GDP; Spending as % of GDP.

Debt ceiling: Also called the debt limit, it was raised again in January 2013 to allow the government to borrow more to pay our bills. Newly appointed Treasury Secretary Jack Lew now says[171] that due partially to payments made by Fannie and Freddie that the US won't face potential default again on paying its bills until after Labor Day, 2013.

See also Credit rating; Debt; Leadership failure quote.

Deepwater Horizon: See BP oil spill.

Delphi pensions: In 2010, President Obama's scheme to bail out the auto industry (i.e., the United Auto Workers union) decimated[172] the pensions and benefits of about twenty thousand white-collar, nonunion, salaried employees at Delphi, an auto-parts company that was a spin-off of and supplier to GM. Pensions of Delphi union members were not affected. From 30 to 70 percent of salaried Delphi employees' pensions were lost. These nonunion pensioners at Delphi also lost all their health- and life-insurance benefits. The pensions of union members became fully funded, and 90 percent of the union pensioners' health care benefits were retained.

The Obama administration made the choice to favor union members over nonunion members in settling GM's debt. Proving that political favoritism instead of purely business necessity was the driver of the decision may be difficult. However, the decision has been traced to the Treasury Department rather than an independent corporation as originally claimed[173] by the administration. It appears the Obama administration may have violated federal law and the

Fourteenth Amendment (equal protection clause) of the Constitution.

See also Bondholders, secure; GM's CEO fired; TARP; Unions.

Derisive quote: In a speech[174] on April 6, 2009, in Strasbourg, France, President Obama said that "… in America, there's a failure to appreciate Europe's leading role in the world. Instead of celebrating your dynamic union and seeking to partner with you to meet common challenges, there have been times where America has shown arrogance and been dismissive, even derisive."

See also Apology tour.

Disability treaty: The United Nations' Convention on the Rights of Persons with Disabilities[175] was signed by President Obama in 2009 and sent to the Senate on May 18, 2012, for ratification. The Senate Committee on Foreign Relations approved the treaty in July 2012. It still required a two-thirds affirmative vote of the whole Senate to be ratified and put into effect. The treaty demands that we conform to UN standards. Ratification would mean a further loss of US sovereignty.

A much more personal concern is the potential loss of parental rights. Under the treaty, the US government, as directed by the UN, would determine what is best for children with disabilities. The government, not the parents, would decide if a special- needs child should be home-schooled or attend private or public school. Currently, US public schools must offer assistance to special-needs children, but parents are not required to accept this assistance. There is also fear that this treaty could force every home owner to make their home accessible to those with disabilities.

Another more complicated issue is that of abortion rights. The treaty requires those with disabilities to be provided with "the same range, quality and standard of free or affordable health care and programmes as provided to other persons, including in the area of sexual and reproductive health and population-based public health programmes." This language would pressure the United States to liberalize abortion laws or policies. So, Senator Marco Rubio (R-FL) offered[175] an amendment clarifying the US position that the UN language could not be used to support, endorse, or promote abortion. Senator John Kerry (D-MA) then offered[175] a second-degree amendment that eliminated Rubio's clarifying language. It passed. One can only deduce that there is possibly an implicit loosening of abortion constraints in the treaty—otherwise the Democrats would not have objected to the Rubio amendment and voted for Kerry's.

The treaty does not apply only to children with disabilities and has been interpreted[176] to ban the spanking of children by parents. It also demands[176] the complete disarmament of all people!

The United States already has the Americans with Disabilities Act, which became law in 1990. The UN treaty includes many of the same provisions as our current law but goes too far beyond it. Still, Obama signed off on it.

On December 4, 2012, the US Senate rejected the treaty by a vote of sixty-one in favor and thirty-eight opposed. An affirmative two-thirds vote (sixty-six) was required in order for it to pass. So the margin of defeat was not all that great. It is expected to be resurrected in 2013.

See also Agenda 21; Internet control by UN; Ocean control by UN; Small Arms treaty.

Dismissive: See Derisive quote.

Dodd-Frank: The Dodd-Frank Wall Street Reform and Consumer Protection Act of 2010[177] increases government oversight and supervision of financial institutions and creates eleven new agencies. It is more than sixteen hundred pages long and by October 2012 had already spawned more than eight thousand pages of regulations.[178] And that is only a third of the number of regulations expected.

This law is supposed to make another economic crisis less likely by instituting more stringent regulation of financial markets. It presumes to prevent corporations from becoming too big to fail, prevent banks from using depositors money to invest in hedge funds for the banks' profit, require the riskiest derivatives to be more tightly regulated, create an office to regulate credit rating agencies, establish an office to identify companies that pose a risk to the financial system, assure affordable insurance availability to minorities and underserved communities, and prevent the Federal Reserve from making loans to single entities without Treasury Department approval and disclosure of the names of those banks. Some of this regulation was warranted.

However, the unintended consequences have been detrimental to the economy. The law gave big banks a competitive advantage by labeling them as "systemically important financial institutions." This advantage for the big banks conversely puts smaller banks at a competitive disadvantage.[593] For instance, the big banks will be able to borrow money at lower rates[594] because it is known by the lender that they will not be allowed to fail by the US government (we the taxpayers). This puts the smaller community banks at a disadvantage. Rules yet to be promulgated under Dodd-Frank have already caused small community banks to further limit lending due to fear of liability if the loans are not "qualified." This has hindered lending for home mortgages, car loans, and businesses, thus putting a further drag on an already weak economy.

One of the eleven new agencies created is the Office of Financial Research[179], which reportedly has unlimited authority to tax big banks without any congressional oversight and is vested with unlimited subpoena power over the companies.

Another agency created, the Consumer Financial Protection Bureau[180], has also been given excessive authority over consumer credit and other financial products and services. Some of these provisions appear to be either illegal or unconstitutional.

See also Consumer Financial Protection Bureau; Too big to fail.

DOI 30 Day Safety Report: shorthand for the Department of the Interior report of May 27, 2110, titled "Increased Safety Measures for Energy Development of the Outer Continental Shelf[181]." It was written in response to the BP oil spill.

The report said that the authors relied on expertise from within the federal government, academia, professional engineers, industry, and other regulatory programs. It also noted that seven members of the National Academy of Engineering peer-reviewed the recommendations.

At issue was the recommendation to impose a six-month drilling moratorium as a result of the disastrous spill in the Gulf of Mexico on April 20, 2010. This recommendation was inserted into the report after the peer review, and so the reviewers were misrepresented as approving the moratorium. The expert reviewers objected[182] saying, "A blanket moratorium is not the answer. It will not measurably reduce risk further and it will have a lasting impact on the nation's economy which may be greater than that of the oil spill." An Office of Inspector General (IG) investigation ensued but was not able to determine if the report's authors intended to deceive the public. The reviewers did receive an apology. However, Obama proceeded with the moratorium anyway.

See also BP oil spill; Drilling moratorium; BP escrow.

Dream act: see Immigration

Drew, Dr. John C.: He knew Barack Obama in 1980 during Obama's days as a student at Occidental College. Drew was at that time an avowed communist and in his words[183] "had been an angry Marxist revolutionary" earlier. Obama was reportedly[183] (Drew through his girlfriend) a participant in an active group on campus, the Democratic Socialist Alliance. Drew has recounted conversations with Obama during which he tried to convince Obama that politics was a better way than revolution to advance a socialist agenda. He referred[183] to the Obama of 1980 as a "doctrinaire Marxist revolutionary."

Drilling moratorium: In May, soon after the disastrous BP oil spill in the Gulf of Mexico, which started with an explosion on April 20, 2010, President Obama halted[184] all offshore exploratory drilling for oil and gas in more than five hundred feet of water. In June, an injunction[184] was issued against the drilling ban. Judge Martin Feldman called Obama's moratorium "punitive." In July, Obama issued a new moratorium. Under heavy political pressure, the moratorium was rescinded[185] in October 2010. But it was another four months before the first deepwater permit was approved.[186] In December 2010, Obama banned[187] new drilling in the eastern Gulf of Mexico for at least seven years. In February 2011, Seahawk Drilling, the second-largest shallow-water driller in the gulf, filed for bankruptcy[188], blaming the moratorium. By July 2011, ten rigs had left[189] the gulf.

In November 2011, the Obama administration opened[190] six offshore areas in the Gulf of Mexico and off the coast of Alaska. The waters off the entire west and east coasts of the continental United States are still out of bounds[190] to drillers. As of October[191], more offshore drilling permits had been issued in 2012 than in the last two years combined. But production in the gulf is not expected[192] to exceed pre-spill levels until 2019.

In the meantime during the summer of 2012, the Obama administration stopped[193] about eighty-five percent of development of offshore drilling or exploration, which left only two percent of the outer continental shelf available for oil and gas exploration and drilling.

While impeding drilling for oil offshore by American-owned companies, Obama has not stopped $1 billion in loans[194] from the US Export-Import Bank to PEMEX, Mexico's government-owned company, to drill in the Gulf of Mexico. The excuse is that this drilling is not in deep waters. The Export-Import Bank also approved $2 billion in loans[195] to Petrobras of Brazil to drill off of that country's coast. Both Mexico and Brazil are required to use goods and services produced or provided by American workers. That is to our advantage, and there is no reason to judge these Brazilian and Mexican oil drilling ventures in a bad light. The problem lies with the Obama administration. Obama doesn't oppose drilling for oil if it is done by other countries and will even assist it, but he is doing as much as he can to impede drilling by our own companies—onshore and offshore—and that makes no sense at all.

While oil production has increased during the Obama years, it is despite his policies, not because of them. The increase is due to drilling on nongovernment lands such as the Baaken formation where the president has little power. Oil and gas production on federal lands has decreased[196] 15 percent during the two years FY2010 – FY2012. It is estimated[197] that Obama's policies have reduced our gulf oil production by 300,000 barrels per day versus what it would be without his interference.

See also BP escrow; BP oil spill; DOI '30 Day Safety Report; Fracking.

Drilling permits: See Drilling moratorium.

Dunham, Stanley Ann: See Stanley Ann Dunham.

Egypt's Arab spring: On January 25, 2011, generally nonviolent protests against President Hosni Mubarak's thirty-year secularist rule began in cities throughout Egypt. Mubarak made some concessions and pledged not to run for another term, but refused to step down. Confrontations between the protesters and pro-Mubarak groups intensified, and the military did what it could to control the factions. An estimated three hundred protesters were killed by government forces - not the military. On February 11, 2011, Mubarak resigned and announced that the military would assume leadership. He was later sentenced to life in prison. Egypt's blockade at the border with Gaza was eased, and Israel considered this a threatening move. The Israeli ambassador was forced to flee Egypt.

By January 2012, the Muslim Brotherhood won forty-seven percent of the seats in the Egyptian assembly and then nominated a candidate for president after saying it would not. In June 2012, Mohamed Morsi, the Muslim Brotherhood candidate, announced himself the winner of the election.

Mubarak was our strongest Arab ally although he repressed his people. Egypt under Mubarak was also Israel's most important strategic ally. Since the days of Anwar Sadat in 1979, there has been a peace treaty between Israel and Egypt. Mubarak, if not a true friend of Israel, at least was not aggressive against it. He was able to maintain some stability in the Middle East.

The peace between Egypt and Israel has become more tenuous since Mubarak's ouster and even more so since Israel's retaliatory assassination[198] of a terrorist in Gaza in November 2012. Morsi had shown[199] he wanted a strong relationship between Egypt and Iran—something that had not existed for more than thirty years. This was not good news for Israel.

President Obama's repeated and very public insistence that Mubarak step down during the uprisings was seen by some as poorly thought out. That concern was borne out when the Muslim Brotherhood gained control of Egypt's government after Mubarak's departure. Obama said[200] of Egypt, "I don't think that we would consider them an ally. But we don't consider them an enemy." Egypt had been our strongest Arab ally.

In late November 2012, Morsi declared[201] his decisions to be absolute and not subject to review by the Egyptian courts. He made this declaration just two days after receiving praise from Secretary of State Hillary Clinton for his work in brokering a cease-fire between Gaza's Hamas and Israel. Some have surmised that the secretary's public praise may have emboldened him. Major protests of Morsi's power grab caused him to retract[202] the declaration.

In December 2012, a new constitution was passed amid accusations[203] of voter fraud. This was considered a victory for Islamists and the Muslim Brotherhood and a threat to Coptic Christians.

In late June 2013, unrest among a very significant part of the Egyptian population was building over Morsi's handling of the government and the economy. The government and its new constitution were too influenced by sharia law, tourism was down, and the economy was unstable. Millions in the street demanded Morsi step down. Morsi refused. On July 3, 2013, the Egyptian military engineered[204] a bloodless coup d'état and ousted Morsi. The military is considered much more secularist than the Muslim Brotherhood.

President Obama had been publically silent during the days of the unrest in the streets. After the coup on July 3, 2013, Obama issued a statement[205] expressing concern about the military's actions to remove Morsi and suspend the new constitution. Obama also called for them to return authority to a democratically elected civilian government. He avoided the word *coup* because acknowledging it triggers a prohibition of federal aid to Egypt. The aid we give them is seen as the only way we may have any influence.

By mid-August 2013, the bloodless coup had resulted in sit-ins and riots of Muslim Brotherhood sympathizers protesting against the ouster of Morsi. An increasingly forceful Egyptian military killed over six hundred protesters in a few short days.

The interim vice president, Mohamed ElBaradei abruptly resigned over the military's brutal handling of the protesters.

The rioting crowds were accused of acts of violence against Coptic Christians, their businesses and places of worship. Many Christian churches have been burned, not just the two or three that the mainstream media has reported. Indeed, the National Review recounting[654] information in the Asia News, reports seven Catholic churches and fifteen religious structures of the Coptic-Orthodox Church and Protestant church that have been attacked. Another source[662] reported as many as thirty-eight churches burned-out across Egypt and others looted in the week following August 14, 2013 when so many protesters were killed by the military.

The uprising is being portrayed as a populist movement that wants Morsi returned to power and the attacks of churches merely to be payback for ousting Morsi. But, the Christians are not responsible for the coup. That portion of the population is not well-organized and appears not to have a voice except possibly through the military which may reflect their position – at least more than the Muslim Brotherhood does. The current clash is between the secularist military and the Islamist Muslim Brotherhood.

President Obama in his taped comments[655] on August 15 from Martha's Vineyard where he was vacationing indicated a very weak repudiation (merely just a phrase) of the attacks on churches and avoided using the word "Christian." He also seemed to side with the Muslim Brotherhood forces contrasting the rights to peaceful protest with violence against civilians by the military. Because of the military's violence, he cancelled military exercises with Egypt and that too was seen as a signal of his favoring Morsi's return to power. He has stopped short of cancelling aid to Egypt which goes overwhelmingly to the military.

On August 20, 2013 Obama enjoyed a photo op while feting[663] the Miami Dolphins team from 1972? Does he not have anything better to do? Three of the championship team members apparently thought so and refused the invitation. Good for them.

Mubarak's Egypt was a much more stable country and a better US and Israeli ally. What did Obama gain by insisting that Mubarak step down? Why does he appear to be favoring the Muslim Brotherhood's position? Was he influenced by his Secretary of Defense, Hagel and advisors, Abedin, Alikhan, Hussain, Mogahed and Parsi?

Grave potential losses for the US in this upheaval are security for Israel and use of the Suez Canal.

See also Green movement; Abedin, Huma Mahmood; Alikhan, Arif; Hagel, Chuck; Hussain, Rashad; Libya's Arab spring; Mogahed, Dalia; Parsi, Trita; Syria's Arab spring.

Election campaign fraud: During 2008, the Obama presidential campaign accepted[206] untraceable electronic donations. Although federal election law does not require the credit verification value (CVV)—the three- or four-digit security code on credit cards—for making online donations, its use helps prevent fraud and large numbers of small and automatic donations (robo-donations) made online to evade federal reporting requirements.

The DOJ overlooked this irregularity, and the Federal Election Commission (FEC) considered it only a loophole.

In 2012, the Obama campaign persisted in this ill-advised online procedure. In addition, the nonpartisan Government Accountability Institute could not ascertain whether Address Verification System (AVS) software was used by the official campaign donor website, Obama for America. This software verifies that the address provided by the donor matches the address on file with the credit card company.

Without the CVV and AVS verification of address—which are legal to omit—Donald Duck, Osama bin Laden, and Minnie Mouse, all living in Tehran and using the same credit card number, can make multiple donations under two hundred dollars (the limit[207] under which names need not be provided to regulators) if they claim to live at any made-up US address. FEC rules prohibit contributions from foreign nationals to US presidential campaigns. But, under current regulation, foreigners would never be caught.

At least one fund raising email for Obama urged[208] donations of "$190 or whatever you can afford."

During the 2012 campaign, an important domain name, Obama.com, was owned by a third-party Obama bundler in Shanghai, China. This site was reported to have heavy traffic and to have redirected 68 percent of its foreign traffic directly to the official Obama for America donation page.

The Obama campaign may have violated federal law by taking contributions that could easily have been rejected by using controls (CVV and AVS) used by 90 percent of e-commerce, nineteen of twenty top charities, and the Romney campaign. Instead, the Obama campaign paid[209] millions in fees for the privilege of accepting unsecured contributions. Why would it do this?

Federal election laws need to be updated. In the meantime, it appears possible that the Saudis may have contributed enough to the election of President Obama in 2008 and 2012 to affect our foreign policy. It is posited[210] that Obama is funneling help to the rebels in Syria through the CIA because the Saudis who are Sunni and to whom Obama may be beholden for his elections, want the Assad regime which is Shiia/Alawite to fall.

See also Benghazi; Syria's Arab spring; Voter ID.

Elibiary, Mohamed[211]**:** Born in Alexandria, Egypt, he founded the Freedom and Justice Foundation in Plano, Texas, in 2002. It no longer exists because its 501(c)(3) status was pulled when the foundation refused to provide documents required by the IRS. Freedom and Justice is the name of the political party of the Muslim Brotherhood in Egypt.

In 2004, Elibiary spoke at a conference honoring the "Great Islamic Visionary Ayatollah Khomeini." He is said[212] to have been an active promoter of Sayyid Qutb, a jihadist ideologue.

In 2010, Homeland Security Secretary Janet Napolitano appointed Elebiary to the Department of Homeland Security's Advisory Council. He has also been a member of the department's Countering Violent Extremism Working Group.

Elibiary had a secret security clearance and illegally accessed a state and local intelligence community database from his home computer. He was the only member of the committee to have such access. His security clearance was reportedly revoked, but as of July 2013 he was still listed as a member of the Homeland Security Advisory Council.

Enough money: See Redistribution.

EPA's CO2 regulations: In March 2009, Dr. Alan Carlin, an EPA employee, produced a ninety-eight-page draft report[213] titled "Comments on Draft Technical Support Document for Endangerment Analysis for Greenhouse Gas Emissions under the Clean Air Act." The document was suppressed[214] and its author gagged by EPA Administrator Lisa Jackson because of pressure on her to support the Obama administration's agenda to regulate CO2. Carlin has a Bachelor of Science degree in physics from Cal Tech and a PhD in economics from MIT. He was a thirty-five-year veteran of the EPA and left the agency shortly after the incident.

Carlin's report accused the EPA of relying on outdated research, ignoring recent declines in global temperatures, and ignoring the moderating influence of natural atmospheric water vapor. New data that showed ocean temperature and solar activity to be more important than CO2 concentrations in determining global atmospheric temperatures, were also ignored.

Suppression of the Carlin report allowed the EPA to declare[215] CO2 to be a poison—"a threat to public health and welfare." This declaration cleared the way for the EPA's regulation of industrial and vehicular CO_2 emissions. These regulations will be so punitive on industries such as coal-fired power plants that "electricity rates would necessarily skyrocket." In January 2008, presidential candidate Obama admitted wanting just this outcome.

In September 2011, the EPA inspector general issued a report that vindicated[216] Carlin and accused the EPA of conducting a shoddy scientific review and rushing to conclude that CO_2 was an endangerment.

After retiring, Dr. Carlin published[677] a significant rebuttal to EPA's position on anthropogenic global warming in a peer-reviewed journal.

EPA's shoddy review has not stopped the Obama administration. On June 25, 2013 in a speech[217] at Georgetown University, Obama directed the EPA to complete performance standards for both new and existing power plants. He was referring to emissions of carbon dioxide.

Newly appointed and confirmed EPA chief Gina McCarthy on August 14, 2013 in remarks[656] at the University of Colorado in Boulder stated that Obama had said "... it is time to act," and that "he wasn't going to wait for Congress" citing what he called his "administrative authorities."

Obama and McCarthy need to be reminded that the Senate defeated the Cap and Trade bill in 2009 when the Democrats were in control of that house. He does not have the authority to ignore Congress and skin the cat any way he wishes.

If Obama and his EPA are allowed to pursue this false crusade against fossil fuels, electricity rates will "necessarily skyrocket."

See also Cap & Trade bill; Coal industry; EPA's crucifixion example; Skyrocket quote.

EPA's crucifixion example: Alfredo Juan Armendariz, the EPA's regional administrator for the nation's south central region— five states where there is a lot of oil and gas—was captured on video[218] giving a speech to residents of a small Texas town concerned about fracking. In answering a question from his audience about enforcement of environmental law, he said, "It is kind of like how the Romans used to conquer little villages in the Mediterranean. They'd go into a little Turkish town somewhere, they'd find the first five guys they saw, and they would crucify them. And then you know that town was really easy to manage for the next few years." And, "You make examples out of people who are not complying with the law."

The comments were made in 2010, but video taken by an audience member didn't surface until much later. EPA Administrator Lisa Jackson at first distanced[219] herself from his comments, which she said were "a poor choice of words," but declined to say disciplinary action would be taken or that Armendariz would resign. Days later, he did.

Armendariz was a political appointee by the Obama administration and considered an environmental activist. Although the comments of one young, overzealous environmental activist should not be used to indict the whole EPA, they are consistent with the heavy-handed measures for which the agency and the administration have become known.

See also Bankrupt quote; Cap & Trade bill; Coal-fired power plants; Coal industry; EPA's CO2 regulations; Fracking.

Exceptionalism quote: On April 4, 2009, in Strasbourg, France, in response to a reporter's question about whether he believed in American exceptionalism, President Obama replied[220], "I believe in American exceptionalism, just as I suspect that the Brits believe in British exceptionalism and the Greeks believe in Greek exceptionalism."

Fair share: One of President Obama's favorite chants is that rich Americans have to pay their "fair share." We already have a very progressive federal income tax structure. If one's household income is $114,000 or more, it is in the top 10 percent and that small portion[221] of the U.S. population pays 71 percent of the federal income tax revenue although they earn only 43 percent of all income. The top 1 percent of earners pays[222] 38 percent of the total federal income tax bill. They also are not the recipients of Medicaid, food stamps, housing subsidies or other federal entitlement programs. This means that in addition to paying the lion's share of the tax burden, they are taking much less from the federal government. The top 51 percent of earners pays[223] the entire US tax burden. That means the remaining 49.5 percent doesn't pay any federal income tax at all. In September 2013 that number was revised[719] to about 43 percent who do not pay federal income tax. The reduction is attributed to expiring tax cuts instituted during the recession that are now expiring and to increased economic activity. It is still a very large number and has risen from only 14.8 percent in 1984.

Obama has stated that those households making more than $250,000 annually ($200,000 for individuals) should pay more in federal income taxes.[224] The president repeated this mantra incessantly in the months before his reelection. He was at least partially responsible for inciting the class envy of the financially disadvantaged, thus encouraging them to vote for him. If Obama were honestly concerned about fairness, he would insist that the bottom 49.5 percent of income earners pay at least some small portion of the nation's tax burden so that they too would have some skin in the game.

Falklands: An archipelago 290 miles east of South America, these islands have been colonized by the French, British, Spanish, and Argentines. The British reestablished rule of the islands in 1833 and then again in 1982 after Argentina's military junta invaded them. The population of the Falklands is 90 percent British and only 0.1 percent Argentine.

Recently, tensions between Britain and Argentina over the Falklands have been rising. In January 2012, Prime Minister David Cameron made it very clear to the House of Commons that the sovereignty of the Falklands would be defended[225]. The Obama administration intervened[226], but not to support Britain. The administration's statement was titled "U.S. Position on the Falklands (Malvinas) Islands." The use of the Argentine name Malvinas was taken as a signal that President Obama recognized

Argentina's claim to the islands. The statement itself said that this was a problem for Britain and Argentina to solve. In 2010, Secretary of State Hillary Clinton sided with Argentina. Obama echoed her the following year.

Fannie & Freddie: This is shorthand for Fannie Mae and Freddie Mac, which are short for the Federal National Mortgage Association and the Federal Home Loan Mortgage Corporation. Fannie was established in 1938 as a government-sponsored enterprise (GSE) to reduce risk in the mortgage market through mortgage-backed securities, thus expanding the market. Freddie, also a GSE, was created in 1970 to expand the mortgage market by pooling and selling mortgage-backed securities to investors.

Although the political left generally blames the greedy private sector and banks, along with lack of regulation, for the financial crisis in 2008, the role of subprime mortgages played a big part. Just before the housing bubble broke, about 30 percent of mortgages on the books of Fannie and Freddie were considered[227] to be subprime at best. It has become increasingly obvious that these GSEs were not just encouraged, but required—especially under demands of President Clinton's attorney general, Janet Reno—to promote mortgages to and reduce lending standards for people who could not financially qualify for mortgages. Therefore many were destined to be unable to make their mortgage payments.

There were warnings[228] about Fannie and Freddie's insolvency as early as 2001. Starting in 2003, President George W. Bush did repeatedly try to increase regulation of Fannie and

Freddie but was unable to push the increased scrutiny through Congress. Representative Barney Frank (D-MA), the ranking Democrat on the House Financial Services Committee, famously said[229] in 2003, "These two entities—Fannie Mae and Freddie Mac—are not facing any kind of financial crisis," and "The more people exaggerate these problems, the more pressure there is on these companies, the less we will see in terms of affordable housing." Representative Maxine Waters (D-CA.), offered[230], "Mr. Chairman, we do not have a crisis at Freddie Mac, and in particular at Fannie Mae, under the outstanding leadership of Mr. Frank Raines."

In 2008, the government bailed[164] out the GSEs by taking ownership of most of their common stock in exchange for keeping them solvent with government loans. This was a huge government intervention into private financial markets. The bailout consisted of $188 billion, and as of November 2012, only 27 percent of the value of that loan had been earned by the Treasury as dividends on its investment in the GSEs. But, the GSEs had not made any payments on the principal of their loan.

The Federal Housing Finance Agency (FHFA) has been the overseer of the GSEs since they were put in conservatorship in 2008. Under the leadership of acting Director Edward J. DeMarco[231], the FHFA has recently tried to shrink Fannie and Freddie, lure private capital back into the system, and get them working together instead of competing.

The Democrats don't think DeMarco is doing enough to refinance the loans of homeowners whose homes are under water or to help those at risk of foreclosure. DeMarco rejected[232] President Obama's proposal to forgive some of the principal that borrowers owe on their underwater mortgages. If the move had been approved, it would have cost the taxpayers $70 billion to $90 billion over about a year.

Senate Republicans have[233], as of July 18, 2013, been successful in blocking White House attempts to install Mel Watt to replace DeMarco. The Senate vote to confirm Watt is scheduled for September. Watt is expected to be in favor of forgiving principal to borrowers in trouble.

During the 2008 presidential campaign, then Senator Obama was the recipient of the second-greatest amount of contributions[234] made by Fannie and Freddie—just behind Chris Dodd. The top three were all Democrats.

See also Federal Housing Authority.

Fast and Furious: The name given to an ill-conceived program of the Department of Justice (DOJ), ineptly executed by the Bureau of Alcohol, Tobacco, Firearms, and Explosives (ATF), ostensibly intended to identify leaders of major gun trafficking rings supplying guns to Mexican drug cartels. There was also the rumored[235] intent to blame loose regulation of US weapons on the havoc that would result, thus paving the way for stricter control of firearms in the United States.

Operation Fast and Furious backfired when border agent Brian Terry was murdered in December 2010 and two guns found at the site were identified as weapons that were allowed to walk across the border under the Fast and Furious program. Fast and Furious guns were also implicated in at least 150 murders of Mexican civilians, according to an unconfirmed report.[236] It was later learned that there was no attempt[237] made to trace the arms after the ATF had let them walk across the border although the DOJ claimed[238], in a letter to Congress, that every effort had been made to "interdict weapons that have been purchased illegally and prevent their transportation to Mexico." The DOJ was later conveniently allowed[238] to withdraw the letter.

In response to loud criticism of Operation Fast and Furious, the DOJ assigned one of its inspectors general, Michael Horowitz, to investigate. This move was criticized as the fox watching the chicken coop. However, Horowitz did conclude[239] that the White House had obstructed his investigation and that although he had no evidence that Attorney General Eric Holder knew of the operation or was involved in a cover-up, five high-ranking DOJ officials were implicated. On September 19, 2012, Deputy Assistant Attorney General Jason Weinstein resigned. The report indicated that he had not adequately shared critical Fast and Furious information. Kenneth Melson, who had been the acting director of the ATF during the operation, resigned from the DOJ on the same day. Kevin O'Reilly, a White House National Security Council staffer who was directly involved in Fast and Furious, refused to cooperate with Horowitz and was reassigned[240] to a State Department position in Iraq just after Fast and Furious became a scandal. His friend, ATF agent Bill Newell, testified to Congress that he had shared information with O'Reilly. O'Reilly's new Iraq position had already been filled by someone else. Although this all smells, because O'Reilly is no longer a DOJ employee, he is supposedly not subject to inquiry.

To the discredit of the IG report, they implied[605] the operation was the result of a few rogue agents in Arizona.

Holder was finally found in civil and criminal contempt[241] of Congress by a vote of two hundred and fifty-five to sixty-seven over documents requested and not provided. Seventeen Democrats voted for the contempt measure and one Democrat voted present. President Obama claimed[241] executive privilege and that has stopped Congressman Issa's investigation.

Fat-cat bankers quote: On the TV program *60 Minutes* on December 13, 2009, President Obama said[242], "I did not run for office to be helping out a bunch of, you know, fat-cat bankers on Wall Street."

Federal Housing Authority: Commissioner Carol Galante reportedly[243] is pushing banks to make bad loans again. She has been "urging the Justice Department to provide assurance to banks ……… that they will not face legal or financial recrimination if they make loans to riskier borrowers who meet government standards but later default."

Haven't we already run this experiment with Fannie & Freddie?

See Fannie & Freddie.

Federal Housing Finance Agency: See Fannie & Freddie.

Fiscal cliff: a term that refers to a potentially recession-inducing situation should the Bush tax cuts be allowed to expire and the spending cuts required by the Budget Control Act take effect.

The spending cuts were to be divided equally between defense and domestic programs. This across-the-board spending reduction was referred to as sequestration. It was supposed to be so undesirable that neither party would let it happen.

In addition to the spending cuts, President Obama's administration wanted to raise revenues by not only letting the Bush tax cuts expire, but letting the capital gains tax rise and the alternative minimum tax go unchecked, repealing inventory valuation rules, restarting the inheritance tax, imposing a bank tax, increasing the taxes on dividends, death, unemployment insurance, and energy companies, and reducing charitable deductions and home mortgage deductions.

The deadline for stopping these onerous actions was January 1, 2013. Each party played chicken on the cliff's edge—again. The Republicans wanted deductions for the wealthy cut but no increase in the marginal tax rate for the wealthy or anyone else. The Democrats wanted to raise the tax rate on the wealthy—defined as households making $250,000 or more or individuals making $200,000 or more. Neither side seemed anxious to cut entitlement spending, although a budget plan by Representative Paul Ryan (R-WI), passed by the House, did make a good run at it. Social Security and Medicare obligations are the greatest problem, long-term.

On January 1, 2013, sequestration was delayed another two months while more reasonable budget cuts were argued. The so-called Bush tax cuts were preserved for all making $400,000 or less, but no spending cuts were included in the package and the wealthy were hit with an additional six hundred billion in taxes. Payroll tax cuts were allowed to expire, causing a 2 percent rise in paycheck deductions. This hit everybody with a paycheck (77 percent of households), not just the wealthy. This compromise package resulted in forty-one dollars of increased taxation and spending for every dollar cut.

See also Bowles-Simpson; Budget; Budget Control Act.

Fisker: Fisker Automotive[244], an American automaker, was promised $528.7 million in TARP funds for development of electric plug-in hybrid cars, the Karma and the Atlantic (originally called the Nina project). Fisker Automotive was already considered a borderline failing company when the loan was made. Hundreds of Karmas (retailing for $97,000) had to be recalled due to a potential fire hazard, and the Department of Energy (DOE) stopped distributing TARP funds after $193 million of the original $528.7 million loan had been doled out. Fisker had been expected to open a plant in Delaware to produce the less expensive version Atlantic (retailing for $55,000) but decided to produce the car in Finland instead.

More recently, Fisker still trying to avoid bankruptcy has been offered to Chinese automaker, Geely, for about 13 percent of its 2011 value. The deal was not consummated in part due to complications of its US government loan.

Fisker has spent more than $1.4 billion in taxpayer and private funds in less than six years. So much for US job creation and millions of taxpayer dollars down the drain.

It has more recently been determined[597] that over the life cycle of an electric car including its manufacture, it may be responsible for more emission of CO_2 than a conventional gasoline powered car. That provides even less justification for subsidies.

See also A123;TARP.

Flag pin: In October 2007 when asked why he did not wear the American flag pin on his lapel, then presidential candidate Barack Obama said[245] that he stopped wearing it after 9/11 because he thought it had become a "substitute for true patriotism." He was criticized, and in May 2008 he began wearing the flag pin again.

Flexibility quote to Medvedev: See Missile defense shield.

Food Stamps: The food stamp program no longer relies on paper vouchers (stamps) exchanged for food, but employs an electronic benefit transfer (EBT) card and the program is officially titled the Supplemental Nutrition Assistance Program, or SNAP. However, it is still commonly called the food stamp program.

As of December 2012[246], 47.8 million Americans were on food stamps. That is a new all-time record, and is a 70% rise since 2008. The cost has doubled[640] under Obama, but also doubled under Bush. The number is dramatically increasing even though the unemployment rate is decreasing, partially because Obama[641], as part of the Stimulus package, relaxed some requirements such as the income ceiling for recipients and eliminated the work requirement.

The Obama administration withheld[247] bad statistics on the SNAP program from the public until after the November, 2012 election.

Food stamps are not supposed to be available to illegal aliens, and eligibility is supposed to be checked through the government database, Systematic Alien Verification for Entitlements. However, not all states use this database, and the Obama administration is encouraging[248] use by the illegal immigrants and others[652] who traditionally have been reluctant to take advantage of them because of pride or self-reliance.

See also Unemployment rate; Welfare.

Fort Hood: On November 5, 2009, Major Nidal Hassan, an Army psychiatrist and American-born Muslim, opened fire on troops in a medical building at Fort Hood in central Texas. Thirteen adults and one unborn child were killed. Thirty-eight people were wounded. Hassan had shouted[249] "Allahu Akbar" (God is great) just before opening fire.

The Department of Defense defined this incident in the context of workplace violence.[250] Because the Department of Defense and Attorney General Eric Holder have not declared this a terrorist attack, the soldiers injured or killed are not eligible for the Purple Heart and the wounded and the survivors of the dead are not eligible for certain benefits.

In 2011, a Senate report[251] on the incident said that Hassan had become an Islamic extremist and a "ticking time bomb." US officials believe that Hassan was inspired by Anwar al-Awlaki.

President Obama's first public statement[252] after the incident, which came just hours later and while the death toll was still rising, started with a roughly two-minute "shout-out" to an audience member and comments about the necessity of health care reform. His demeanor and focus were inappropriate; he appeared unconcerned and passionless. "Inappropriate" is a charitable description. The following day, November 6, Obama cautioned[253] Americans not to jump to conclusions.

The military court-martial of Hassan for murder began August 6,2013, and Hassan defended himself. He was found guilty on all counts and sentenced to death.

Now it is time for our government to change the description of the event from workplace violence to an act of terror.

See also Anwar al-Awlaki.

Fox News Channel, attack on: In May of 2013 it was learned that James Rosen, a FOX News correspondent had been investigated to determine the source of his information about North Korea's arms testing in 2009. To do this, the FBI got a search warrant[254] from a judge to search his personal e-mail account, and that of his parents without his knowledge. The first two judges turned down the request. The third judge approved. In order to get this search warrant, the FBI had to claim that Rosen was potentially involved in a criminal conspiracy and that he was a flight risk.

Even the New York Times editorial board considered[255] this a threat to the fundamental freedoms of the press to gather news.

Attorney General Eric Holder had signed[254] off on the paperwork to obtain the search warrant and yet testified under oath to the House Judiciary Committee on May 15, 2013, "this is not something I've ever been involved in, heard of, or would think would be wise policy." He testified to that before it became public that he had signed off on the investigation of Rosen.

See also AP leak investigation.

FOX News/Limbaugh quote: In an interview[256] on January 27, 2013, President Obama said, "If a Republican member of Congress is not punished on FOX News or by Rush Limbaugh for working with a Democrat on a bill of common interest, then you'll see more of them doing it."

Fracking: A shorthand term for the hydraulic fracturing[264] of rock formations. The technique is used to increase the volume of fissures, which then collect oil or gas for delivery to the wellbore for extraction. Fracking has become so successful[257] that it has opened up vast new reserves, such as those in the Baaken and Marcellus shale formations, for significant production.

Such success means not just lots of good product recovered, but lots of good jobs, as well. It is estimated in one report[258] that for each producing well in Marcellus shale (Pennsylvania and New York), $5.5 million is directly injected into the economy and sixty-two mostly good-paying, private sector jobs are created.

An EPA report[259] released in December 2011 indicated its test drilling in Wyoming showed evidence of groundwater contamination because the aquifer sampled contained compounds associated with fracking. As it turns out, the EPA had, in fact, drilled into a natural gas reservoir. But, in addition to the natural organic compounds expected in a gas reservoir, there were also several man-made chemicals detected in the samples. This would seem to indicate contamination by the fracking process. But these man-made chemicals were also detected in the "blank" samples that were supposed to analytically represent the "pure" baseline sample. Blanks are part of standard procedure used to help validate results of sampling and analysis techniques. So the blank results of the testing, along with inadequate review of the report, invalidated the EPA's findings.

Canada has been using fracking for thirty-five years[260], and more than 90 percent of its oil and gas wells involve fracking. North Dakota, where drilling in the Baaken formation has exploded, now (June 2013) has the nation's lowest unemployment rate.[261]

In February 2012, officials of the New York Department of Health officials learned that a report[262] had shown fracking could be done in the state with no hazard to public health. The findings of the report were not released at that time but were leaked to the public in January 2013 – almost a year later.

Under the Clean Air Act, the EPA will tighten regulation of methane, a greenhouse gas, released from the wells. A state study[263] near Marcellus Shale drilling sites in Pennsylvania found no water contamination that could be attributed to fracking.

Lisa Jackson, EPA administrator, acknowledged[257] to Congress that there had been no confirmed cases of contamination of water supplies by fracking.

In June 2013, the Democrat-dominated California State Assembly voted overwhelmingly to defeat[619] a fracking-ban bill. They are getting smarter.

A final EPA report mandated by Congress is expected in 2014. Expect it to support regulations that will promote President Obama's green agenda whether or not there is sufficient justification. Stay tuned.

See also Cap & Trade bill; Coal industry; Drilling moratorium; EPA's CO2 regulations; EPA's crucifixion example.

Frank Marshall Davis: See Davis, Frank Marshall.

Fundamental Transformation quotes: On October 30, 2008, in Columbia, Missouri, presidential candidate Barack Obama said[265], "We are five days away from fundamentally transforming the United States of America."

This was not apparently just a poorly thought-out line spoken off the cuff. Eight months earlier, In Milwaukee, Wisconsin, on February 16, 2008, then-Senator Obama said[266], "And together you and I we will change this country and we will transform the world." And a full year prior to that, in announcing his run for the presidency, he said[267], "I'm in this race not just to hold an office but to gather with you to transform a nation."

Gaspard, Patrick: See ACORN.

Gates, Professor Henry Louis: See Beer summit.

GDP: Gross domestic product is defined as the market value of all officially recognized goods and services produced in a country. It includes all consumer, government, and business spending on capital and all net exports. The GDP is used to define whether or not we are officially in recession. Recession is defined as two successive quarters of contracting (negative) GDP. The latest recession officially ended in June 2009 with two successive quarters of positive GDP.

Our GDP was up 1.70 percent[678] in the second quarter of 2013 over the previous quarter and this was later revised up to 2.5 percent.[687] Overall this is good news and shows that the sequester did not hurt the economy. But imports are rising[679] faster than exports and the first quarter's advance was revised down from 1.8 percent to 1.1 percent. We need instead four to six percent growth as in the 80s after the last deep recession. The average GDP growth rate from 1947 to 2013 was 3.23 percent.

See also Gross debt/National debt/Spending as percentage of GDP; Sequestration.

General Carter Ham: he was relieved[268] as commander of Africom (Africa) just after the Benghazi debacle. Leon Panetta, Secretary of Defense, said "... you don't deploy forces into harm's way without knowing what's going on; without having some real-time information about what's taking place, and as a result of not having that kind of information, the commander who was on the ground in that area, General Ham, General Dempsey and I felt very strongly that we could not put forces at risk in that situation." Panetta said Ham had advised against intervention.

There is another take on that. Reportedly General Ham received an order to stand down and refused. His second in command apprehended him and told him he was relieved of command.

The administration's story is that General Ham's normal rotation out of that position was scheduled.

See also Benghazi.

Gibson Guitars: In August 2011, Gibson Guitars in Nashville and Memphis were raided[269] by armed federal agents. Why? They were in potential violation of using foreign endangered exotic woods (ebony and rosewood) that had been certified to have been legally harvested and exported by the supplier, in making their guitars. Even if the charge had some validity, was all the drama and intimidation of a SWAT operation necessary?

Gibson CEO Henry Juszkiewicz is a known contributor to Republican candidates. C.F. Martin, also a fine guitar manufacturer, uses these same woods but they were not raided. C.F. Martin CEO, Chris Martin IV, is a known contributor to Democrats.

There was some limited outrage regarding this incident at the time but it quickly died out. However, in light of the May 2013 revelations of the IRS targeting of Conservative groups and the Justice Department's snooping into the press, suspicion[270] that the raids on Gibson were more than just over-reaction and poor judgment by the Justice Department gained traction.

The Justice Department finally dropped criminal charges against Gibson in August 2012 but only after Gibson agreed to pay $300, 000 to the US Government and make a $50,000 "community service payment" to the National Fish and Wildlife Foundation. They may continue to use ebony and rosewood, but this seems like extortion.

See also AP leak investigation; Corporate culture; IRS scandal.

Global Counterterrorism Forum: Established by President Obama in September 2011 and co-chaired by the United States and Turkey, this is a group of thirty countries seeking to enhance global cooperation in preventing terrorism. The group includes representation of eleven Arab or Muslim countries, but Israel was excluded although it sought membership. It has been reported[271] that Israel was excluded because of fierce objection by Obama's friend[87] Turkish Prime Minister Tayyip Erdogan. Turkey co-chaired the Forum with Secretary Hillary Clinton. Not only does Israel have no membership in the group, but it has not been invited to attend and has not even been mentioned at the meetings.

Under pressure, the Forum has agreed to discuss the possibility of involving non-members such as Israel, but not including them as members of the Forum.[272]

Global Poverty Act: The bill, introduced[273] in 2008 by then Senator Barack Obama, would provide the United Nations with 0.7 percent of the US gross national product—a donation estimated to be worth $845 billion. It was approved by voice vote in the House and then died in the Senate.

This bill was directly tied to the UN's Charter for Global Democracy and the UN millennium development goals that followed.

Almost immediately after Obama's inauguration in 2009, the bill was resurrected[274] as H.R. 2639, the Global Poverty Act of 2009. It died in the House Foreign Affairs Committee.

In November 2011, Bill Gates, representing his foundation, presented[275] to the G20 summit his plan to eradicate world poverty. It included taxes on financial transactions (the Tobin tax), tobacco, aviation fuel, and carbon. Collectively these are sometimes referred to as the Robin Hood tax. These taxes would be enforced by all of the G20 nations. This was the Global Poverty Act resurrected in a different, more global venue. The proposal had insufficient support and failed.

Though this policy has not become law, Obama's relentless pursuit of the plan illustrates just how committed he is to redistribution of US wealth not only to the poor of America but to the poor of the world and his willingness to engage in policies that relinquish our sovereignty in order to accomplish that.

See also Agenda 21.

GM's CEO fired: In March 2009, the Obama administration fired GM's CEO, Rich Wagoner. It may not have been a firing in the strict legal sense, but Wagoner himself said[276] that administration officials "… requested that I step aside as CEO of GM, and so I have." This was done as part of the government bailout and restructuring of GM under TARP. Although there was little sympathy for Wagoner, since GM had reportedly been poorly managed, the federal government's autocratic move to force his leaving was, if not unprecedented, at least very heavy-handed.[277] A company in financial crisis typically goes through bankruptcy court where a judge may fire management. This would have kept politics out of the process, but President Obama bypassed[278] this process. This degree of government intervention in US industry is chilling and possibly illegal, if not unconstitutional.

Part of the reason for GM's financial problems was, supposedly, its emphasis on trucks and SUVs instead of more fuel-efficient small cars and hybrids. However, it is just as plausible to posit that GM had stayed alive because of its trucks and SUVs and that Obama just wanted to change the product line to be more in keeping with his green agenda. He was able to do this and bail out the UAW pension fund, thus rewarding union support for him in the 2008 election.

See also Bondholders, secure; Delphi pensions; Green agenda; TARP.

God damn America quote: See Wright, Reverend Jeremiah.

Green agenda: Green energy companies received $90 billion as part of Obama's stimulus package in 2009. The House Oversight Committee found[279] twenty-two of twenty-six companies that received DOE loan guarantees had junk ratings at the time of the loans.

As of November 2012, the Heritage Foundation reported[279, 280] that nineteen "green" companies that received DOE loan guarantees were now bankrupt including: Abound Solar, Beacon Power, Ener1, Energy Conversion Devices, Evergreen Solar, Mountain Plaza, Olsen's Crop Service and Olsen's Mills Acquisition Co., Range Fuels, Raser Technologies, Solyndra, Spectrawatt, and Thompson River Power.

In addition, A123 Systems, Willard & Kelsey Solar Group, Solar Trust of America, LSP Energy, Uni Solar, and Azure Dynamics have filed for bankruptcy despite infusions of taxpayer dollars. Many other "green" energy companies are closing plants, laying off workers, reporting financial losses, and/or expected[281] to fail despite taxpayer largess.

The DOE's failed stimulus loan program for renewable energy companies has cost[282] $9 billion. But, as much as $48 billion in subsidies and incentives to green energy companies was allocated just in 2011 and 2012. A National Academy of Sciences study[283] determined the government help to have done little or nothing to reduce the US carbon footprint and that it isn't likely to before 2035 —less than 1% reduction over the next twenty-five years. The jobs "saved" have been tallied; many companies failed; the jobs evaporated. What good did taxpayers' dollars do?

In addition, Obama and his administration have made a point of impeding oil, gas, and coal production apparently wherever they could get away with it.

In his remarkable arrogance, Obama is clearly trying to pick and create winners. Free-market capitalism has a much better record of accomplishing this. The other possibility is that he is purposefully wasting money to weaken the economy.

See also A123; Agenda 21; Bankrupt; BP oil spill; Cap & Trade bill; Cash for clunkers; Coal industry; Drilling moratorium; EPA's CO_2 regulations; Fisker; Fracking; Green jobs training program; mpg; Skyrocket quote; Solyndra; Stimulus.

Green jobs training program: The Department of Labor inspector general's report[284] of October 25, 2012 states that the department's $595 million green jobs training program, financed with stimulus money, successfully placed just eleven thousand people in permanent jobs – defined as lasting six months or longer. That is only 16% of those completing the training. Another estimate[285] of the green jobs training effort indicates only a 55% success rate for target placements as of July 2013.

Green Movement: This is the name given to a very large peaceful protest in Iran that started in June 2009 against the rigged election of Mahmoud Ahmadinejad as president. The protesters knew the election to be fraudulent, and it dashed their hopes of a more democratic government. Over the following months, these dissidents became angry and periodically took to the streets. The protesters appealed[286] directly to

President Obama, "Obama , you are either with us or with them." Instead of supporting them, Obama said[287], "I've made it clear that the United States respects the sovereignty of the Islamic Republic of Iran and is not interfering with Iran's affairs."

Many demonstrators were killed, tortured, or raped by the brutal Ahmadinejad regime; the most important activist leaders were put on trial and made to confess on TV; the United States offered no help—even after what some analysts described as a clear call for help from the Green Movement leaders in a long memo[288] sent through channels to Obama. In that memo, the opposition leaders rhetorically asked of the Obama administration, "Will they continue on the track of wishful thinking and push every decision to the future until it is too late, or will they reward the brave people of Iran and simultaneously advance the Western interests and world peace?" The memo also pointed out that the Islamist regime "with its apocalyptic constitution will never give up the atomic bomb."

It seemed to many that this upwelling of democratic sentiment in Iran was a missed opportunity by the Obama administration to advance democracy in the Middle East, pull away from a theocratic dictatorship, put a wrench in Iran's nuclear program, and stop its aggression against Israel.

It later came to light that administration advisers cautioned[289] against supporting the Green Movement and that one of those advisers was Trita Parsi, president of the George Soros-funded[440] National Iranian American Council (NIAC), a powerful Iranian lobbying group.

See also Egypt's Arab spring; Libya's Arab spring; Parsi, Trita; Syria's Arab spring.

Griffin, Richard: see NLRB.

Gross debt as percentage of GDP: Gross debt-to-GDP is the ratio of a country's total debt to its productivity expressed as a percentage. The figure for the United States began to rise steeply in 2007. As President George W. Bush was leaving office and President Obama was starting his first term, the US gross debt-to-GDP was 69.5 percent. It had exploded to 104.8 percent just four years later. That is a 50.8 percent increase in our debt-to-GDP ratio in just 4 years. Passing the 100 percent milestone marker means we are officially bankrupt, since we owe more than our economy is generating. Our gross debt as a percentage of GDP is expected[290] to be 107 percent throughout the rest of the decade. That is almost as high as it was just after World War II. We appear to be on the road to modern day Greece or maybe ancient Rome.

See also Debt; GDP; National debt/spending as percentage of GDP.

GSA scandal: In 2010, the General Services Administration held a conference in Las Vegas that cost the taxpayers $823,000. Jeff Neely, region nine commissioner for the GSA, organized the gathering. Included in the tab were a clown, a mind reader, a bicycle-building exercise, and coins specially made to commemorate the event. The GSA is charged with eliminating wasteful government spending.

In May 2011, well before the scandal broke, Inspector General Brian Miller briefed[292] the GSA administrator, Martha Johnson, on his preliminary findings of inappropriate GSA spending. Johnson was handpicked[293] by President Obama for the GSA Administrator slot. At this point, Obama's staff is reported[292] to have been informed of the questionable expenditures. The warning of the preliminary report was not heeded. In November 2011, Neely took a seventeen-day trip to Hawaii, Guam, and Saipan with his wife. It was billed as official business, of course. But in Neely's own words[294], the trip was to be his wife's birthday present.

In February 2012, the final inspector general's report was released. Johnson, who had taken no action after the preliminary report's findings and instead swept the Las Vegas conference under the rug, resigned.[295] She first fired two officials and put ten others, including Neely, on administrative leave. Two employees are susceptible to criminal charges, but nothing is expected to come of it.

Gun control: In the presidential debate on October 16, 2012, President Obama said[296] that he believed in the Second Amendment but admitted wanting to introduce an assault weapons ban and implied that he would act against "cheap handguns" as well.

See also Small-arms treaty.

Guns or religion quote: At a fund-raising event in San Francisco on April 11, 2008, presidential candidate Barack Obama in Pennsylvania spoke about people in small towns who were frustrated about the state of the economy. He said[297], "And it's not surprising then, they get bitter, they cling to guns or religion or antipathy to people who aren't like them or anti-immigrant sentiment or anti-trade sentiment as a way to explain their frustrations."

Hagel, Chuck: A Republican US senator from Nebraska from 1996 to 2008 and later co-chair of President Obama's Intelligence Advisory Board, he was nominated by Obama on January 7, 2013, to replace Leon Panetta as secretary of defense, but his views on Israel and the Arab/Muslim world were questioned by many including some in his own party.

He was endorsed[298] by People's World, the official magazine of the Communist Party USA. Claire Lopez, senior fellow at the Center for Security Policy, asserted[299] that although Hagel was not directly tied to the NIAC, founded by Trita Parsi, he was affiliated with groups that were.

Hagel was quoted[300] as saying, "The Jewish lobby intimidates a lot of people" and "I'm not an Israeli senator. I'm a United States senator."

In 2000, he was one of only four senators who refused[301] to sign a pro-Israel statement. In 2001, he was one of only two senators who opposed[302] additional sanctions on Iran. In 2005 Senator Hagel opposed[301] requiring the Palestinian Authority to disqualify terror groups from participating in elections. In 2006, he said[303] of our relationship with Israel that "…. it need not and cannot be at the expense of our Arab and Muslim relationships"—almost the exact opposite of what Israeli Prime Minister

Benjamin Netanyahu said in the spring of 2011. In 2007, Hagel voted[304] against designation of the Iranian Revolutionary Guard Corps as a terrorist group.

In spite of his background, Hagel was confirmed as Secretary of Defense.

See also Corporate culture; Israel; Parsi, Trita

"Hard-wired" quote: In Massachusetts in October 2010, President Obama said[305] of his political opponents that they were "hard-wired not to always think clearly."

Hassan, Nidal: See Fort Hood.

Hussain, Rashad: He is the Muslim son of Indian-born American citizen parents. He is a Yale-educated attorney and has been outspoken on the need to combat terrorism. Hussain has a Master of Science degree in Arabic and Islamic studies from Harvard. In 2009, he served[306] as deputy associate counsel to President Obama. In 2010, Obama appointed[306] him as US special envoy to the Organization of Islamic Cooperation.

See also Organization of Islamic Cooperation.

Ibrahim, Samira: an Egyptian activist[649] who has made anti-Semitic and anti-American statements on her social media account and elsewhere. The US State Department rescinded its offering[650] of the *International Women of Courage Award* when her prejudicial statements were publicized.

Ibrahim had first claimed her account had been "stolen," but later stated, "I refuse to apologize to the Zionist lobby in

America regarding my previous anti-Zionist statements under pressure from American government ......"

Ideals quote: In Cairo, Egypt, on June 4, 2009, President Obama said[307] 9/11 had led America to "act contrary to our traditions and our ideals."

See also Apology tour.

I'll walk the picket line quote: In a 2007 campaign speech, then-Senator Barack Obama said[308], "And understand this, if American workers are being denied their right to organize and collectively bargain, when I'm in the White House, I'll put on a comfortable pair of shoes myself. I'll walk that picket line with you as president of the United States."

See also Card check; NLRB; Unions

Immigration: The Development, Relief and Education for Alien Minors (DREAM) Act was first introduced in 2001. Various versions of the bill have failed through the years to get the necessary votes to pass. The legislation stalled in the Senate in May 2011 because Republicans wanted more control of our borders before passing it.

On June 15, 2012, President Obama signed[309] an executive order to be implemented by his Department of Homeland Security that stops deportation of illegal immigrants if they entered the United States before age sixteen, have lived here for five years, are under thirty-one, have a high school diploma or a GED, or have been honorably discharged from the military unless they have committed certain crimes, are national security threats, or lie on a form for application to this "deferred action." This action, called the Dream Act executive order, was expected to apply to 700,000 thousand to 1.4 million people currently in the country and is seen as an overreach of executive power.

In late August 2012, ten federal immigration agents of ICE sued[310] Janet Napolitano, secretary of the Department of Homeland Security (DHS), because the executive order forced them to break the law and ignore their duties. The suit also charges that the directive "unconstitutionally usurps and encroaches upon the legislative powers of Congress." In April 2013, Chris Crane, an ICE agent and union president and other ICE agents won[311] this case. In the decision, Judge Reed O'Connor ruled that DHS had no power to refuse to deport illegal aliens and that the plaintiffs had standing and could proceed in federal court.

The following week, Crane testified[312] before the Senate Judiciary committee regarding the immigration reform legislation drafted by the gang of eight. He pointed out that the legislation was written with input representing illegal aliens but excluded law enforcement from providing input. Taken from Crane's testimony[313] and paraphrasing only slightly for sake of brevity, Crane indicated: agents can't arrest for entering the US illegally or over-staying visas; agents are prohibited from enforcing laws regarding fraudulent documents and identity theft; agents can't arrest for public charges; agents must apply the DREAM act to those in prison thus releasing criminals; ICE deportation numbers have plummeted since 2008 contrary to the opinion of presidential appointees at ICE and DHS.

In January 2013, Obama's administration announced[314] a new DHS rule that would greatly reduce the requirements for illegal immigrants wanting to become US citizens. Under the new rule they would be allowed to stay in the United States during the application and waiting periods, and would have to return to their native country only for an interview and to pick up a visa. This could reduce the period during which families are disrupted from as much as ten years to about a week.

This may be a just rule, but the administration should not have bypassed Congress. This was another overreach by the executive branch.

According to Judicial Watch[696] in early 2012, the Obama administration created a "public advocate" job to help illegal immigrants. The person named to the position confirmed that he would enhance the open borders movement. Tennessee Congresswoman, Diane Black, introduced[697] a bill to prevent ICE from funding the position. It passed both the House and Senate without opposition. President Obama signed the bill and then created the same position under a new name and retained the same employee with the same job description even though congress had specifically de-funded it. Obama has again done an end run around congress.

In June 2013, DHS and the Obama administration came up with another way of confounding the system in their favor. They published[646] the phraseology on line that can be used by illegal aliens wanting to gain access to this country. Illegal aliens are merely walking through border crossings telling the guards that they seek asylum because they have *credible fear* of persecution or torture. They say their fear is of the drug cartels. What a lovely, legal scam. Hundreds per day are now just walking across our southern border. Because it will take years to schedule and process them properly by granting them a hearing to prove that their need for asylum is valid, they are set free and will just blend into society and never turn up for their hearing when it is finally scheduled.

In the meantime, the Obama administration is planning to help[673] Mexico secure its southern border to the tune of almost $2 billion of our tax dollars. Does this make any sense?

See also Arizona.

IPAB: The Independent Payment Advisory Board, commonly called the death panel, created by the Obamacare law, has unfettered power to impose taxes and ration health care. It may issue edicts through the health and human services secretary without congressional approval or even oversight. Other than during a narrow seven-month window in 2017, Congress may never alter an IPAB proposal. This essentially amends the Constitution by statute! The IPAB is not beholden to Congress, the president, the judiciary, or the people. It will effectively ration health care by limiting reimbursements to health care providers. So, in effect, it does become a death panel.

As of May 2013, President Obama had not appointed members of the board and they will probably be none until 2019. Although checks and balances were built into Obamacare which provide for an override of IPAB decisions with a two-thirds vote of each congressional body, with no IPAB appointed, the HHS Secretary (Kathleen Sebelius for now) can make[315] these decisions totally un-checked.

Even Howard Dean, former Governor of Vermont, former Democratic National Committee chair, and an MD himself has problems[634] with this board and acknowledges that it has too much authority and probably will not save any money.

See also Contraceptive mandate; Obamacare.

Iran: This Middle East Arab country does business as Hezbollah in Lebanon, is allied with Syria, supports the Taliban, supplies rockets to Hamas in Gaza that are being used against Israel, is stirring up trouble among the Shiites in Bahrain, continues to enrich uranium for nuclear weapons, and has called[316] for the elimination of the Zionist regime (Israel).

On May 18, 2008, presidential candidate Barack Obama characterized[317] Iran as one of the "tiny" countries that "don't pose a serious threat to us…." While technically true, this statement signaled Israel and Israel's friends in the United States that an Obama administration might not treat Iran as a serious threat to the Jewish state either.

Iran has failed to cooperate with the International Atomic Energy Agency, which continues to doubt Iran's contention that its uranium enrichment program is for only peaceful purposes. The agency strongly suspects[318] that Iran is developing nuclear arms. Iran's development and operation of new centrifuges and a uranium enrichment program are in violation[319] of several UN Security Council resolutions.

At the United Nations on September 27, 2012, Israel's prime minister, Benjamin Netanyahu, expressed[320] a sense of urgency over Iran's accelerating progress toward nuclear weapons. He was said to be considering a preemptive strike. The US defense secretary, Leon Panetta's comments on the subject have been weak if not disingenuous[321].

See also Green Movement; Missile defense shield.

IRS scandal: On Friday afternoon, May 10, 2013, the current head of the determinations unit of the tax exemption division of the IRS, Lois G. Lerner, in response to a question planted by the IRS with one of the IRS lawyers, apologized[322] for inappropriately targeting groups with "tea party, patriot, or 9/12" in their names.

As information would later reveal, this targeting caused many conservative groups to give up on requesting tax-exempt or 501(c)(4) status. Alternatively their applications were greatly delayed. Before the IRS began targeting such groups, a Tea Party group in Illinois received[323] approval of their tax exempt status in ninety days. After targeting began there wasn't a tea party group granted[323] that same status for twenty-seven months and some have waited a full three years. The targeting included very lengthy questionnaires requiring answers to intrusive, personal questions that are illegal for the IRS to ask.

Within about a month it became known[324, 608] that Lerner knew of this practice as early as six months before the 2012 national election, but did not report it and that it was revealed recently (the planted question) only because IRS inspector general J. Russell George's report[325] was about to be made public. The report exposed the unlawful practices.

Lerner was asked to resign. She refused. She was granted leave with pay – a six figure salary. Nice paid summer vacation.

Over the ensuing months and investigations it was claimed[326] that only a few rogue agents in Cincinnati were acting on their own. Then it came out that many others were involved including some in California and Washington, D.C. but nobody knew anything about who gave the orders. The IRS claimed[325] that liberal groups were also targeted. Then it was learned[327] that 292 conservative groups had been culled and submitted to harassment with excessive and personally invasive questions and unreasonable delays, while only six to nineteen (the numbers vary depending on the source) liberal groups were culled and subsequently "processed" with no indication so far that any was subjected to the same delays and invasive excesses.

It has also been revealed that the IRS gave[603] not-yet-approved applications for tax-exempt status of nine Conservative groups to ProPublica, a very liberal organization funded[607] by George Soros; that the application of Z-street, a pro-Israel group, has been delayed/denied[604] because it has a policy that does not comport with Obama's policy regarding Israel; and that Frank Vandersloot[606] who contributed $1 million to Romney's campaign was audited twice by the IRS and once by the Labor Department at a cost to him of $80 thousand in attorney and accountant fees. He was found guilty of nothing and was assessed no penalties. Other Conservative donors[612] have also been audited. This is harassment.

Lerner under oath before Representative Issa's investigative committee professed her innocence and <u>then</u> claimed fifth amendment privileges. If she was going to claim those privileges, she should not have said anything else. She was dismissed but because of the illegal procedure she enlisted, is still under oath and will be re-called.

Sara Hall Ingram was in charge of this tax exempt unit between 2009 and 2012 when most of the screening occurred before Lerner took over. Ingram has not yet been called to testify and has now been promoted[328] to head the office in charge of the Affordable Care Act (Obamacare) enforcement. She received[328] more than $103 thousand in bonuses during the past three years.

Douglas Shulman was the IRS Commissioner from March 2008 until November 2012 and visited the White House 157 times[329] from September 2009 through January 2013 – many more times than any other cabinet member. HHS Secretary Sebelius visited only forty-eight times.[329] In a May 2013 congressional hearing Shulman claimed[330] not to know anything about the targeting although most of it occurred while he was in charge of the IRS.

When President Obama was asked if anyone in the White House knew about the IRS actions before April 22, 2013, his response[331] was a very Clintonian, "I can assure you I certainly did not know anything about the IG report before it was leaked through the press." His parsed and disingenuous answer did not go unnoticed. On May 13 he had said[601], in answer to a question, "I first learned about it from the same news reports that I think most people learned about this. I think it was Friday." Really, Mr. President?

By July 18, 2013 it was revealed[332] in the testimony of Carter Hull that William Wilkins, an Obama administration political appointee and chief counsel in the office that led the targeting, was implicated. Wilkins met with Obama on April 23, 2012 – two days before IRS agents were provided with new guidance on how to scrutinize tea party and conservative groups. Just one day later, Wilkins' boss, Doug Shulman (IRS commissioner at the time) met with Obama. The day after that, Wilkins issued new guidelines on how to process tea party applications. The cast of actors is moving closer to the White House[615].

The targeting appears to be vengeful and unlawful. It was clearly not due to the bad judgment of just a few rogue agents in Cincinnati. If the rogue agent excuse sounds familiar see the entry for Fast and Furious.

Islamic Society of North America: see Magid, Mohamed; Mattson, Ingrid; Mustapha, Kifah.

Israel: President Obama's relationship with Israel and its prime minister, Benjamin Netanyahu, has been chilly at best.

In July 2009, *The Washington Post* reported[333] that in a closed meeting between President Obama and select Jewish leaders, President Obama said to them, "Look at the past eight years; during those eight years, there was no space between us and Israel, and what did we get from that? When there is no daylight, Israel just sits on the sidelines, and that erodes our credibility with the Arab states."

In November 2009, Obama made it clear he opposed[334] Israel's plan to build dwellings in a section of the West Bank that Israel had captured in the 1967 war and made part of Jerusalem – east Jerusalem. Again[335] in 2010, presumably with Obama's blessings, Vice-President Biden, Secretary of State Clinton, and chief presidential adviser David Axelrod separately and strongly criticized Israel's plan to build apartments in Jerusalem. The construction site was not disputed territory but a Jewish neighborhood under construction since the early 1990s. Very soon after the criticism, Obama snubbed[336] Prime Minister Netanyahu at a White House visit, abandoning the prime minister to have dinner with his family; the prime minister got not even a photo-op. The shabby treatment of the Israeli leader was seen as retaliation for not yielding on the building of settlements in east Jerusalem.

In 2010, Israeli Ambassador Michael Oren said[337], "Israel's ties with the United States are in their worst crisis since 1975 … a crisis of historic proportions."

In May 2011, Obama called[338] for Israel's return to the borders existing before the 1967 Six-Day War. He said "… the borders of Israel and Palestine should be based on the 1967 lines with mutually agreed swaps so that secure and recognized borders are established for both states." Netanyahu responded[338] the next day in a press conference held jointly with Obama that a return to those borders would leave Israel "indefensible" and that "the viability of a Palestinian state cannot come at the expense of Israel's existence."

In September 2012, Obama refused[339] to meet with Prime Minister Netanyahu during the UN General Assembly session. Netanyahu volunteered[340] to go to the White House if that would better accommodate Obama's schedule. Obama did not agree to the meeting and instead appeared that evening on *The Late Show with Dave Letterman*. His priorities are questionable.

In June 2013, the US government published[614] on-line about one thousand pages of construction details of a top secret Israeli missile base the US was helping them expand. Supposedly, this was done to give potential contractors enough detail to bid or so the story goes. It was later described as a mistake. What is wrong with providing information by special courier or even snail mail if potential construction firms are interested in bidding? This is inexcusable.

There have been many other situations in which the President has implied his dislike or disrespect of Prime Minister Netanyahu, or Israel. There is a pattern that is undeniable.

See also Apology tour; Hagel, Chuck; Iran.

Joe the Plumber: See Redistribution quotes.

Jones, Van: In March 2009, President Obama appointed Van Jones to the newly created czar position for green jobs. Jones was an attorney and well-known activist for the environment and civil rights.

It did not take long for his radical connections and sentiments to surface. He had been a self-avowed[341] communist, allegedly for ten years; was a signatory to a 9/11 "truther" petition; formed[342] a socialist group, Standing Together to Organize a Revolutionary Movement (STORM), in the 1990s, and publicly called[343] the previous President George W. Bush and the Republican Congress "ass holes" in a speech at Berkeley University just a month before his appointment by Obama.

Jones could also be called a racist for some of his statements.[344] He has said that only suburban white kids shoot up schools, and "You've never seen a Columbine done by a black child." He also claimed[341], "The white polluters and the white environmentalists are essentially steering poison into the people of color communities, because they don't have a racial justice frame."

Jones generated so much criticism and controversy that he resigned in September 2009, just six months after his appointment. He remained politically active, became a vocal advocate of the Occupy Wall Street movement, and has done work with the George Soros-funded MoveOn.org.

See also Czars; Occupy Wall Street.

Kenya funding: There is a law referred to as the Siljander Amendment (an amendment to the FY 2006 Appropriations Act) which restricts US funds from being used to "lobby for abortion or the liberalization or legalization of abortion in foreign countries."

117

Twenty-three million in taxpayer dollars was given to the US Agency for International Development (USAID) to support the "yes campaign" in favor of Kenya's new constitution, designed to curtail the excessive powers of the country's president. However, some of this money went toward lobbying[345] for more liberal abortion provisions in the new constitution. In 2010, four Republican representatives questioned this expenditure, citing the Siljander Amendment in a letter to USAID's inspector general. The IGs report dismissed the abortion lobbying allegations.

In 2011, a subsequent GAO report[346] by the Government Accountability Office (GAO) revealed that USAID granted some of the money to the International Development Law Organization, which advised the committee writing the Kenyan constitution that it "might consider adding language to make clear that the fetus lacks constitutional standing, and that the rights of women under these articles therefore take priority." This same GAO report revealed that $18 million went to a number of groups, at least one of which openly worked to reverse Kenya's anti-abortion law.

Vice President Joe Biden visited Kenya in 2010 to promote the new constitution. He said[347] that Kenyans had to adopt the new constitution in order "to allow money to flow" to Kenya. Quid pro quo? President Obama's undersecretary of state for democracy and global affairs did not cooperate[348] with the GAO investigation. President Obama's administration may have violated the Siljander Amendment by indirectly suggesting relaxation of Kenyan anti-abortion law and advocating the new Kenya constitution.

118

In addition to being pro-abortion, the new Kenyan constitution is pro-sharia. It provides for sharia courts throughout Kenya and grants them a degree of legal authority over Muslims. These courts threaten Christians, who do not have a similar court system, and moderate Muslims, as well. Why would the United States spend millions to promote such a constitution?

An interesting sidebar to these issues is that Kenyan Raila Odinga, who claims to be President Obama's cousin, was promoted[349] for president of Kenya by then-Senator Barack Obama in 2006. Odinga lost the election but was made prime minister in 2008. He is described as a communist with ties to Abdulkader Al-Bakri of Saudi Arabia, who is a sponsor of al-Qaeda. Odinga has also reportedly[349] signed an agreement with a Muslim group to be of no assistance in the apprehension and extradition of terrorists.

Keystone XL pipeline: In January 2012, President Obama rejected[350] rapid approval of the oil pipeline from northwest Canada to Texas refineries on the Gulf Coast although it had been studied for three years. The reason given for the rejection was that Congress had forced the administration to decide on a permit in too short a period of time to adequately examine alternative routes to avoid traversing real estate above the Ogallala aquifer.

The potential environmental impact had been studied for three years and found to be benign. Although considered shallow, the Ogallala aquifer is nonetheless one hundred to four hundred feet below the surface. That is a lot of buffer in case of a pipeline breach or a spill.

The decision to reject construction was seen as a tactic to delay approval past the November 2012 election so as not to upset the Democrats' base of environmentalists who oppose it. It has been estimated that construction of the pipeline would create at least twenty thousand direct and indirect jobs, reduce our dependence on other foreign oil, and generally stimulate the US economy. Without assurance of a US market for its oil, Canada is exploring the possibility of another pipeline to the Pacific to accommodate oil tankers for export to China.

In March 2012, under criticism and pressure, President Obama yielded just enough to approve[351] the 485-mile leg of the pipeline south from Cushing, Oklahoma. This section of pipeline would alleviate a choke point for oil produced domestically but would do nothing to get Canadian oil to our refineries. It turns out that this southern leg did not even need Obama's approval, since the only federal permits required for this part of the pipeline are typically handled by the Army Corps of Engineers, not the president. However, this move allowed Obama cover from those accusing him of pandering to the environmental lobby for votes and from charges that he was causing increases in gasoline prices. Completion of the Keystone XL pipeline, would require an additional 1,179 miles of construction, and is still obstructed by the Obama administration.

The pipeline builder, TransCanada, has submitted a new application to the Obama administration. There have now been almost five years of review, a new route avoiding the more sensitive areas of the aquifer has been established, and there are no more bureaucratic hoops left.

On June 25, 2013, in a speech at Georgetown University, Obama said[352] that the pipeline would be approved, "only if this project does not significantly exacerbate the problem of carbon pollution. The net effects of the pipeline's impact on our climate will be absolutely critical to determining whether the project is allowed to go forward."

Americans stand to lose jobs, oil that will make us more independent, oil that will help control gasoline prices, a competitive advantage with China, and a shot in the arm to our economy if the pipeline is not approved.

See also Climate change; Drilling moratorium; EPA's CO2 regulations; Fracking; Green energy program.

Kick ass quote: In an interview aired on national television on June 8, 2010, President Obama said[353] he had been talking to experts regarding the BP oil spill "so I know whose ass to kick."

See also BP oil spill; Drilling moratorium.

Khalidi, Rashid: See Arab-American Action Network.

Kill list: President Obama has a list[354] of targets (people) whom the military is authorized to kill. Anwar al-Awlaki was reportedly put on this kill list in April 2010. The kill list is secret, and the public is not privy to the criteria used for being put on the list;

nor is Congress. The list is reviewed every Tuesday morning when President Obama is in Washington.

Under the Constitution, it is not lawful for the president to order any killing by the military except when the United States has been attacked or attack is imminent or Congress has declared war. Under federal law, civilians can be ordered to kill only if someone has been sentenced to death by a court of law, and the sentence is upheld on appeal.

CIA personnel are civilians. Therefore the excuse that drones used in these assassinations are CIA-operated is not justification under the Constitution or federal law for this use.

Obama is alone acting as judge, jury, and executioner. For all of President George W. Bush's overreach during his war on terror, President Obama has taken this to another level and may be guilty of an impeachable offense.

See also al-Awlaki, Anwar.

Kimathi, Ayo: a Department of Homeland Security[670] employee, described as a small business specialist, Kimathi runs a website, www.waronthehorizon.com as a part time endeavor. He uses the nom de plume of the "Irritated Genie" and his website is dedicated to "properly educating Black people to prepare for racial warfare."

The DHS has purchased abnormally large amounts of ammunition – so large that the House of Representatives voted, June 5, 2013, to block[672] further funds for ammunition purchase until there is an accounting and history presented to them. One of Kimathi's tasks[671] at DHS is procurement of guns and ammunition for ICE.

What is this man doing anywhere near DHS?

Labor force participation rate: See Unemployment rate.

Law: Tax law apparently applies only to those not of political privilege as shown by the fact that Obama's executive office staff owed[355] $833, 970 in back taxes.

Lawsuits against Obamacare: Many Catholic institutions, organizations, and hospitals, including the Archdiocese of New York and Notre Dame University; one evangelical college, and at least seven Christian-owned businesses have filed[152] lawsuits against the Obama administration over Obamacare's mandate to purchase health care insurance and/or abortion-inducing drugs. The mandate is seen by many as an infringement on religious freedom.

Ironically, the Religious Freedom Restoration Act[150,151] of 1993, introduced by two Democrats, Senator Edward Kennedy and then-Representative Chuck Schumer, is at the heart of the lawsuit. This act protects religions from laws that impose restrictions on religious practices.

In February 2013, the Obama administration, under pressure, dropped[356] the requirement of religiously affiliated hospitals, universities, and social service agencies to directly provide contraceptive insurance coverage to its employees even if those institutions provided services to those not of their religion. However, the insurance companies, according to the

Obama administration, would pick up that part of the insurance so that the employees would still be covered. The Catholic hierarchy still objected because the result was the same and the relaxation of the rules merely obscured who was paying for the coverage.

Religious, not-for-profit institutions are not the only objectors to the contraceptive mandate. Some private, for profit businesses whose owners object on religious grounds are also suing. Among these is Hobby Lobby which describes[357] itself as a "biblically founded business." The lower court decision went against Hobby Lobby. However, the 10th Circuit Court of Appeals on June 27, 2013, sent the decision back to the Oklahoma lower court saying it was wrong not to grant Hobby Lobby an injunction. Hobby Lobby has more than five hundred stores and was facing a fine on July 1, 2013, of one hundred dollars per day per employee for thirteen thousand employees if it had not received the injunction. The case will now proceed without the company's having to pay the fines.

Some of these lawsuits are likely to be dismissed in lower courts; some could make it to the Supreme Court. The issue is not resolved.

See also Contraceptive mandate.

Leadership failure quote: In 2006, then-Senator Barack Obama said[358], "The fact that we are here today to debate raising America's debt limit is a sign of leadership failure. It is a sign that we now depend on ongoing financial assistance from foreign countries to finance our government's reckless fiscal policies. ... America has a debt problem and a failure of leadership. Americans deserve better." Yes they do.

See also Credit rating.

Lew, Jack: Nominated in January 2013 to replace the departing Timothy Geithner as treasury secretary, Lew was most recently President Obama's chief of staff and before that was director of the Office of Management and Budget (OMB). In 2008, while at Citigroup[359], he received a greater than $900 thousand bonus (that is in addition to his greater than $1 million salary) after Citi received a $45 billion TARP bailout by US taxpayers.

At a 2011 Senate hearing while OMB director, he was challenged by Senator Jeff Sessions (R-AL) with his own words[360]: "Our budget will get us over the next several years to the point where we can look the American public in the eye and say we are not adding to the debt anymore." Mr. Lew was given several opportunities during the hearing to retract that statement. He did not. According to the administration's own numbers, the budget in question (which received zero votes in the Senate) would have added $13 trillion to the debt.

Lew has also asserted[361] that Social Security is "entirely self-financing," and he is widely suspected[362] of being behind the last-minute $400 billion tax hike requested by Obama in 2011. That surprise proposition killed the deficit deal that House Speaker John Boehner had hammered out with Obama. Agreement was very close when the deal-breaker was popped.

Confirmed as treasury secretary in February 2013, Lew is likely to perpetuate the policies of the president's first term:

higher taxes, more spending, and no entitlement reform, thus leading to more debt—not less as Lew disingenuously suggested in 2011.

See also Budget; Debt ceiling.

Libya's Arab spring: Mass demonstrations were probably triggered by the self-immolation of a Tunisian street vendor on December 17, 2010, after his government took his job away. In February 2011, protests started in Benghazi, Libya, against Moammar Gadhafi's dictatorship. Gadhafi responded with brutal force against his people, and the UN Security Council imposed sanctions on him and his family.

In March, a coalition[363] of many countries, led by France and the United Kingdom and including the United States, was formed around a UN authorizing mandate to protect the Libyan people from attack by their government. A NATO committee had control of the no-fly zone to prevent Gadhafi's attacks from the air on the rebels. NATO alone was responsible for military action, with a Royal Canadian Air Force lieutenant-general in command. This meant that the US military was under command of NATO, operating with a UN mandate. The US assets committed to the joint effort included eleven ships, attack aircraft, stealth bombers, F-16 fighters, missile-armed drones, and tanker aircraft.

By the end of August 2011, rebel protesters had taken control of Tripoli. In October, Gadhafi was captured and killed and the war ended.

Throughout the Libyan uprising, President Obama was operating without the approval[364] of Congress. It is not clear that the War Powers Act gave him the authority to participate in this NATO action. But it is reported[365, 366] by a knowledgeable source and widely accepted that Obama, in addition, secretly transferred arms to rebel forces in Libya to aid in Gadhafi's overthrow although it was known that al-Qaeda had infiltrated those forces. This would seem to violate[367] the War Powers Act.

According to that act, clearly after sixty to ninety days of involvement, even the NATO-led mission had to be terminated unless Congress authorized our participation in it to continue and of course it did not.

Furthermore, the goal of the mission changed from defending civilians to forcing Gadhafi from power. Gadhafi had given up his quest for nuclear weapons development and was not an immediate threat to the United States. In using the UN authorization and the cover of a NATO coalition, Obama relinquished our national sovereignty and bypassed the constitutional authority of our Congress.

Asked to explain why he had circumvented Congress, Obama asserted that our military involvement was not restricted under the War Powers Act because it fell short of full-blown hostilities. This was seen by some as a creative argument at best, but, more importantly it is a precedent for future presidents' unilateral war-making powers.

Obama's justification for US intervention was that Gadhafi threatened the imminent massacre of his people—

essentially the same justification as the UN mandate. This justification for action begs comparison with our inaction during the anti-Assad uprising in Syria and with our inaction during Iran's Green Movement uprising.

The overarching concern surrounding the Arab spring uprisings is whether bad, authoritarian dictators will be replaced with bad, autocratic theocracies not friendly to the United States instead of by a more democratic style of governance.

See also Benghazi; Egypt's Arab spring; Green Movement; Syria's Arab spring; War Powers Act.

Magid, Mohamed: Sudanese by birth but a US resident since he was very young, Magid[368, 369] is an imam and a member of the Department of Homeland Security's Countering Violent Extremism Working Group. He also worked with Secretary of State Hillary Clinton and her office and the National Security Council. Magid is also the president of the Islamic Society of North America, a Muslim group reported to be the largest Muslim organization in North America, claiming four thousand members in 2008. This organization occupies a headquarters complex valued at more than $49 million. The cost of this facility was borne, in part, by financing from international sources. The stated goals of this organization sound reasonable, but the group is nonetheless a subject of controversy and criticism. It has been investigated and found to have no ties to terrorism. Magid is also the leader of the five thousand-member All Dulles Area Muslim Society.

See also All Dulles Area Muslim Society.

Mattson, Ingrid: Asked by President-elect Obama to speak at his 2009 inauguration prayer service[370] at Washington's National Cathedral, she is a Muslim convert and was at the time president of the Islamic Society of North America, a Muslim Brotherhood-linked group. Her selection sent a message to the Muslim world.

See also Magid, Mohamed; Mustapha, Kifah.

Missile defense shield: Part of a US ballistic missile defense capability first scheduled for Poland and the Czech Republic under President George W. Bush, the system was intended to protect against missiles from Iran. Russia opposed the system. The plan was canceled[371] on September 18, 2009 (the anniversary of Poland's invasion by the Soviet Union in 1939) by President Obama, who appeased Russia and apparently got nothing in return. The action to kill the program caused mixed reactions in Poland. The preponderance of Poles supported Obama's decision. Many Polish leaders opposed it. The sentiment in the Czech Republic was similarly mixed.

New plans announced in 2011 called for missile defense installations in Romania and Turkey to defend against potential Iranian attacks. However, on March 26, 2012, Obama, speaking unguardedly in the presence of an open microphone, told[372] Russian President Dmitri Medvedev, "This is my last election. After my election I have more flexibility." Medvedev's response was, "I understand. I will transmit this information to Vladimir," referring to Vladimir Putin, Russia's prime minister. This exchange concerned "particularly missile defense."

This could not please Israel or any other country feeling threatened by Iran.

See also START.

Mogahed, Dalia[373, 374]: Born in Cairo, she is a pro-sharia adviser to President Obama. She is a leader of the US-Muslim Engagement Project, which favors outreach to the Muslim Brotherhood. Mogahed is also a senior analyst and executive director of the Gallup Center for Muslim Studies. In 2009, she was appointed to Obama's Advisory Council on Faith-Based and Neighborhood Partnerships. She has also contributed to the DHS Advisory Council's Countering Violent Extremism Working Group.

Over a nine-month period, Mogahed neglected[375] to sign a letter from Former Muslims United pledging to honor the freedom of former Muslims to choose a personal belief other than Islam. She also apparently did not sign[376, 377] a fall 2009 pledge from the same organization that repudiated the sharia law consensus permitting execution of apostates from Islam.

Mosque restoration: US funds have long been contributed to help preserve the cultural heritage of foreign lands. However, the Code of Federal Regulations states that USAID funds "may not be used for the acquisition, construction or rehabilitation of structures to the extent those structures are used for inherently religious activities." The US Ambassadors Fund for Cultural Preservation, operated out of the State Department, allows funding of religious structures if they have cultural importance.

So giving money to mosques, churches, or temples is a gray area due to separation of church and state considerations.

However, as reported by one source[379] "the specific funding of mosques appears to be directed since 2009." Although USAID allocated $18.8 billion[378] for cultural heritage projects in 2010, they have not provided the amount spent on mosques. It is, however, strongly suspected that more has been spent on mosques than on churches. Only one synagogue could be identified that may have received funding from the Ambassadors Fund for Cultural Preservation and that was in Turkey; President Obama has a special friendship with Turkish Prime Minister Tayyip Erdogan. On the other hand, a State Department report[380] shows "zero construction efforts on historic Jewish synagogues." Good data seem hard to come by on this subject.

It appears that some cultural heritage funding actually was used to purchase computer equipment for mosques in Mali and Tajikistan. Where is the quality control on spending of US tax dollars? These funds are supposed to go for preservation of cultural heritage. Does anybody care?

Whether it is legal or not to provide taxpayer money to religious institutions, it is difficult to swallow that many millions of our dollars are going to restore Muslim mosques while Muslims are persecuting and killing Christians (thousands since 2009), destroying Christian homes, and burning Christian churches in many of the same countries and even the same areas where we are helping to restore their mosques. Atrocities have occurred[381] against Christians in Egypt, Nigeria, off the coast of Tanzania in Zanzibar, Pakistan and other countries.

mpg: The EPA's fuel economy standards, published in the Federal Register on May 7, 2010, called for greenhouse gas/fuel economy standards for new, model year 2010–16 motor vehicles. These standards will cost the auto industry an estimated $51.7 billion. Just two weeks later, the White House announced[382] plans for even tougher standards for model years 2017–25.

The new rules require new passenger vehicles sold in the United States to average 54.5 mpg by 2025, up from 29 mpg today—an 88 percent increase in fuel economy.

See also Climate change; Green agenda; EPA's CO2 regulations; Cash for clunkers.

Muslim Brotherhood: Also called the Society of Muslim Brothers, it was established in Egypt in 1928. It is a worldwide Islamic movement of Muslims that encompasses religious, political, and social beliefs and behaviors. It has grown to become the Arab world's most influential movement and is the parent of the Sunni terrorist groups al-Qaeda and Hamas.

The Muslim Brotherhood's credo states, "Allah is our objective; the Quran is our law; the Prophet is our leader; Jihad is our way; and death for the sake of Allah is the highest of our aspirations." The movement's goals include the imposition of sharia law on society and the liberation of Muslims from foreign imperialism.

In Egypt, the Muslim Brotherhood had been illegal as a political party since 1954, and this suppression was reinforced in 1981 when President Anwar Sadat was murdered because the Brotherhood opposed his 1979 peace treaty with Israel. Although technically not a political party, the Muslim Brotherhood has found its way into politics—for example, through Hamas and Egypt's Freedom and Justice Party. The Muslim Brotherhood was recently legalized in Egypt after President Hosni Mubarak's forced resignation, and the new president (under house arrest and then to a hospital), Mohamed Morsi, is a member of the Brotherhood.

In January 2012, the deputy leader of the Freedom and Justice Party, an Egyptian Islamist political party with strong ties to the Muslim Brotherhood, and Muslim Brotherhood member said[383] that Egypt's Muslim Brotherhood will not recognize Israel "under any circumstances." In this same interview with an Arabic newspaper, he doubled-down, calling Israel "an occupying criminal enemy."

Ayman al-Zawahiri, Osama bin Laden's deputy, was a Muslim Brotherhood member; Khalid Sheikh Mohammed, mastermind of 9/11, was a Muslim Brotherhood member. In Syria, the bloody uprisings against Bashar al-Assad could well result in another coup for the Muslim Brotherhood.

See also Abedin, Huma Mahmood; Egypt's Arab spring; Syria's Arab spring.

Muslim call to prayer quote: In February 2008, in an interview[384] with a *New York Times* reporter, presidential candidate

Barack Obama the Muslim call to prayer was "one of the prettiest sounds on earth at sunset." He is also reported to have recited the first few lines of the prayer with a first-class Arabic accent:

> Allah is Supreme! Allah is Supreme!
>
> Allah is Supreme! Allah is Supreme!
>
> I witness that there is no god but Allah.
>
> I witness that there is no god but Allah.
>
> I witness that Muhammad is his prophet.

Muslim country quote: On June 3, 2009, in a French interview, President Obama said[385] that based on population, the United States would "be one of the largest Muslim countries of the world." According to estimates of the US Muslim population (there are no hard numbers available), this is not true. However, Obama did say it and was apparently trying to appeal to the Muslims in Europe.

See also Apology tour.

Mustapha, Kifah: A Chicago imam[386] and a fund-raiser for Hamas with ties to the Muslim Brotherhood, he was named as an unindicted co-conspirator during a 2004 trial targeting the Holy Land Foundation for Relief and Development, a front group for Hamas, but was never charged.

In 2009, Mustapha graduated[387] from the FBI's "citizen academy." As part of that program, he toured[657] the top secret

134

facility of the National Counterterrorism Center. In 2010, his appointment to the Illinois State Police as its first Muslim chaplain was revoked after a background check. In 2012, he spoke[388] at the Countering Violent Extremism Workshop for the National Capitol Regions. He has also spoken[389] about the All Dulles Area Muslim Society partnering with local law enforcement.

See also All Dulles Area Muslim Society.

NASA: The National Aeronautics and Space Administration was established by President Dwight Eisenhower in 1958. Its mission was to "pioneer the future in space exploration, scientific discovery and aeronautics research." NASA has been responsible for landing the first man on the moon, the international space station, Skylab, and the space shuttle.

When President Obama took office, he appointed Charles Bolden as NASA administrator, killed[390] the moon-mission program, and shifted[390] the mission from space exploration to Muslim diplomacy.

In February 2010, Administrator Bolden confirmed[390] that the president wanted him to "find ways to reach out to dominantly Muslim countries." Months later, in an interview[391] with Al Jazeera, Bolden elaborated, ".... he charged me with three things. One was he wanted me to help re-inspire children to want to get into science and math; he wanted me to expand our international relationships; and third, and perhaps foremost, he wanted me to find a way to reach out to the Muslim world and engage more with dominantly Muslim nations to help them feel good about their historic contribution to science and engineering—science, math, and engineering."

A former NASA administrator called[391] this a "perversion of NASA's purpose."

National Counterterrorism Center: This government organization operates in an unmarked building in McLean, Virginia. Established in 2003 under a different name, it is responsible for our national and international counterterrorism efforts.

As reported[392] in mid-December 2012, Attorney General Eric Holder gave the center sweeping new powers to store dossiers on US citizens, even if they are not suspected of crimes. Earlier in 2012, Holder granted the agency the authority to copy entire government databases holding flight records, casino employee lists, the names of Americans hosting foreign exchange students and other data and to store them for up to five years. That gives the center the ability to mine these databases for suspicious patterns of behavior. The databases on US citizens may also be handed over to foreign governments. What?

See also NSA.

National debt as percentage of GDP: The national debt-to-GDP ratio, expressed as a percentage of GDP, is the amount of government debt (borrowing) of a country in relation to its GDP. In general, the lower the ratio, the better the economy's health. Our national debt-to-GDP ratio was 72 percent in 2011 and is estimated[393] to be 72.5 percent of GDP in 2012. For comparison, expected 2012 figures for Spain = 84.1 percent, France = 90.2

percent, and Greece = 156.9 percent. As this number increases, the value of the dollar is likely to decrease, which may cause interest rates to rise and thus slow the economy. It has been estimated[291] that a national debt-to-GDP ratio above 90 percent could slow the economy by 1.3 percent per year.

Our national debt-to-GDP ratio was just 36 percent[394] at the end of 2007 before the most recent recession.

See also GDP; Gross debt/spending as percentage of GDP.

New Black Panthers: On Election Day 2008, two members of the New Black Panthers Party, dressed in military-style black uniforms, berets, and boots, stood outside a polling place in Philadelphia intimidating voters. One brandished a nightstick. Sometimes they blocked the entrance to the poll and made incendiary comments. This was documented[395] on videotape. The Justice Department, still under President George W. Bush, filed charges against three Black Panthers. They did not respond, and the court entered a default judgment against them.

After President Obama was elected, his Justice Department under Eric Holder dismissed[396] the charges and imposed a sham restraining order on Malik Zulu Shabazz, chairman of the New Black Panthers Party, ordering him to refrain from displaying a weapon within one hundred feet of a Philadelphia polling place for the next three years—something that is already illegal.

The case was dismissed although an eyewitness, former civil rights attorney and Democratic activist Bartle Bull, testified[397] that this was "the most blatant form of voter intimidation I've ever seen." Six DOJ lawyers reportedly recommended[398] continuing to pursue the case. An Obama administration political appointee, Associate Attorney General Thomas Perrelli, overruled their recommendations and the case was dropped by the DOJ.

The DOJ's decision led to accusations of bias against white victims of civil rights violations. J. Christian Adams, an attorney in the DOJ, resigned his post in 2010 over the department's handling of this case. He held a voting rights enforcement position in the civil rights division, and he and his supervisor, Christopher Coates, both testified[399] against the handling of the case by DOJ.

DOJ attorney Thomas Perez gave false testimony[400] before the US Commission on Civil Rights about political involvement and pressure in the case. In fact, there is strong evidence[400] that AG Holder and the White House were involved in the decision to drop the case.

Even the original Black Panther Party denounced[401] the New Black Panthers Party for operating on hatred of white people.

In March 2011, at a House oversight hearing about the DOJ's decision to drop the case, Attorney General Eric Holder referred[402] to the black population of this country as "my people." This would tend to confirm a suspicion of bias by a man who is supposed to be the attorney general for all Americans, not just his people.

It would appear that our attorney general is guilty of violating the equal protection clause of the Constitution (Fourteenth Amendment, section 1).

See also Trayvon Martin.

NLRB: The National Labor Relations Board, acting on behalf of the International Association of Machinists union, sued Boeing because it wanted to open a new plant in South Carolina, a right-to-work state, instead of Washington State where the union had gone on strike against the company. The plant did open in South Carolina in June 2011 while hearings proceeded. Six months later, the NLRB ended its legal pursuit when the union withdrew charges because it had reached a four-year collective bargaining agreement with Boeing that guaranteed the 737 MAX aircraft would be produced in Washington, not South Carolina. There was reportedly[403] jubilation among the NLRB members over this outcome, which does not connote impartiality.

The five-member NLRB is charged with administering the National Labor Relations Act. The board acts in a judicial capacity to assure the propriety of labor practices and is charged to take sides with neither management nor union. However, recent appointments to this board have cast even more doubt on its ability to be impartial.

Certain presidential appointments must be confirmed by the Senate. NLRB appointments are in this category. President Obama, knowing that his desired appointments to the NLRB would be controversial, waited until January 4, 2012, during a twenty-day Senate break for the holidays to make recess appointments[404], supposedly in accordance with provisions of article II, section 2 of the Constitution.

But the Senate was not technically in recess. It was convened every few days for a short period of time to avoid just such appointments. Although provided for in the Constitution, Obama's recess appointments appear to have circumvented the intent as explained in Federalist Paper 67 and denied the Senate its constitutional authority.

Two of these nominations, Richard Griffin and Sharon Block, were not even nominated until two days before lawmakers left town, were so rushed that they did not make the administration's tracking list of appointees, and were referred to the Senate for confirmation with insufficient time for routine civil and criminal background checks.

Griffin was an attorney for the 400,000-member International Union of Operating Engineers, a union with documented[405] connections to the mob and corruption. He also served on the board of directors for the AFL-CIO's Lawyers Coordinating Committee.

Block's independence was questionable, because she served as deputy assistant secretary for congressional affairs in the Department of Labor under Secretary Hilda Solis, an advocate of forced unionism.

The Obama administration and its appointments to the NLRB are obviously pro-union and are seen as abusing federal labor law to discourage job providers like Boeing from locating in right-to-work states. Obama's action was challenged[406] in a lawsuit joined by forty-two Republican senators alleging that the president operated outside the Constitution in making the appointments and that subsequent decisions by the board are therefore invalid.

The US Court of Appeals for the D.C. Circuit heard arguments on December 5, 2012, and ruled on January 25, 2013 that Obama's three appointments were unconstitutional because the Senate was technically in session. If the ruling stands, 218 decisions made by the illegally appointed board should also be invalidated. The Obama administration has decided not to invalidate the decisions and has petitioned the Supreme Court to overturn the decision.

In the meantime, another appeals court, the US Court of Appeals of the Third Circuit, has upheld[407] the D.C. Circuit Courts decision in a separate case involving the same issue.

Senate majority leader, Harry Reid threatened to change the Senate's rules to employ the nuclear option to push through President Obama's appointments to the board and other appointments. This option would require only a simple majority instead of a two-thirds vote.

On July 16, 2013, the Senate GOP came to agreement with Reid and the Democrats that Richard Cordray's appointment to head the Consumer Financial Protection Bureau would be approved along with six other appointments and that these two appointments to the NLRB would be denied. In exchange, Reid would not institute the nuclear option.

See also Consumer Financial Protection Bureau; Perez, Thomas; Unions.

NSA: Edward Snowden, whistle-blower or traitor, depending on your point of view, exposed the National Security Administration's program of data (metadata) collection. Metadata includes the phone numbers called; when the call was made; the initiating phone number; and how long the calls lasted but supposedly not actual eavesdropping for content. This was initially reported to be from only Verizon subscribers. Very soon, however, it was determined[408] that this data collection included phone records from phone companies AT&T and Sprint, and Nextel as well and emails, web searches, and credit card transactions without a FISA court-ordered search warrant on all US residents.

Snowden[409] was only a data analyst working for a contractor, but he had a top secret clearance and access to NSA secrets. He revealed NSA's program through The Guardian[410], a London newspaper and fled to Hong Kong then Russia. He appealed to Russia for asylum which was granted for one year.

William Binney[411], who worked in the intelligence community for over thirty years and blew the whistle on NSA in 2001, believes the government has used data collected on US citizens who are political opponents against them. Although NSA claimed they checked metadata of less than three hundred telephones in 2012, Binney counters[411] that it is "hard to believe that they have on the order of ... ten thousand people looking at three hundred phone calls."

As the story has unfolded it has been reported that the NSA is not authorized to listen in on conversations unless one conversant is presumed to be outside the US. If that is the case, it is legal for NSA to listen in for content. If it is later found out that both conversants were inside the US, but information "inadvertently" picked up indicated criminal activity, intelligence information, of potential harm to a person or property (this could be something as innocent as a demonstration by an activist group), any information that is encrypted, or anything related to cyber security, it can be used – that means acted on without a warrant from the FISA court. It is referred to as the inadvertent rule[412].

Our National Intelligence Director James Clapper when asked at a hearing in June 2013 if the NSA collected any type of data on millions of Americans, replied[620], "No, sir." When queried again, he responded, "Not wittingly. There are cases where they could inadvertently perhaps collect, but not wittingly." Days later he said it was the "least untruthful" answer he could give.

Attorney General Eric Holder signed[410] off on two documents in July 2012 that detail the above circumstances under which the content of communications within the US can be obtained, retained for up to five years and used. This is an expansion over what was permitted by the George W. Bush administration.

Different from other privacy invasions suffered by Americans such as pat-downs at airports and drug testing of some employees in critical positions where public safety is a concern, this privacy invasion of metadata collection is being accomplished secretively and without probable cause. This likely is in violation of the fourth amendment of the Constitution.

In addition, although the analysts are required to have probable cause and FISA court approval to eavesdrop for content between two American residents, it is not clear that they can't and don't do it without approval. There is a big difference between these analysts having the ability to listen and being authorized to listen. Politicians in favor of the program emphasize the analysts don't have the authority. That may be correct as far as it goes. However, the temptation to snoop whether on a girlfriend or a presidential candidate of the opposing party is probably too great to deny by many for personal, political or financial gain. Eventually the NSA admitted that *love interest* snooping had occurred[685] but, of course, on a very small scale. Most of the incidents uncovered were self-reported. How many went undetected?

By mid-August 2013 suspicions were confirmed[651]. Documents leaked to the Washington Post by Snowden showed NSA personnel were directed to remove information from reports to the DOJ and the Office of the Director of National Intelligence. The NSA also failed to notify the FISA court of a new collection method until long after it had been used. The court found the method to be unconstitutional. An audit of the NSA from May 2012 reported 2,776 incidents in just the preceding twelve months and from just the Washington D.C. area that represented "unauthorized collection, storage, access to or distribution of legally protected communications." This number apparently does not even include the records of innocent Americans that get caught in authorized sweeps for information. Those records are considered "incidental" and do not have to be reported to the NSA inspector general as it is not considered a violation by NSA.

But, due to a lawsuit it was revealed[676] that NSA admitted to the FISA court the collecting of 56,000 emails of Americans over a three year period starting in 2008. These Americans were suspected of nothing but were caught up in a "sweep" – at least that is the official position. The FISA court ruled in October 2011 that NSA had misrepresented its operations and that some of its data collection was unconstitutional. The Administration would probably not have declassified this information were it not for a 2011 lawsuit. "Officials" also indicated that it was not clear whether any NSA analyst had actually read the content of the emails.

It was also revealed in August 2013 that two years earlier in October 2011 the administration had obtained approval, through an amendment to FISA, to search for phone calls and emails by the name[702] of the author without a warrant. This is no longer a matter of collecting just metadata and should be a violation of section 702 of FISA. It makes William Binney's accusation much more plausible than the righteous protestations of President Obama and James Clapper.

The eleven-member FISA court never hears an opposing opinion. They get one side only of the argument – the government's side. This may explain why no government requests[413] for eavesdropping out of 1,789 were turned down in 2012 by the FISA court.

This operation could be legal and still unconstitutional. Apparently the ACLU agrees as they have sued[621] the Obama administration over this. In early September 2013, the National Rifle Association (NRA) filed[698] an amicus brief in support of the ACLU lawsuit. The NRA's contention is that a gun registry could be constructed from the data collected by the NSA and that the mere knowledge such data were being collected would chill communication between the NRA and its members. Politics does indeed create strange bedfellows. The First and Fourth Amendments to the Constitution are at stake.

See also National Counterterrorism Center.

Obamacare: The Patient Protection and Affordable Care Act (PPACA or sometimes just ACA) was signed into law in March 2010 after a bitterly partisan fight and vote in both the House and Senate. Not one Republican voted in favor of it in either chamber and thirty-four Democrats opposed it in the House. The vote was taken on Christmas Eve, 2009.

The greater than 2,500-page bill, which creates 159 new federal agencies, was not fully read or understood by anyone voting on it. And, who can forget Speaker of the House Nancy Pelosi's instructions[414] that, "... we have to pass the bill so that you can find out what is in it, away from the fog of the controversy."

The legislation passed, at least in part, due to some very attractive, well-publicized provisions: mandated coverage for children up to the age of twenty-six under their parents' policy; no denial of insurance coverage to those with pre-existing conditions; a requirement that employers of fifty or more full-time workers (defined as thirty or more hours per week) provide them health care insurance or pay a fine; extension of health care insurance to 30 million who would not otherwise have it.

However, there are many defects in the law, beginning with the unpopular provision requiring everyone to purchase health insurance or pay a fine. Unpopular as it was, the Supreme Court upheld the validity of the individual mandate as a tax. Those who don't want insurance will game the system by waiting until they need it and will opt to pay the fine until then because it is much cheaper than purchasing insurance.

Accepting pre-existing conditions while the healthy opt out until they need it will likely bankrupt insurance companies, leaving only a government plan. This is probably by design and that notion is supported by Obama's preference for single-payer government insurance (see Single payer quotes). Senate majority leader Harry Reid recently admitted[658] that indeed the Democrats did want a single-payer plan.

Some insurance companies have already elected[636, 637, 638] to not participate at least for the first year in some state or federal health care insurance exchanges because they have determined they can't make a profit.

Small companies will be reluctant to expand and hire more than forty-nine full-time employees, will hire more part-time employees, and may convert full time jobs to part time jobs to avoid buying health care insurance for them. As of

August 2013 this was already beginning to occur[675] with Red Lobster and Olive Garden restaurants in some test markets. The retail clothing firm Forever 21 is reducing hours[683] to 29.5 per week. The University of Virginia and UPS will no longer cover spouses.[683] Subway[684] is cutting hours.

The Obama administration says the information about companies' efforts to avoid Obamacare is anecdotal. However, by early September 2013, over two hundred and fifty businesses had declared[699] a cut in hours or jobs to avoid the extra expense of Obamacare.

The punitive cost to employers is not limited to private business. City and county governments are also feeling the pressure enough to cut[682] some of their employees' working hours to less than thirty hours per week. Although employers have been given a waiver until after the 2014 elections, many are implementing cuts now because of contracts that must be negotiated well in advance. This is not good for our economy.

The IPAB often referred to as the death panel, was unconstitutionally created and has unconstitutional powers. A shortage of medical doctors—particularly specialists—will result because they will be reimbursed by the government at the same low rate regardless of specialty. A brain surgeon, for instance, will be reimbursed at same rate as a general practitioner. Medicare recipients will find treatment less available because doctors are refusing new patients due to reduced government reimbursement under the PPACA (and Medicare).

The cost of the law to the taxpayer was first promised[415] by Obama in September 2009 to be "around $900 billion over ten years." But by March 2012 the cost was revised upward to $1.76 trillion, double what was originally touted and more recently is estimated[416] to be $2.6 trillion. What happened to his 2009 pledge[417] not to sign a bill "that adds one dime to our deficits?" Another broken promise.

The overall dollar cost is not the only cost consideration. Data available[418] for California, one of the first to publish policy rates under Obamacare, show a tremendous premium cost. There are four levels of insurance plans available through exchanges: bronze, silver, gold, and platinum. For the three lowest silver plans in California, the premium would be an average of $321 per month per individual with a $2,000 annual deductible. This would put the annual premium cost for a family of four at $15,400. The cost of the deductible would be additional. This is not affordable for most people.

It must have been recognized that many could not afford this and so there is a provision in the Act that allows a government subsidy to help cover the premium cost for those earning less than four hundred per cent of the poverty level. Of course, the taxpayers will pick up the tab for this. More redistribution.

Analyses show that without Obamacare, the greater the income, the lesser the percent of income spent on health care. With Obamacare[419], the greater the income, the greater the percent of it is spent on health care. In addition, insurance companies will no longer be able to give breaks[420] (non-smoking is the exception) to those with healthy histories. They must instead average out costs in a market pool resulting in the healthy subsidizing the unhealthy. So, not only do the healthy/well-off individuals not get the benefit of subsidies, they pay for those who do. Very redistributive.

Emergency room medical services will continue to be provided to all non-US residents even if they are here illegally. However, illegal immigrants are exempted[421] from the individual mandate and so are not required to buy insurance. They also are not subject to a fine for not having health care insurance under the ACA. More redistribution.

All personal bank accounts will be accessible and subject to electronic withdrawals by the government.

Employers opposed to birth control and abortion on religious grounds are required to provide insurance that pays for these treatments and procedures for their employees. These provisions have generated many lawsuits already.

States' Medicaid rolls will increase drastically on January 1, 2014, with no provision of federal funds. The budget cuts to Medicare are severe and will decrease the availability of care to seniors. There is enough to keep this law and its regulations in the court system for many years.

As of mid-August 2013, there were already 17,900 pages of regulations to implement the act. Even the Obama administration appears to realize there will be severe problems driven by this law. On July 2, 2013, just before the long fourth of July holiday, the administration announced[422] they will institute a one year's delay (until 2015) the requirement that employers of fifty or more full-time employees provide insurance for their employees or pay a fine of as much as three thousand dollars per employee. It is certainly not coincidence that the delay is timed to expire after the 2014 elections. The Democrat Senators and Representatives who voted for Obamacare and are up for re-election needed some protection from the adverse effects of some of the law's provisions and the subsequent expected reaction of their constituents.

Just three days later on Friday July 5 the Obama administration announced that they would temporarily drop the provision that individuals verify eligibility for receiving a subsidy for their health insurance purchase. Individuals would be on an honor system. Of course everybody is so honest they won't take advantage of this. This is pure and simple and invitation to fraud.

Representative Diane Black of Tennessee recognized this and sponsored[718] a bill, the "No Subsidies without Verification Act. It passed the House on September 12, 2013. However it probably will not see the light of day in the Senate and Obama has said he would veto it.

It was announced during the Labor Day weekend, 2013 that forty thousand members of the ILWU (longshoremen) will disaffiliate[694] from the AFL-CIO because that federation misled their membership about the negative implications of Obamacare. There is more, specifically about the Cadillac tax which is the bone of contention, in the following section on exemptions. This is a big blow to the private sector union management which is dependent on the dues of their members. Anything that hurts the unions, by extension hurts the Obama administration as they seem to be co-dependent.

IBM will give 110,000 retirees a subsidy and shunt them from its company sponsored health care plan to an Obamacare exchange plan. Time Warner is doing the same with its retirees[701].

See also mandate; IPAB; Obamacare exemptions; Lawsuits against Obamacare; Single payer quotes; Unemployment; Unions.

Obamacare exemptions: The PPACA exempts[423] members of religions that bar the acceptance of benefits from any private or public insurance group and do not pay Social Security taxes or receive Social Security benefits. Members of such religions are exempt from "minimum coverage and annual shared responsibility payments" (i.e., they are not required to buy health care insurance). The exemption covers the Amish, the Mennonites, and the Scientologists and is called the "religious conscience exemption." Whether it covers Muslims is not yet clear, since they do not accept insurance, but do pay for and receive Social Security benefits. This issue will probably be resolved in the courts. Other groups exempted from the PPACA are prisoners, illegal aliens, foreign nationals, and Indian tribes. Those who can't afford insurance on their own will get a subsidy.

In addition to exemptions specified in the law, the Obama administration had, as of early January 2012, granted[424] temporary waivers to employers of almost eight times as many union-represented workers as nonunion workers.

By January 2013, unions which overwhelmingly supported Obama and Obamacare, had discovered that the health care
insurance would cost their employers so much more that it
could jeopardize their forty-hour work week. Employers of less
than fifty full time (defined as thirty hours or more per week)
workers do not have to provide health care insurance for them
under Obamacare. So the answer for them is to make part-time
jobs out of what used to be full-time jobs.

Some unions have now asked[425] for subsidies to union
workers who already have health care insurance benefits but do
not meet the eligibility requirements (their salaries are too high
to qualify) for subsidies under Obamacare. Others including the
union that represents many IRS employees[427, 623] just want to
keep the insurance plan they already have. The so-called
"cadillac" plans that many of these union members have as part
of their union-negotiated contracts will be subject to a cadillac
tax and employers are going to be hard pressed to pay it. Some
are considering dumping their employees onto the insurance
exchanges where union employees will have to pay just like the
rest of us and get less luxurious plans than what they currently
have. They want to be exempt from having to do this. If the
requests for special treatment were granted, it would transfer a
large share of the cost of millions of people whose health care
insurance costs are currently borne by employers to the
taxpayer. More redistribution.

In April 2013, it was reported[426] that congressional leaders of both parties were talking secretly about how to exempt
members of congress and their aides, numbering in the
thousands, from an Obamacare requirement that they join

health insurance exchanges. This would cost them thousands of dollars out of pocket. Public indignation ensued when the information leaked and supposedly the idea was dropped.

Dropped only for a short time as it turns out. Announced on Friday, August 2, 2013, Obama granted[616,617] a carve-out to Congressional lawmakers and staffers so that, although most have to participate in the health care exchanges to get their insurance, the US taxpayer will provide a 75% subsidy to help them with the cost, although they do not qualify under the ACA for a subsidy. Some apparently do not even have to participate in the Exchange.

Senator Charles Grassley (R. IA) had tried to forestall this situation by inserting a requirement[618] into the ACA requiring Senators, Representatives and staffers to go by the same rules as would apply to the rest of us. It is being circumvented to the detriment of the rest of us.

States such as Georgia[428] are having so much difficulty implementing reasonable options for their exchanges that they too are requesting special considerations.

Although published in February 2013, a "rule" regarding the caps on out-of-pocket expenses of health insurance policy holders was not really noticed until August.[647] The rule delays for one year until 2015 the Obamacare requirement that caps the amount of out-of-pocket expenses such as deductibles and co-payments. Without the temporary exemption, the insurance companies would have to raise premiums dramatically. This would not be expedient for the Obama administration and

Democrats – especially before the November 2014 elections. Ergo, another politically-driven exemption from Obamacare.

See also Contraceptive mandate; Lawsuits against Obamacare; Obamacare.

Occupy Wall Street: The name of a movement (also referred to as OWS) that began in the fall of 2011 in Zuccotti Park in the financial district of New York to protest social and economic inequality, greed, corruption, and what demonstrators saw as the unfair influence of big corporations on government. Their slogan[429], "We are the 99 percent," was supposed to call attention to the growing gap between the wealthiest 1 percent and the rest of the population.

Mayor Michael Bloomberg did not require that protesters disband, and since they were on private property and the owner of that property did not object, they were allowed to continue to protest for more than two months. The demonstration was ugly, dirty, noisy, and ill-mannered but legal—except for the occasional assault[430] – sexual or otherwise.

The protesters tended to be young (at least as compared with Tea Party demonstrators), with an average age of thirty-three.[431] One survey found that 80 percent of the protesters identified themselves as slightly to extremely liberal. By November 15, 2011, they were prevented from staying overnight at the park. By New Year's Day 2012, the protest had run its course and died out. It cost[431] New York City an estimated $17 million in overtime pay for police.

Zuccotti Park was trashed. It is suspected that the reason the owners, Brookfield Asset Management, permitted the protesters access was that President Obama had just given[432] the firm a $168.9 million loan guarantee. The Department of Energy finalized the loan less than a week after the crowd camped out at Zuccotti. Bloomberg's domestic partner is on the board of directors at Brookfield Properties.

There were also connections between OWS and ACORN and SEIU through their organizers and community groups.

Obama tacitly endorsed[433] the protesters and compared them to the Tea Party demonstrators. He must have forgotten that he had earlier mocked the Tea Party movement although they were tidy and law-abiding.

See also ACORN; Jones, Van.

Ocean control by UN: The United Nations' Law of the Sea Treaty (LOST) proposes[434] to control mineral and oil exploration in oceans, oceanic passage, biosphere land preserves and corridors, population density, rezoning of inhabited areas, use of fossil fuel, and fishing. This is all proposed under the guise of supporting "healthy and sustainable oceans." It is more honestly Agenda 21 repackaged.

A companion bill to LOST is the Consolidated Land, Energy and Aquatic Resources (CLEAR) Act passed by the House on July 30, 2010, which requires membership in LOST. This bill could easily have been killed[435] in the House if just seventeen of the twenty-one Republicans who were too chicken to show up for the vote had appeared and voted "nay."

In another very politically adroit move, President Obama issued an Executive Order[435] just eleven days before the CLEAR Act's passage in the House that cleared the way for approval in the Senate without the two-thirds vote that has always been necessary for treaties. A provision bypassing the treaty approval process was not included in the House bill, and Obama would have done another end run around Congress if the legislation had been passed in the Senate. Thankfully, it died in the Senate.

If this bill had passed and been fully implemented, it would have driven out American drilling in the Gulf of Mexico, delayed drilling in general, increased our dependence on foreign oil, and implemented climate change legislation.

The bill also provided for a conservation tax on every barrel of oil and BTU of natural gas produced. That would have caused our energy prices to "necessarily skyrocket." The taxes collected by the UN would have been redistributed as the UN saw fit—presumably to poor, underdeveloped nations. More redistribution.

Just as important as the impact on our economy and the violation of the Constitutional separation of powers is the fact that this legislation would have given away our sovereignty to the UN in exchange for a more global governance model in keeping with Agenda 21.

See also Agenda 21; Cap & Trade bill; Skyrocket quote.

Organization of Islamic Cooperation: This group of fifty-seven Islamic states is the collective voice of the Muslim world. The organization has a permanent delegation to the UN, and its parliamentary union of member states has headquarters in Tehran, Iran. The group has successfully fought in the UN to shield its member states from civil rights criticism but takes a different stance with regard to criticism of Israel.

Palestine: On November 29, 2012, the UN General Assembly upgraded[436] Palestine from "entity" to nonmember state by a vote of 138 to 9 with 41 abstentions. Although this was not an obvious substantive change, it gave the Palestinians more credibility to challenge Israel in the International Criminal Court. The United States, Israel, and Canada were among those opposing the move. France, Spain, Italy, and Switzerland voted for it.

The uppermost issue for the Palestinians involves the borders established by the 1949 armistice after the first Arab-Israeli war. The Palestinians want to return to those borders, negating the terms of the 1967 armistice ending Israel's Six-Day War with Egypt, Syria, and Jordan. After the war, Israel had full authority and security control over much of the West Bank.

The Obama administration, Russia, and the European Union want Israel to return to the pre-1967 borders, and President Obama stated[338] this publicly on May 19, 2011. Israeli Prime Minister Benjamin Netanyahu, visiting Obama the very next day, rejected this solution as "indefensible," since it would leave Israel only nine miles wide at the narrowest point and would jeopardize the security of Jewish settlements in the West Bank.

Israel maintains a military presence in the West Bank and has established settlements with as many as forty thousand people there since 1967. Israel insists this military presence is necessary to protect itself.

Considering Obama's desire for Israel to return to pre-1967 borders and the Palestinians' desire for the same, it seems inconsistent for the United States to oppose UN recognition of Palestine as a state, since that would inch Palestine toward a border resolution in its favor. So it appears possible that the US vote in opposition to Palestine's increased recognition by the UN was disingenuous and that we knew the vote would give increased status to Palestine without our help.

In April 2012, Obama waived[437] the Palestinian Accountability Act's freeze on US funding of the Palestinian Authority, thus providing $192 million to the Authority.

The 2012 Democrat Party platform shifted[438] very obviously toward Palestinian positions, even deleting reference to Jerusalem as the capital of Israel. After strong objection, this language was reinserted but with loud protest from the floor. Pro-Palestinian positions had been implied by removing pro-Israel statements from the 2004 and 2008 platforms.

See also Egypt's Arab spring; Israel.

Parsi, Trita: He was born in Iran and is the founder and president of the National Iranian American Council (NIAC)[439], which is at least partially funded[440] by George Soros. Parsi earned a PhD from the Johns Hopkins School for Advanced International Studies and is a permanent resident of the United States although he is not a citizen.

A critic of Parsi and the NIAC was sued by Parsi for defamation, and in the discovery process, documents provided by the NIAC brought to light many things not advantageous to Parsi's case. Documents[447] showed that Parsi and the Iranian ambassador to the UN had exchanged e-mails[443] and that Parsi had secret meetings with Iranian officials[444]. It also appears that the NIAC lied to members of Congress[444]; falsified membership numbers[443]; violated tax law[443], the Lobbying Disclosure Act[443], and the Foreign Agents Registration Act[443]; defrauded federal funds[444], and bribed witnesses[444]. Judge John Bates dismissed[441, 442] the case brought by Parsi and ordered him to pay a large part of the defendant's costs. So none of the accusations of the defendant was proven but none was disproven. The case none-the-less backfired on Parsi as he and his NIAC are more suspect of questionable activity than before because of the information that came forward during the discovery process and NIAC attempts to foil it.

Parsi has openly opposed[443] sanctions against Iran and favors diplomatic engagement. He has been seen[445, 446] as an apologist for Mahmoud Ahmadinejad in the past.

In October 2010, in an open letter[446] to Secretary of State Hillary Clinton, the Pro Democracy Movement of Iran called Parsi a lobbyist for the Iranian regime who should be considered a "nonregistered foreign agent" and accused him of having an anti-Semitic, anti-Israel agenda. The letter protested Clinton's sending Parsi at US taxpayers' expense to represent the United States at talks in Saudi Arabia.

It is reported[447] that President Obama turned over virtually all responsibility and authority for foreign policy negotiations with Iran to Parsi.

See also Green Movement.

Perez, Thomas[596]: This Assistant Attorney General in the Justice Department was able to get St. Paul Minnesota to drop a pending case[448] in the Supreme Court shortly before the scheduled oral argument. The case revolved around racial discrimination that had it been decided against the plaintiffs would have limited the justice department's rationale of "disparate impact" for bringing housing discrimination suits.

St. Paul had decided to increase enforcement of housing code standards for rental properties. Some owners of these properties sued St. Paul claiming that enforcement would have a disproportionately large impact on minorities (disparate impact) because it would decrease the amount of affordable housing.

Disparate impact was the rationale that the justice department did not want challenged and feared that if the plaintiffs lost, a valuable tool used in more than just housing might be lost as well. They did not want to take the chance.

Perez was able to cut a deal with one of St. Paul's attorneys such that if St. Paul would drop the case, the Justice Department would drop their plans to sue St. Paul for two false claims act violations, one of which involved their not providing job training, employment and contracting opportunities to low income residents as required by law.

This quid-pro-quo came to light on April 15, shortly before confirmation hearings for Perez's appointment by President Obama for Secretary of Labor. The House Committee on Oversight and Government Reform and the House and Senate Judiciary Committees had been investigating this for over a year and had produced a damning report[449, 450]. Perez was confirmed anyway in the Senate by a vote of fifty-four to forty-six.

Much more well-known is the case in which, under the previous administration, four New Black Panthers were charged with intimidating voters in the 2008 presidential election at a Philadelphia polling place. After Obama was elected, his justice department dropped[396] the case against three of them after the New Black Panthers had already lost the case by default.

An investigation into the matter by Inspector General Mike Horowitz, determined that Perez's testimony that the decision to drop the case did not involve political appointees was not true[451] and that Attorney General Eric Holder[452] "was briefed and generally indicated his approval."

Perez has also been accused of using a personal e-mail account for government business. This is against the law. A subpoena of these e-mails has been ignored[596] by Perez.

See also Corporate Culture; New Black Panthers; NLRB.

Petraeus, David: A highly popular former four-star general responsible for the successful surge in Iraq under President George W. Bush, he was considered by many Republicans to be a potential presidential candidate in 2012. Democrats feared his popularity as evidenced by the full-page "General Betray Us" advertisement in the September 10, 2007, *New York Times*, paid for by the George Soros-funded MoveOn.org.[453]

President Obama nominated him in June 2010 to succeed General Stanley McChrystal as commanding general of the International Security Assistance Force in Afghanistan. This was seen as a step down from being commander of the United States Central Command and an attempt by the president to keep a potential competitor out of the political limelight. In August 2011, Petraeus retired from the Army. He had been confirmed as director of the CIA in June.

On November 9, 2012, just three days after Obama's reelection and six days before a formal inquiry into the Benghazi attacks by the Senate Intelligence Committee at which CIA Director Petraeus was scheduled to testify, he resigned[454] his CIA post due to an extramarital affair—an affair of which the Obama administration surely had knowledge before November 6. It was concurrently announced that Petraeus would not be testifying about Benghazi. However, he voluntarily stepped forward.

One has to wonder if the resignation of Petraeus from his appointment as Director of the CIA had more to do with his distaste for the final version of the Benghazi talking points than the discovery of his extra-marital affair. In fact, when the ninety-four Benghazi e-mails were released on May 15, 2013 it was found that Petraeus, after much editing of the talking points said[455], in an e-mail dated September 15, 2012 to his deputy, that because so much information was removed, "Frankly, I'd just as soon not use this, then."

As another aside, those personal e-mails that revealed Petraeus' affair were accessed how and why? Recent questions about NSA's possible illegal access of our personal information raise doubts.

See also Benghazi; NSA.

Pfleger, Father Michael: A Catholic priest at St. Sabina Church on Chicago's South Side, he was a longtime friend of Barack Obama and a defender of Louis Farrakhan, leader of the anti-Semitic and racist Nation of Islam. He and Farrakhan had visited[456] each other's homes, and Farrakhan had lectured from the St. Sabina pulpit. Father Pfleger has lectured at the Reverend Jeremiah Wright's Trinity United Church of Christ where he preached[457] about what he called "white entitle-ment"—especially with regard to Hillary Clinton's expectation of being elected president in 2008. His message was racist and anti-capitalist. After Pfleger's mocking of Clinton at Wright's church, Obama expressed disappointment in the comments and distanced himself from him.

See also Wright, Reverend Jeremiah.

Poland: See Missile defense shield.

PPACA: See Obamacare.

Private sector doing fine quote: In June 2012, President Obama said[459], "The private sector is doing fine. Where we're seeing weaknesses in our economy have to do with state and local government—oftentimes cuts initiated by governors or mayors who are not getting the kind of help they have in the past from the federal government." Economist Paul Krugman chimed[460] in and covered for the president saying that "the private sector is doing better than the public sector. Cutbacks of the public sector are what's hurting recovery."

Both Obama and Krugman were apparently basing their comments on the fact that while the private sector was adding jobs, the public sector was losing jobs. True. However, the national unemployment rate was 7.8 percent while the unemployment rate for government workers was only 3.8 percent. The public sector needs to lose jobs. It is bloated.

The contribution of the public sector component[461] of our GDP has risen significantly during the Obama administration. Yet government jobs produce nothing of substance, nothing that can be used, bought, and sold by consumers. They contribute very little to the overall health of the economy.

See also Stimulus.

Punish our enemies quote : On October 25, 2010, just prior to the midterm elections, a Univision radio interview aired in which President Obama said[462], "If Latinos sit out the election instead of saying, 'We're going to punish our enemies and we're going to reward our friends who stand with us on issues that are important to us,' if they don't see that kind of upsurge in voting in this election, then I think it's going to be harder and that's why I think it's so important that people focus on voting on November 2."

QE3: See Quantitative easing.

Quantitative easing: This is an unusual process used by the Federal Reserve to essentially print money (increase the money supply) to buy up financial assets (usually government bonds) from commercial banks. It is done to stimulate the economy.

Stimulation is more commonly done by lowering interest rates. But when short-term interest rates are already so low that they can't go any lower and the economy is still weak, quantitative easing may be employed. The Fed's purchase of the bonds, using money that it generates out of nothing, keeps the yield low and thus makes borrowing money attractive. The banks, which have received the money from the Fed, get more to loan out to stimulate business. At least that is the theory. Quantitative easing is usually restricted to a dollar amount.

The first recent quantitative easing (QE1) occurred in late November 2008. By June 2010, $2.1 trillion had been pumped into the system and the pump was turned off. QE1 probably kept the economy from going into a deep depression. But, by the summer of 2010, the economy was again weakening and so the Federal Reserve chairman, Ben Bernanke, started buying bonds again in August 2010 with funny money. This was QE2, and it is much less clear that it helped much.

On September 13, 2012, the Fed not only began QE3, but planned to keep buying assets with funny money, including mortgage-backed securities, until the labor market improves substantially. In other words, it is an open-ended move—the pump is on continuously, full throttle. To carry the analogy to its limit, the mechanical pump will eventually burn out. Is that what our economy is in for? The Fed has also indicated[463] it will keep short-term interest rates low until mid-2015.

Although this process of quantitative easing guards against deflation and can stimulate the economy, it is a balancing act and if done too aggressively can cause inflation— the more money that is created, the less it is worth and so prices rise. There is also no guarantee the banks on the receiving end will use the money obtained from sale of bonds and other securities to make loans that will stimulate the economy. These banks are nervous about the ability of their clients to repay their loans in such a weak economy, and they are hamstrung by the specter of Dodd-Frank regulations yet to be written. If the money stays in the banks, it does the economy no good.

See also Credit rating; Dodd-Frank.

Recess appointments: See Consumer Financial Protection Bureau; NLRB.

Redistribution quotes: In a radio interview[464] in 2001, Obama, then a state senator, said "economic rights" could be attained by gaining legislative control through an "actual coalition of powers through which you bring about redistributive change." In 1998, in a speech[465] at Loyola University, state senator Obama said, "I think the trick is figuring out how do we structure government systems that pool resources and hence

167

facilitate some redistribution, because I actually believe in redistribution, at least at a certain level, to make sure that everybody's got a shot." On October 12, 2008, presidential candidate Obama, responding to a question by Samuel Joseph Wurzelbacher (Joe the Plumber) about taxes on small businesses said[466] "... when you spread the wealth around, it's good for everybody." As president, speaking on April 29, 2010, in Quincy, Illinois, regarding Wall Street reform, he said[467], "I do think, at a certain point, you've made enough money."

See also ACORN; Bondholders, secure; BP escrow; Cap and Trade bill; Collective salvation quotes; Delphi pensions; Fair share; Fannie & Freddie; Food stamps; Obamacare; Obamacare exemptions; Ocean control by UN; TARP; Unemployment rate; Welfare.

Right-to-Work: This phrase refers to a statute that prevents the imposition of union membership and union dues as a condition of employment and also refers to the states in which these laws exist. There are twenty-four such states.[468] The other twenty-six are known as "forced unionism" or "collective bargaining" states.

One study[469] comparing counties close to the border between states with and without right-to-work laws (thus correcting for factors such as geography and climate) found that growth of employment in manufacturing was 26 percent higher in the right-to-work counties. The National Institute for Labor Relations Research using Bureau of Labor Statistics data reported[470] that for 2000 to 2010, employment growth for the non-farm private sector was an average of 5.8 percent higher in right-to-work states than in forced-union states.

Over the past decade, right-to-work states have had a net gain of 3.6 million jobs while unionized states have lost 900,000 jobs, according to payroll surveys.[476]

A report[471] by the US Commerce Department's Bureau of Economic Analysis showed that from 2001 to 2011, inflation-adjusted, private-sector wages grew four times more in right-to-work states than in forced-union states and nearly double the national average. Another study[472] from the University of Colorado found a $4,300 advantage in right to work states for purchasing power[473] over forced unionism states. In October 2012, the average unemployment rate[474] in right-to-work states was 6.9 percent. In non-right-to-work states, unemployment was 0.7 percent higher at 7.6 percent.

Based on a 2011 Bureau of Labor Statistics report, median wages are 9.4 percent lower in right-to-work states than in states that have unionized labor requirements. However in 2011 the cost of living was an average of almost 20 percent lower[475] in right-to-work states and the unemployment rate was an average of 0.6 percent lower. This explains the increased purchasing power in right to work states.

In April 2012, President Obama said in a speech[477] at an AFL-CIO conference that he thinks "the economy is stronger when collective bargaining rights are protected." Obama has repeatedly made it clear that he is against right-to-work laws and has disparagingly referred to them as "right-to-work-for-less" laws. His opposition is consistent with his NLRB's attempt to keep Boeing from opening a new manufacturing plant in South Carolina, a right-to-work state, instead of the state of Washington, a forced-union state.

Obama is in favor of unionized collective bargaining even for public-sector workers, as exemplified by his opposition to Wisconsin Governor Scott Walker's successful fight to strike down collective bargaining for much of Wisconsin's public-sector workforce. Walker's move remains successful at least for now. It is being challenged in the court system.

On December 11, 2012, a bill passed both houses of congress in Michigan making it the twenty-fourth right-to-work state despite the fact that Obama had injected[478] himself into the fray in opposition to the bill.

See also Assault on unions quote; NLRB.

Rosen, James: see FOX News channel, attack on.

Rugged individualism quote: In a speech[479] in Osawatomie, Kansas, on December 6, 2011, President Obama said, "It's a simple theory—one that speaks to our rugged individualism and healthy skepticism of too much government. It fits well on a bumper sticker. Here's the problem: it doesn't work. It never worked." He was speaking of free-market capitalism. He was wrong.

Rules of engagement: Although officially secret, the new military rules of engagement issued by President Obama through General Stanley McChrystal have become known from interviews with the troops. They were issued[480] in late summer or early fall 2009 and are just short of criminal.

Reportedly included among them: unless our troops are absolutely certain no civilians are present, they're denied artillery air support; if any civilians appear where we meet the Taliban, our troops are to retreat; night surprise searches are not permitted; villagers are to be warned prior to searches; firing at insurgents is not permitted unless they are preparing to fire first; men are not permitted to search women; troops can fire on insurgents if they catch them in the act of placing an improvised explosive device, but not if the insurgents walk away from where the device is located.

These rules of engagement were put in place because of Afghan President Hamid Karzai's complaints about civilian deaths during firefights. The rules apply to all coalition forces of the US and NATO.

Levels of approval required before military action is taken are unreasonable and not timely in many cases. These are not rules of war but of some political game.

See also Benghazi.

School vouchers: The DC Opportunity Scholarship Program[481] was signed into law by President George W. Bush and was the first federally funded school voucher program in the United States. It provided low-income DC families help in paying for private school tuition for their children.

In 2009, President Obama signed a spending bill that phased out the program the following year, and Secretary of Education Arne Duncan rescinded scholarships for children already admitted for that next year.

This expiration of the program was allowed despite the fact that the Obama administration had in hand a Department of Education report[482] showing the per-pupil cost of the program was a third of what DC public schools spent and that the students who received the vouchers were nineteen months ahead of their public school counterparts in reading skills.

Obama had made a point[483] of not prejudging the DC voucher system experiment, of letting the results speak for themselves, and of doing "what's best for the kids." But he ignored the results of the report quite possibly because they were good and undermined the argument of teachers unions against the program.

Although phased out in 2009, the program was revived[484] in 2011 as the Scholarships for Opportunity And Results (SOAR) Act through the efforts of House Speaker John Boehner (R-OH) and Senator Joe Lieberman (I-CT).

In 2012, again President Obama's budget proposal for 2013 did not include funding for the program. Supposedly, the 2012 budget had enough funding to cover vouchers for 2013. But Education Secretary Duncan, speaking for the president about the future of the program, said[485], "we remain convinced that our time and resources are best spent on reforming the public school system...."

The DC public schools have a terrible record—among the highest dropout and therefore lowest graduation rates in the country. It was reported[482] in 2007 that fourth- and eighth-graders scored lower than children from all fifty states. No wonder there are roughly four applicants for every slot available in the voucher program.

In August 2013, the Obama Department of Justice sued[680] the State of Louisiana to prevent thirty-four of its public schools that have been under desegregation orders from giving school vouchers to students. The vouchers make it possible for students from poor families who are currently enrolled in failing public schools to attend private independent schools. About 90 percent of the children taking advantage of the program are black and the program is popular. The Obama administration's excuse for the lawsuit is that the voucher system is destroying the racial balance in the public schools. So, for the sake of the race numbers game, Louisiana is supposed to deny underprivileged minority students from getting a better education. It appears to be more a situation of favoring the wishes of the teachers unions than good education for children. What has happened to "what's best for the kids," Mr. President? Governor Jindal was correct when he said of our federal government's action, "shame on them."

See also Unions.

Sea Treaty: See Ocean Control by UN.

SEIU: See Unions.

Sequestration: This provision of the Budget Control Act was to take effect on January 1, 2013, if Congress couldn't forestall it before then. Under sequestration an equal percentage of across-the-board cuts to defense (excluding war), nondefense discretionary programs, a little from entitlements, and interest reduction would occur. Although it sounds quite equitable, defense programs provide 42.6 percent of the total sequester cuts—and that is on top of a $407 billion cut from defense spending caps already in place. By comparison, entitlement program cuts contribute only 14.8 percent to the total sequester cuts. These cuts as proposed were not truly cuts in spending, but merely a cut in the rate of increase of spending. The budget would still increase by trillions over ten years.

A deal was not reached by January 1, 2013, and sequestration was delayed for another two months before finally taking effect on March 1.

Sequestration was clearly proposed by the president to be so onerous that even the Republicans would not allow it to happen. He was probably counting on the cuts to defense to kill it. But, once it appeared that the Republicans were considering it, the president, although it was[486] his and Jack Lew's idea, said[487] that sequestration was not his idea but Congress' idea – and a bad one at that.

Republicans wanted to give the president total authority to pick and choose which cuts to make so as to avoid the most critical services and not do an across-the-board cut. Obama said[488] that if a bill requiring that of him came before him, he would veto it. He would rather blame[489] the Republicans refusal to cut loopholes for the "well-off and well-connected" and the resulting sequester for any bad economic news than take responsibility for reasonable decisions on cuts.

Instead, according to Obama's campaign organization, Organizing for Action, "On the chopping block are 10,000 teaching jobs, more than 70,000 kids' spots in Head Start, thirty-five million dollars for local fire departments, forty-three million dollars to make sure seniors don't go hungry, and access to nutrition assistance for sixty thousand women and their families." President Obama also cancelled[491] all White House tours. All of this is pure political gamesmanship not leadership and expected of only the most petty of politicians.

See also Budget Control Act; Fiscal cliff.

Shora, Kareem: Born in Damascus, Syria, he describes[493] himself as a Muslim American (rather than an American Muslim). He has close ties[492] with Columbia University's Rashid Khalidi through the American-Arab Anti-Discrimination Committee for which he was national executive director. The organization has a reputation of defending Hamas and Hezbollah as non-terrorist, legitimate organizations. It opposes[494] US aid to Israel.

In 2009, he was sworn in by Secretary Janet Napolitano to serve on the Homeland Security Council of the Department of Homeland Security.

See also Arab-American Action Network.

Shovel-ready projects: This is a term for infrastructure construction projects funded by the Recovery Act of 2009, commonly known as the stimulus. President Obama first used the phrase[495] on December 6, 2008, to describe an immediate good use of stimulus funding expected to help jump-start the economy. The phrase became a main selling point in getting the stimulus passed. The law set aside $48.1 billion for transport and infrastructure projects. This included $27.5 billion specifically for highways and bridges.

Of course, the infusion of stimulus money to states did initiate projects and create some jobs. However, many construction projects were of very short duration—days or weeks, not months—and were not as labor intensive as construction projects of the past. This was due to the replacement of large construction crews by heavy construction equipment and other technological advances.

The construction projects were also slow in being implemented due to normal bureaucratic red tape of the contracting and approval process and sometimes died on the vine before expiration of the date by which the money had to be committed. So, the states sometimes used[496] the funding to cover what they considered to be more pressing budget shortfall issues— for instance, the costs of public employees' salaries and pensions. This explains how some of the infrastructure money bolstered the employment of public employees and did less than expected to promote new private-sector jobs. The shovel-ready part of the stimulus was not well thought out. Even Obama eventually realized this and joked[498] to a friendly audience on June 13, 2011, that "shovel-ready was not as shovel-ready as we expected."

Yet the president did claim[498] in June 2011 that 2.1 million private-sector jobs had been created by the stimulus. This does not square with the fact[499] that at this same point in time, the United States had 1.9 million fewer people employed than when the stimulus passed and that construction jobs were estimated[500] to plunge by nearly 700,000 from 2008 to 2010.

The one construction project that could have had a big positive impact on employment, the Keystone XL pipeline, was approved only in part (less than 30 percent) by Obama, and he did not put his imprimatur on it until March 2012.

See also Keystone XL pipeline; Stimulus.

Siljander amendment: See Kenya funding.

Simpson-Bowles: See Bowles-Simpson.

Single payer quotes: In 2003, speaking at an AFL-CIO conference, Barack Obama, then a state senator, said[501], "I happen to be a proponent of single-payer, universal health care plans ... a single-payer health care plan, a universal health care plan. And that's what I'd like to see. But as all of you know, we may not get there immediately."

In August 2008, presidential candidate Obama said[502], "If I were designing a system from scratch, I would probably go ahead with a single-payer system."

Of course "single payer" is a euphemism for a system provided and controlled by the US government. The problems of implementation of Obamacare, possibly designed into the act, make a single payer system more likely.

See also Obamacare.

Skyrocket quote: In January 2008, then-presidential candidate Barack Obama said[72], "Under my plan of a cap-and-trade system, electricity rates would necessarily skyrocket."

Small Arms Treaty: Officially called the Arms Trade Treaty (ATT) of the United Nations, it would regulate the import and export sales of conventional arms. President George W. Bush opposed it because he thought national control was better. President Obama overturned[503] that decision in 2009, making it possible for the UN to advance a draft in September 2012. He delayed[504] his approval of the draft until just hours after his re-election. The ATT went to the UN General Assembly on April 2, 2013 where it passed.

The ATT ostensibly would help prevent the illicit international trade of firearms. It also includes a program to implement the provisions of the act in all countries and track ownership of guns imported and exported. Governments would be required to keep records for twenty years. This treaty would be implemented in all countries over the next six years.

The ATT purports to support collective rights of defense but does not emphasize (mention?) individual rights. There would be meetings every year starting in 2014 to assess each country's progress—expected to be federal statutes further limiting the right to keep and bear arms.

Although the ATT requires ratification by fifty nations before going into effect and in the US requires a two-thirds majority in the Senate for ratification, it may not be necessary for this treaty to be ratified by a two-thirds majority in the Senate for ratification. It is feared that Obama might merely sign an executive order implementing it or work through the ATF to reach the same goals. In fact, Secretary of State John Kerry said[505] on June 4, 2013 that President Obama would sign the treaty in spite of congressional opposition.

The horrific massacre of school children in December 2012 in Newtown, Connecticut, led to emotional prejudice against firearms[595]. Colorado along with other states passed stricter gun laws. But two Colorado state senators were punished for their anti-gun votes by being recalled[706].

In addition to the threat that more of our sovereignty would be ceded to the UN under the ATT, our Second Amendment rights would be sorely weakened.

On August 13, 2013, the Senate voted[653] in favor of a bill that states its purpose "to uphold Second Amendment rights and prevent the United States from entering into the United Nations Arms Trade Treaty." Yes, the Senate passed this bill, but only by a margin of seven votes: 53 to 46.

See also Disability treaty; NSA.

SNAP: See Food Stamps.

Socialist/Communist connections: Barack Obama has been endorsed by or endorsed the Democratic Socialists of America[507], the Communist Party USA[506], and Senator Bernie Sanders (D-VT)[508], who calls himself a socialist.

Solis, Hilda: See Unions

Solyndra: a manufacturer of cylindrical solar panels and the first company to receive loan guarantees under President Obama's stimulus program. Solyndra[509, 510] received $535 million, and when it declared bankruptcy on September 1, 2011, it had $875 million to $975 million in net operating losses. The company also received $12 million in solar tax credits, reducing its future tax liabilities dollar for dollar. These tax benefits were granted to delay Solyndra's demise. But the company failed anyway, and the tax benefits simply increased taxpayers debt.

In 2011, the Department of Energy waived its privilege as first creditor in the event of Solyndra's bankruptcy. That is taxpayer money – our money – to which the Energy Dept. waived its rights as first creditors. George Kaiser's Argonaut Investors, which was heavily invested in Solyndra, would be paid off first. Kaiser bundled $50,000 to $100,000 for Obama in 2008.

A US bankruptcy court decided on October 22, 2012, that Solyndra's owners, 360 Degree Solar Holdings, would realize tax benefits of between $875 million and $975 million for net operating losses; the investors, Argonaut Ventures and Madrone Partners, would benefit with up to $341 million in future tax deductions, while others including the DOE (that's us, the taxpayers) would receive almost nothing.

On November 1, 2012, the IRS appealed[511] the bankruptcy court decision, asserting that the principal purpose of Solyndra's bankruptcy plan was tax evasion.

If ever there were a poster child for Obama's failed green energy agenda, it is Solyndra. But this is also a shining example of cronyism at its worst and of the president's arrogance in interfering with free-market capitalism.

See also Green agenda; Stimulus.

Spending as percentage of GDP: Total government spending is federal, state and local government spending. Government spending is just federal spending. Each of these numbers as a percent of GDP is instructional.

The Obama administration will take credit for decreasing government spending as a percent of GDP but it was during a Republican-controlled House of Representatives that this statistic decreased the most and it is the House, not the president that controls the budget.

Government spending as a percent of GDP[512] was 25.2 during FY 2009. By FY 2012 when the Republicans held the majority in the House, federal government spending had dropped to 22.8 percent of GDP.

President Franklin D. Roosevelt spent enormous sums to win World War II, and the figure reached 24.8 percent of GDP in 1946. But never since then has any president spent at so high a rate until very recently. Exorbitant spending started up again in 2008 when George W. Bush was president. However, Congress controlled the budget process and Democrats were in the majority. House Speaker Nancy Pelosi and Senate Majority Leader Harry Reid were able to end-run President Bush's budget and pass continuing resolutions until Obama could take office. They then passed an Omnibus Spending Bill to increase FY 2009 spending. Although President Obama was not to blame for all the spending, it is estimated[513] that he was responsible for about 38 percent of it. However, Obama was totally responsible for spending in the years that followed. Each of those years saw a higher rate of spending expressed as a percentage of GDP than in any year since 1946. Federal spending as a percentage of GDP was under 10 percent until 1934 and under 12 percent until 1941.

Total government spending as a percent of GDP is a little different. It has risen quite steadily[514] since just after World War II when it peaked. It is now even higher than during WWII (1945). The two notable exceptions to the moderate but steady increase are periods of deep recession (1929-33 and 2007-09) when shrinking GDP caused a noticeable bump up in the ratio. (If GDP goes down, the ratio of spending to GDP goes up).

See also Budget; Debt; GDP; Gross debt/national debt as percentage of GDP.

Stand with Muslims quote: On page 261 of his book *The Audacity of Hope*, Barack Obama states[515], "I will stand with them [Muslims] should the political winds shift in an ugly direction."

Stanley Ann Dunham: Insofar as she[516] was Barack Obama's mother and a strong influence on him, it is instructional to explore her background. She married two Muslim men, one of whom was Obama's father and the other his stepfather. Dunham's biography is fascinating and impressive. Extremely well educated, with a PhD in anthropology, she did her doctoral field work on blacksmithing in Indonesia, which has the world's largest Muslim population. Her interest in social issues and concern for the Indonesians' quality of life caused her to become an activist.

When Barack was just ten years old, Ann Dunham (she had dropped the name Stanley) sent[517] him back to Hawaii to be raised by his grandparents, preferring that he not be influenced by her second husband, Lolo Soetoro, who had been hired by a Western oil company. Capitalism was rearing its ugly head.

According to the adult Obama[516], his mother was "the dominant figure in my formative years. The values she taught me continue to be my touchstone when it comes to how I go about the world of politics."

START: The acronym stands for Strategic Arms Reduction Treaty. A new treaty, intended to replace one that had expired, was signed by President Obama and Russian President Dimitri Medvedev in April 2010 but required ratification by the Senate. The aim of the original START was to reduce the number of strategic nuclear weapons held by the Soviet Union and the United States.

Russia made[518] US abandonment of an antiballistic missile defense shield planned for Poland and the Czech Republic a precondition for START renewal. Obama complied.

Under terms of the new treaty, both countries would reduce the number of strategic nuclear missile launchers, but were not obligated to reduce the number of stockpiled warheads. Each country would monitor the other's arsenal although Republicans considered[519] verification procedures weak.

Prior to ratification, Republicans proposed an amendment to the treaty preamble that would have required continued Russian compliance with the treaty even if the United States were to set up a missile defense system. The Democrat-majority Senate voted[520] down the amendment. The new START took effect in January 2011 after Senate ratification on December 22, 2010.

This treaty was pushed through a lame-duck Senate session with less than half the number of hearings normally held for international treaties. In addition, the Obama administration withheld[521] key documents, including the records of the treaty negotiations.

See also Missile defense shield.

Stern, Andy: See Unions.

Stimulus: The common name for the American Recovery and Reinvestment Act of 2009. The cost to taxpayers was first reported as $787 billion. The final pricetag[522] turned out to be

$862 billion. The stimulus was supposedly necessary in order to get the economy going again and guarantee that the unemployment rate would stay below 8 percent. This was to occur by cutting taxes, extending unemployment benefits, preserving the solvency of state budgets, augmenting health care, and funding shovel-ready infrastructure projects and renewable energy development and conservation.

In August 2010, a $26 billion bill – called the jobs bill - was enacted[523] to save the jobs of teachers and other civil employees - many in New York - and to plug more holes in state budgets. President Obama said this was an emergency measure.

Our Stimulus money given to green companies such as Solyndra, A123, and Evergreen Solar was ill spent. They bankrupted.

In 2009, 80 percent of stimulus dollars allocated went to five programs: Medicaid, unemployment compensation, Social Security, grants to state and local governments, and student aid. Some of the grants were for things like nutrition, anti-salt, anti-smoking, pro-breast feeding, anti-tobacco, and anti-obesity campaigns. It is unlikely that funding such things created many jobs or were intended to.

An AP study[524] concluded that there was no effect of the more than $20 billion for road and bridge construction projects as of early 2010 on local unemployment. The jobs were not shovel-ready and the president joked about it on June 13, 2011. Not funny.

State and local governments were to receive $90 billion to cover their budget shortfalls that were often caused by their unwillingness to cut bloated payrolls. Such fiscal irresponsibility should not have been rewarded with federal handouts that would only put a patch on the problem for one more budget cycle. Teachers, firefighters, and police are not the only public employees, as we are led to believe and they are generally funded by local tax dollars not federal tax dollars. Administrators and managers and their secretaries, motor pool employees, public park personnel, motor vehicle department staff, sanitation workers, and restaurant inspectors are also at risk— or should be. The critical services of teachers, police, and firefighters need not be in jeopardy. But, of course, the threat to the more critical services was a good selling point and has much greater political impact. If local governments are not collecting enough taxes to support the budgets they need (not want), maybe it is because businesses have closed and the people who pay taxes have moved elsewhere to find work. Fewer individuals and businesses to serve should dictate fewer public employees to serve them— not federal handouts to maintain bloated payrolls.

In February 2009, when the stimulus was passed, the unemployment rate was 7.6 percent. It hit 10.2 percent just eight months later in October 2009 and was at 7.8 percent in December 2012 and 7.3 percent by August 2013.[686] Even if one accepts the premise that the stimulus saved or created 3 million jobs, that computes to a cost to the taxpayer of $296,000 per job created.

It was estimated[525] from CBO data that 39 to 44 percent of the $862 billion would go toward "government transfer payments" including tax refunds to people who don't earn enough to pay taxes. A lot of the money funded unemployment payments. So the stimulus may have been less about job creation and more about the redistribution of wealth.

Many studies have been done on the effectiveness of the stimulus. Some say it failed and some say it succeeded. But we didn't get even close to as many jobs as were promised; our highways are still badly in need of repair; local governments are still going bankrupt; unemployment is still very high; the employment rate is lower than when the recession began; the number of people on food stamps has more than doubled and is at an all-time high; and the taxpayer is left with the $888 (862 + 26) billion debt liability, a drag on the economy that probably erases any benefit from the few jobs saved or created.

See also A123; Food Stamps; Redistribution; Shovel-ready projects; Solyndra; Unemployment.

Syria's Arab spring: As with other recent Mideast uprisings, this one too was probably triggered by the December 2010 self-immolation of a street vendor in Tunisia who lost his job because of government harassment. The uprising against Bashar al-Assad's dictatorship began in March 2011 with protesters calling for release of political prisoners and an end to corruption. Soon they demanded Assad's resignation.

Assad's retaliation against his people has been brutally bloody. Estimates[708] vary but are as high as 100,000 killed as of

June 2013. Although Assad released some prisoners, ended emergency law, and made changes in government positions, he has refused to step down. Many in the Syrian army defected to join the rebels and the protests escalated into civil war.

President Obama has been publicly weak in support of the rebels, saying[526] only things like, "Assad's days are numbered." He has made tepid statements such as this for two years. We and the rest of the West have been reluctant to commit to physical intervention—possibly because the Assad regime is allied with Iran, Hamas in Gaza, the Lebanese Hezbollah, China, and Russia and because our allies are waiting for the United States to do the heavy lifting.

The rebels are backed by Turkey and Qatar reportedly because these countries want some of Syria's natural gas riches delivered to the Mediterranean, not to China and Russia. Israel has thrown in with Turkey and Qatar to help prevent Iran from benefiting. Saudi Arabia is also backing the rebels.

Obama opposed military involvement in Syria and did not, at least at first, supply weapons to the rebels for fear that arms would fall into the hands of militant Islamists who have infiltrated the opposition ranks. Several proposed cease-fires, including one brokered[527] by Kofi Annan on behalf of the UN, have failed.

Russia and China have vetoed UN attempts to intervene, and Russia is supplying the Syrian army with weapons. Russia also has a military installation in Syria on the Mediterranean coast which it wants to protect. So it appears that if the West is to exert influence against Assad, the United States may be the only option left. However, it is probably too late in the game, and politically, military intervention has not been an acceptable approach for the Obama administration – that is until he backed himself into a corner with his "red line" statement.

Obama said[528] on August 20, 2012, that if Assad used chemical weapons against his people it would be crossing a red line for us. In April, 2013 US intelligence reported that analysis of Syrian rebel blood samples revealed exposure to the chemical warfare agent, Sarin. Obama, through his Secretary of Defense Chuck Hagel, downplayed[529] the importance of the report. A weak Obama response reaped[666] more aggression by Assad. On the anniversary of Obama's red line comment, the Assad regime killed another two hundred to as many as one thousand[667] by chemical gassing (later reported[689] to be 1,429). The anniversary is probably not just coincidence. There is also a possibility that the poison gas stockpiles in Syria came from Iraq.[681] If true, it is ironic that President Bush was accused of lying about the WMDs at the time.

Obama should never have made the red line comment. It appears he painted himself into a corner with that statement and because of it he couldn't even take the chance of having our UN Ambassador, Samantha Power, show up at the emergency UN Security Council meeting[667] to discuss the gassing in Syria. It is apparently better to wimp out than take a stand and face opposition.

The UN and a NATO coalition approved intervention in Libya to protect civilians. What about the over one hundred thousand Syrian civilians who have already been killed without chemicals? Apparently without the political protection and approval of the UN, or NATO, or England and France, the President won't act. Apparently slaughter with conventional weapons is acceptable. However, the use of poison gas is against international standards[622].

These situations raise questions of morality and sovereignty. Who is pulling the strings of US foreign policy? What drives our decisions?

President Hosni Mubarak of Egypt was our strong ally, yet we supported the uprising to depose him. Gadhafi of Libya was causing us no trouble yet we helped the movement to depose him – probably in violation of the Constitution and the War Powers Act.

Iran is our enemy and Israel's enemy, yet we made no attempt to encourage Iran's populist Green Movement in 2009 against undemocratically elected Ahmadinejad.

Assad has never been our friend or ally and yet we did not support the movement against him. It is possible that Obama is reluctant to get more involved[530] because his suspected covert operations in Libya backfired and his support of Morsi has not worked out well in Egypt. It is not argued here that we should have interfered in Iran or should interfere in Syria. But merely that our foreign policy, at best, is feckless and lacks consistency.

Clearly President Obama should not have drawn the red line[528] in August 2012. However, since he stuck the US with this off-the-cuff foreign policy, he should have followed through by building a coalition to be drawn upon should the unthinkable happen. He did not do his job to build a coalition.

The unthinkable happened. It actually happened as many as fifteen times[688] since 2012 but the chemical attack of August 21, 2013 killed a reported[689] 1,429 including over four hundred children. It was no longer possible to ignore it and it may not have been coincidence that it happened on the anniversary of Obama's red line statement. Obama's immediate response was reportedly[707] to explore a strike on Syria that would be "just muscular enough not to be mocked."

Obama had painted himself into a corner with his red line; Assad thumbed his nose at us; and so Obama was forced to react. He talked tough[690], sent war ships to the eastern Mediterranean and trotted out Secretary of State, John Kerry who dutifully presented and impassioned justification[691] for taking action against Assad. Obama had indicated[710] that he had the authority to act without congressional approval and many thought a strike was imminent. Obama then backed off within twenty-four hours and declared[693] he would petition congress for approval of a limited strike against Syria.

Obama then retreated[695] from his red line statement by saying, "I didn't set a red line; the world set a red line." And emphasized it by adding, "My credibility is not on the line; the credibility of the international community is on the line." How embarrassing and weak.

Of course the supposition is that the United Nations would not be with us in any military strike because Russia and China would veto any action against Syria. The British parliament turned down[692] a request from Prime Minister Cameron to help us retaliate and the Arab League and the Organization of Islamic Cooperation (OIC) equivocated and wanted a diplomatic solution. The French were with us in principal but stopped short of committing any resources. There are other potential allies in principle such as Turkey and Saudi Arabia. Many condemn the use of chemical weapons. However, so far, none has pledged to participate in a strike[704]. The American people were against[711] military action by about a 60 percent majority.

Obama had no substantive support and so, as a last resort and the very day after Kerry's strong speech, Obama backed off and requested[693] congressional authorization. But, he didn't call congress out of their summer break and back into session and then he immediately went golfing[712] with vice president, Joe Biden. What sort of message does this send about our sense of urgency or the importance of the situation?

Besides humiliating himself and Kerry, Obama has weakened the US in the eyes of the world, disappointed our allies, and emboldened Assad and more importantly, Iran. As Stephen Hayes of the Weekly Standard put it, Obama has again voted, "present" (FOX discussion just after Obama's 8/31/13 speech).

On September 9, 2013, in another apparently off-the-cuff foreign policy statement, Secretary of State John Kerry posited[709] a rhetorical argument to a question asked of him at a news conference. His response was that a strike on Syria could be averted if Assad were to give up all his chemical weapons to the international community. He quickly followed up with his disbelief that this could happen.

Within just a few hours of Kerry's statement, the Russian foreign minister proposed[703] that the UN secure all war chemicals in Syria; the Syrian foreign minister accepted the idea; and Ban Ki Moon agreed to present the idea to the UN. Credit for the proposal was given to President Putin of Russia. This proposed operation sounds better than are its chances of actual implementation during a civil war. Nonetheless, if Obama thought it to be such a good idea, why couldn't he have proposed it to Assad or at least have Samantha Power propose it at the emergency UN Security Council meeting? Her vacation[713] was apparently more important.

September 10, just one day later, Russia withdrew[714] its proposal from the UN and issued an ultimatum[714] that securing chemical weapons in Syria would not happen unless the US gave up any option for military action against Assad. Putin is now calling the shots. Obama delayed[715] the vote in congress to see how the Russian proposal develops. However, that proposal served another very useful purpose because Obama was likely[716] to lose the vote in congress. Putin has given Obama a way out, knowing that Obama would jump at the opportunity to crawl out of the corner into which he had painted himself and defer to "diplomacy."

The diplomatic solution to declaring, verifying, moving and neutralizing or destroying vast stores of very hazardous chemicals involving Syria, Russia, the US, and the rest of the UN

Security Council will take forever and has little hope of being comprehensive and effective. As a first step[717], Russia and the United States under the guidance of Secretary of State John Kerry have laid out a framework for the destruction of the chemicals and come to a consensus regarding the quantity of them. How could this occur without Syria as part of the conversation? Are we really going to believe that Russia has intentions advantageous to us in mind when it is they who are providing arms to Assad? In the meantime Assad will proceed as he wishes -- a masterful stroke by Putin.

The Russian proposal makes a vote in congress highly un-likely because the Representatives and Senators don't want to vote on such a politically hot issue if there is a chance the chemical hazard in Syria could be administratively neutralized or removed by the UN. Putin wants Assad to remain in power and has upstaged Obama and we have prostituted our foreign policy to Russia and the UN.

It appears Obama is much more concerned about impact on politics and his legacy than in doing what is right. If a potentially escalating tit-for-tat military confrontation is avoided and at least some token amount of poisonous war chemicals are neutralized or destroyed, both sides can and will claim victory. Don't expect anything substantive to happen in a timely manner. The handling, however, of the whole affair has made the US, through President Obama, appear indecisive and weak and conversely has strengthened the Russian position and its power in the Middle East.

We no longer "speak softly and carry a big stick." We are now trying to attain peace through the UN's weakness instead of peace through our own strength. The whole "leading from behind" approach isn't leading and it won't work.

See also Benghazi; Egypt's Arab spring; Election campaign fraud; Green Movement; Israel; Libya's Arab spring; Parsi, Trita; Shora, Kareem.

TARP: The first half of $700 billion for the Troubled Asset Relief Program came at the end of the George W. Bush administration. The second half[59] came under Obama's control. TARP was supposed[624] to buy up troubled assets like bad subprime mortgages and associated instruments from financial institutions or insure them. Under Obama, the focus shifted[624] just a very few days after his election and the money was used instead to bail out[60,61] AIG, Citigroup, small banks, GM and Chrysler. This effectively nationalized the car companies. This bait and switch may have been unconstitutional since no money is to be taken from the Treasury except "in consequence of appropriations made by law" (Constitution, Article I, Section 9).

Neil Barofsky, the special inspector general for TARP (SIGTARP) reported[625] that quick shut down of car dealerships may not have been "necessary or prudent." A disproportionate[62] number of closings were in rural areas not friendly to Obama, yet dealerships in oversaturated metropolitan areas[626] were spared. The IG also pointed out that one of the criteria for choosing which dealerships to close was to avoid those owned by minorities or women[626]. This caused some dealerships that were more profitable to be closed in their stead. According to at least one GM official, it was not clear that the closings saved the car company any money.

The Italian car maker Fiat now,[63, 627] owns the controlling interest in and manages Chrysler. Their debt has at least partially been handled using smoke and mirrors: $4 billion in debt was forgiven and then Secretary of Energy Chu gave Fiat an amount ($3.5 billion) equal to what it owed so it could pay on its debt. Yes, Chrysler is paying off its debt to the US taxpayer with money borrowed from the US taxpayer[628] and it appears GM used a separate pot of TARP money[67] to pay back its TARP loan. It is akin to paying off one credit card with another.

GM is now (July 2013) 16% - 18% owned[64, 629] by the US government. That is a great improvement over the original 60% ownership, but it should have always been zero. GM still owes us almost $20 billion[630].

The portion of TARP that was to help homeowners who couldn't make their mortgage payments is called Home Affordable Modification Program or HAMP. The IG found as of April 2013 and reported in the SIGTARP report of July 24, 2013, that of the 1.2 million homeowners in HAMP who needed and got help to avoid foreclosure, 25.5% have missed three monthly payments and so are out of the program. So far, this is $815 million of taxpayer money down the drain.[631] There is more to come. In fact data show that the longer homeowners are in the HAMP program, the more likely they are to default. Now President Obama wants to give more help to homeowners[632] - more redistribution of wealth. This is not likely to happen under

FHFA's acting director, Ed DeMarco. However, Obama has plans to replace him (see Fannie & Freddie).

A lawsuit[65] against senior members of the Obama administration on behalf of homeowners seeking to stop foreclosures, audit the Fed and all bailout programs, requested the return of $43 trillion. Plaintiffs in the lawsuit asserted that $43 trillion was laundered and invested in an enterprise they consider criminal under racketeering laws. There was a settlement[66] in March 2013. However, payout to individual homeowners appears to be an extremely unlikely and maybe expensive proposition.

Failure is part of capitalism. Capitalism is tough, but it works and its rewards are great. Competition weeds out the inefficient and useless. What TARP did was and is not in the spirit of capitalism and is shifting the risk from the big business owner, to the taxpayer. We now are backing with our tax dollars banks, car companies and high-risk mortgages. We take the risk so they don't have to. But, even though we are taking more and more of the risk, we get none of the profit. This is not capitalism.

See also Bondholders, secured; Delphi pensions; Fannie & Freddie; GM's CEO fired;

Terry, Brian: See Fast and Furious.

Thatcher, Margaret: Former prime minister of England a strong ally of the US during the Reagan administration died and was honored in a very formal funeral on April 17, 2013. Neither President Obama, nor Vice-President Biden nor the first lady, Michelle Obama was in attendance. They were too busy stumping for gun control. Speaker of the House, John Boehner sent two men as private citizens. What a snub!

See also Churchill bust.

Times Square bomber: Faisal Shahzad, a thirty-year-old Pakistan-born resident and citizen of the United States, attempted on May 1, 2010, to detonate a car bomb in Times Square in New York City. Smoke coming from the vehicle alerted two street vendors, who alerted police. The explosives did not detonate. Shahzad was arrested, convicted, and sentenced to life in prison.

Following Shahzad's arrest two days after the bombing attempt, the Obama administration misinformed[531] the public that the terrorist had acted alone. Homeland Security Secretary Napolitano said it was a "one-off" thing and General David Petraeus declared Shahzad to be a lone wolf. The media[532] made excuses for Shahzad of financial pressures and a Spartan existence. Michael Bloomberg[533] attempted to politicize Shahzad's act of terror.

After the event, Shahzad was being tracked by the FBI, but agents lost him on the way to the airport, and although his name was on the no-fly list, he still managed to board a flight to Dubai. It was the work of the New York City Police Department, not the feds that led to his arrest on the plane after he had boarded.

Shahzad admitted the car bombing attempt and said[534] he had been trained at a Pakistani terrorist camp and was inspired by Anwar al-Awlaki. The attack was directed and possibly financed by the Pakistani Taliban, who are closely allied with al-Qaeda. He was not exactly a lone terrorist as the Obama administration had first asserted.

Although Shahzad was quoted[535] as saying, "If I'm given a thousand lives, I will sacrifice them all for the life of Allah," President Obama never mentioned Islam in his remarks about the incident and he was praised[536] by an Arabic newspaper for that.

See also Anwar al-Awlaki, Underwear bomber.

Too big to fail: Remember the AIG bailout of 2008? If we know anything about the Dodd-Frank Act, we know it is supposed to prevent another "too big to fail" crisis that requires another taxpayer-funded bailout.

The Dodd-Frank Act, through its Financial Stability Board, designated eight US banks as "systemically important financial institutions" because they are so large, complex, and interconnected that they must not be allowed to fail. Failure would cause too much financial disruption globally—not just in the United States. The eight institutions are Bank of America, Bank of New York Mellon, Citi, Goldman Sachs, JP Morgan Chase, Morgan Stanley, State Street, and Wells Fargo. So we've moved from "too big to fail" to "too systemic to fail."

No less than Federal Reserve Chairman Ben Bernanke said[537], "A bank which is thought too big to fail gets an artificial subsidy in the interest rate that it can borrow at." That is expected to happen, and it puts non-listed banks at a competitive disadvantage. As a result, the big banks get even bigger than they were before the crisis and the small banks are in jeopardy of being squeezed out of the market. The "systematically important" designation also creates a politically acceptable mechanism for politicians to grant favors to those on the list under the guise of preventing their failure.

However, should one of these banks get into financial trouble, the Federal Deposit Insurance Corporation now has the power under Dodd-Frank to seize the institution and restructure it, wiping out the shareholders and giving first claim on anything the newly structured bank owns to the Treasury. This is better than a bailout? There are severe separation of powers and due process issues here.

Dodd-Frank does explicitly prohibit the Federal Reserve from bailing out individual firms. However, another section of the law declares that any financial institution that is engaged in "clearing, settlement or payment activities" may be designated by the Financial Stability Oversight Council as eligible for a Federal Reserve bailout. This category includes many banks—especially the big ones.

In a speech[538] on November 15, 2012, William Dudley, president of the Federal Reserve Bank of New York, said that "too big to fail" was still with us despite Dodd-Frank because of the market's perception (reinforced by the law) that the US government will protect such institutions.

It has been suggested by a few that big banks be broken into smaller banks that don't mix traditional banking functions with investment services and that this would make them less susceptible to becoming "systemic" and therefore they could be allowed to fail. It seems a suggestion worthy of serious consideration.

Governor Mitt Romney was apparently correct when he said[539] that Dodd-Frank "institutionalized" too big to fail.

See also Dodd-Frank.

Traditions: See Ideals quote.

Transport rule: See Coal-fired power plant.

Trayvon Martin: The seventeen-year-old was killed in Florida by George Zimmerman on February 26, 2012. It was dark; Zimmerman was on neighborhood watch; Trayvon looked "like he's up to no good"; an altercation occurred; Zimmerman killed Trayvon. Zimmerman was charged with murder and went to trial. A jury of six women found him not guilty on July 13, 2013.

The case was emotionally charged, since Trayvon was a black minor and Zimmerman was an adult Hispanic and armed. In a report on March 22, 2012, *The New York Times* described[540] him as a "white Hispanic." It is unlikely that anyone had ever before been described that way.

As the case unfolded, the 911 tapes were reported[541] by NBC on March 19 to reveal Zimmerman's volunteering that Trayvon was black. That report exacerbated an already racially heated situation. However, the complete 911 tape had been injudiciously edited—a generous assessment. The full tape showed that Zimmerman was asked by the dispatcher whether

Trayvon was "white, black, or Hispanic." Zimmerman responded, "He looks black." NBC edited out the dispatcher's question and left only that short response—a good example of mainstream media bias.

The New Black Panthers offered ten thousand dollars for the man who killed Trayvon Martin. The Department of Justice, under Attorney General Eric Holder, did not consider[542] this bounty placed on a yet-to-be-indicted man to be a hate crime.

On March 22, 2012 President Obama injected himself into the controversy by saying[543] in the White House Rose Garden, "If I had a son, he would look like Trayvon," and "I think all of us have to do some soul searching to figure out how something like this happened."

A question for the president: if the young man killed had been white should it have demanded any less soul searching or any less attention from you? How sad the president focused only on Trayvon's blackness. Obama's phantom son comment poured fuel on the fire and it is difficult to believe he did not know exactly what he was doing.

In July during the height of the trial it was made public[544] that FOIA requests had revealed documents showing that the Community Relations Service, a unit of the DOJ had been dispatched to Florida in April after the incident to "help organize rallies and protests against George Zimmerman." They spent tax payers' money doing this.

After the not guilty decision for Zimmerman, the NAACP petitioned the DOJ to bring a federal civil rights case against him. The DOJ is considering it.

See also Beer summit; New Black Panthers.

TSA: The Transportation Security Administration was created by President George W. Bush just after the 9/11 attacks on the U.S. It was charged with protecting US transportation—especially ensuring airport security and preventing aircraft hijacking. It is now a part of the Department of Homeland Security and employs roughly forty-seven thousand screeners, federal air marshals, inspectors, explosives-detection canine teams, and others.

The public's opinion of the TSA is not good. A survey[545] found that 90 percent of frequent flyers asked thought the TSA was doing either a poor or fair job with airport security screenings. Screeners have failed many tests, missing planted mock guns and bombs, and there have been many accusations of pat-down and other abuses.

In 2011, TSA chief John Pistole expressed[546] a desire to build the agency into a "national-security, counterterrorism organization, fully integrated into US government efforts." Since then, the TSA has had a visible presence[547] at unlikely venues including 2012 campaign events and Tea Party rallies in May of 2013 which protested[611] the IRS targeting of Conservative groups. This occurred in multiple states and involved uniformed, armed guards. Their presence at these events is unrelated to transportation and inappropriate.

One has to wonder if these are the seeds of what then-candidate Barack Obama called[548] for on July 2, 2008: a "civilian security force that's just as powerful, just as strong, and just as well funded" as the military. Taken somewhat out of context, this is nonetheless worrisome, and it is not clear—even in context—exactly what Obama meant.

It is clear, however, that the president is trying to diminish the capabilities of our military and restrict private gun ownership. That is consistent with his desire for a strong civilian force.

See also Kimathi, Ayo; Small Arms Treaty.

Underwear bomber: On December 25, 2009, Umar Farouk Abdulmutallab, a twenty-three-year-old from Nigeria, also known as the Christmas bomber, tried to blow up a Northwest Airlines plane headed for Detroit, using plastic explosives hidden in his underwear. The explosives fizzled and Abdulmutallab was arrested, convicted, and sent to prison for life.

Janet Napolitano, secretary of homeland security, said[549] of the incident, "And one thing I'd like to point out is that the system worked." The system did not work. Rather, the terrorist failed, which gave Napolitano cover.

President Obama first addressed[550] the incident three days later while on vacation in Hawaii and referred to the perpetrator of the attempted bombing as an isolated extremist. This turned out not to be the case. Abdulmutallab was trained by al-Qaeda in Yemen, and Anwar al-Awlaki was behind the plot. Al-Qaeda in the Arabian Peninsula claimed responsibility for the attempted bombing.

Whether Obama just used the wrong words, really thought, or wanted us to believe that this was not a terrorist act is not known. But it is consistent with the way he wanted us to perceive the Fort Hood shooting and the attempted bombing in Times Square as well – that is, anything but a result of Islamic extremism.

See also Anwar al-Awlaki, Fort Hood; Times Square bomber.

Unemployment rate: The rate, reported as the U3 unemployment rate (the official figure), is defined as the number of unemployed divided by the number in the labor force. The devil is in the details, however, and the officially unemployed don't include those on disability, in school, retired due to age, moved back in with parents, or just not looking for a job. In fact, the percentage of working age people (16 – 64) employed plus not employed but actively looking for a job (called the labor force participation rate) has dropped[551] from 65.7 percent in June 2009—when the recession officially ended—to 63.4 percent in July 2013, the lowest figure in over thirty years[552]. By August the rate[700] was 63.2 percent, the lowest in thirty-five years.

The long-term unemployed are defined as those out of work twenty-seven weeks or more, and that number is 4.246[553] million for July 2013. The long-term unemployment figure when President Obama took office was 2.6 million. This is a 63 percent increase in long-term unemployment in four years. So the number of long-term unemployed has risen sharply despite the fact that Obama has hired[554] an average of 101 federal employees per day, every day, seven days a week, averaged over the 202 weeks since he was inaugurated in 2009.

Increased long-term unemployment is at least partially due to the administration's repeated extensions of unemployment benefits. In 2008, just before Obama took office, unemployment benefits could be claimed for up to twenty-six weeks. At the height of the economic crisis, individuals were eligible for up to ninety-nine weeks of benefits depending on a state's unemployment rate. That was later reduced to 73 weeks as unemployment rates started to come down. January 1, 2013, Democrats got a year's extension[555] of unemployment benefits for the long-term unemployed as part of the fiscal cliff package.

Looking at the converse, employment (employment-to-population ratio),[556, 557] as of July 2013 is 58.7 percent which is a full four percentage points lower than when the recession began sixty-six months earlier in December 2007 and this number includes those who are employed only part-time.

In fact, 87.5% of the jobs created[639] under Obama (Jan 2009 through July 2013) were part-time jobs. That is 7 out of every 8 jobs created. Part-time employment has accelerated and full-time employment has decelerated[558] due, at least in part, to Obamacare which requires employers of more than 49 employees to provide health care insurance for full-time workers (defined as those working 30 hours or more per week) or pay a fine.

See also Fiscal cliff; Obamacare

Unions: Labor unions in the United States have a long history of association with socialist and communist doctrine. The activist battle cry "Workers of the world unite" goes all the way back to the Communist Manifesto of 1848. President Franklin D. Roosevelt's New Deal liberalism promoted social welfare, labor unions, civil rights, and regulation of business. The teachers' union, the National Education Association (NEA), the country's largest union, has never endorsed[559] a Republican or third party presidential candidate.

Barack Obama said[560] in a speech to union members in 2007, "Your agenda's been my agenda in the United States Senate." It seems he has moved that agenda forward[564] since his inauguration by infusing his administration with pro-forced-unionism thinking and policy-makers wherever it was feasible.

Patrick Gaspard, considered to be Obama's Karl Rove, was formerly executive vice president[561] of New York's Local 1199 —the largest local within the Service Employees International Union (SEIU). Hilda Solis, a forced-unionism partisan[562], ran the Department of Labor. AFL-CIO and SEIU attorney Craig Becker[563] was appointed by Obama to the NLRB in 2010 during a Senate recess although his nomination had been rejected by the Senate the month before; Obama made a recess appointment to the NLRB of Richard Griffin, an attorney for a union with mob connections.[405]

In addition to making union-biased appointments, Obama cut[564] funds from his first budget for the federal agency that enforces union disclosure laws and investigates union corruption. There were speaking slots at the September 2012 Democratic National Convention for three union presidents—those of the SEIU[565], UAW[566], and AFL-CIO[567]. Andy Stern, former president of the SEIU, visited[568] the White House fifty-three times between Obama's inauguration and February 2011, and Obama appointed[569] Stern to his National Commission on Fiscal Responsibility and Reform.

There is an obvious problem with diverting enormous sums of money from taxpayers—who have no choice but to pay union dues (forced-unionism), —into Democratic campaigns. For instance, the two large teachers' unions, the NEA and the American Federation of Teachers, have, over the last twenty years, contributed more than ten times more[570] to Democrats than to Republicans. This does not reflect the demographics of the teachers. The SEIU contributed $85 million to Democrats in 2008. The Obama campaign received $60 million[571] of this. This promotes a quid pro quo situation.

A less obvious problem is that the union employment model fosters the same set of goals as those of socialism/communism—only in microcosm. That is, compensation should be as egalitarian as possible; profits aren't that important; there is more security in seniority than in good job performance; promotion is not necessarily a function of job performance; the collective good is emphasized rather than individual rights and freedoms; health and retirement benefits are liberal and for life; and you can't be fired. The greater these perks are, the more likely their recipients are to vote to perpetuate the power of the providers. It is a cradle-to-grave, we'll-take-care-of-you approach to life. If unionism is forced—that is, no job without union membership—this model is self-perpetuating.

See also ACORN; Delphi pensions; NLRB; Occupy Wall Street; Right to work; School vouchers.

UN Speech: President Obama's 2012 speech to the UN on September 25, 2012, came just two weeks after the jihadist attacks on our consulate and annex in Benghazi where Ambassador J. Christopher Stevens and three other Americans were murdered on September 11. Although it is now known that within two hours it was clear this was a planned terrorist attack involving splinter groups of al-Qaeda, Obama, in his highly public speech[572] to the UN, mentioned the video trailer disparaging Muhammad six times, in such a context as to imply that this was the cause of the attacks. He used the word *terrorist* only once and not in the context of Benghazi, but with reference to Iran's support of terrorism in general. He adopted a tone of apology for US freedom of speech, and his voice reflected no outrage over the Islamic terrorist act.

See also Benghazi.

Voter ID: In our country's not-so-distant past, some states suppressed the minority vote—black, Asian, or Native American.

Passed in 1965, the Voting Rights Act (VRA) required all or parts of sixteen states, mostly in the south, with a history of discrimination to get federal approval (preclearance) before changing the way they held elections. Texas and South Carolina are two of those states.

In 2012, President Obama's Department of Justice cited[573] the VRA in rejecting new voter-ID requirements in South Carolina even though the US Supreme Court had upheld Indiana's photo-ID requirement for voters in 2008. Indiana is not one of the states covered by the VRA.

However, Shelby County in Alabama (one of the sixteen states covered by VRA) challenged[574] the law, arguing that the data on which it was based are now more than forty-seven years old and that the state has come a long way toward anti-discrimination since then.

The Supreme Court agreed on November 9, 2012, to hear the case, *Shelby County v. Holder.* North Carolina and other Southern states brought similar challenges. SCOTUS decided[575] on June 25, 2013, that these states no longer must get preclearance from the federal government to manage their voting process. Many Democrats including Obama[576] claimed that this was a setback in the civil rights movement.

On July 25, 2013, in spite of the Supreme Court decision, Eric Holder announced that the Justice Department believed[577] that Texas should have to petition the federal government in order to change its voting regulations. Texas wants to institute a voter ID requirement and Obama's DOJ is going to make them jump through hoops to get it. It appears to be a stall tactic that could impact the 2014 mid-term elections.

It is difficult to believe that requiring a photo ID of voters is likely to impose an undue burden on minorities and thus suppress their vote, as Democrats argue. Some form of ID and often a photo ID is a requirement for so many daily routine activities[578] that not having one is a major disadvantage, so most people have one. In some states, they are free and in others, inexpensive.

Georgia is one of only four states that requires[579], not just requests, a photo-ID to vote. The requirement took effect in 2007. Many other states are in the process of enacting similar legislation or already have. A study conducted[580] by *The Atlanta Journal-Constitution* and published on September 3, 2012, found that black voting was up 44 percent from 2006 to 2010. Hispanic voting increased 67 percent, and white voting rose 12 percent in the same period. Although black voting dropped in 2010, there were still more black voters in 2010 than in 2006. This indicates that Obama probably was not the only factor driving black turnout and that photo IDs probably did not have a suppressing effect.

On August 12, 2013, Governor McCrory of North Carolina signed[648] a new law requiring photo IDs to vote. The new law also shortens the period of early voting and prohibits same-day registrations. Civil rights groups immediately filed suits against the new law essentially charging that it discriminates against Democrats.

See also Election campaign fraud.

Vouchers: See School vouchers

War Powers Act: This law, a reaction to the Vietnam War, is also called the War Powers Resolution of 1973 or simply WPR. It was passed by a two-thirds vote in each house of Congress after then-President Richard Nixon vetoed it. It requires the president to notify Congress when committing armed forces to military action and requires congressional approval if the forces remain in action more than sixty days (with thirty additional days for withdrawal).

The joint resolution is supposed to prevent the president from assuming more power than has been granted him under the Constitution as commander in chief (article II, section 2). It is generally agreed that the commander-in-chief role gives the president power to defend against attack on the United States and power to lead the armed forces. However, article I, section 8 of the Constitution gives Congress the power to declare war, raise and support the armed forces, and control war funding. There has, therefore, always been tension between the president and Congress on this issue.

Presidents Ronald Reagan, Bill Clinton, and Barack Obama have disregarded the War Powers Act and have not suffered legal consequences. Presidents George H. W. Bush and George W. Bush sought congressional approval before going to war in Iraq and Afghanistan.

The War Powers Act and its violation have been controversial since the law's inception in 1973. It should be amended or enforced as is.

See also Libya's Arab spring.

Waxman-Markey Cap-and-Trade Bill: See Cap & Trade Bill.

Welfare: Considering only means-tested federal welfare expenditures (which exclude Social Security and Medicare), the Congressional Research Service shows[581] that together these entitlement programs were the largest budget item in fiscal year 2011. We are spending more on these entitlements than on Social Security, Medicare, or national defense. Spending on federal welfare programs has increased 32 percent from 2008 to 2011.

As an example of how out of balance things are, consider the situation in Pennsylvania as explained by that state's secretary of public welfare and reported[582] by James Pethokoukis. A single mother of two in that state with a gross income of twenty-nine thousand dollars and income-adjusted welfare benefits is financially better off than a single mother of two with a gross income of sixty-nine thousand dollars and no welfare benefits.

More data on our ridiculous largesse were just recently revealed by a Cato Institute study and reported[659] by Michael D. Tanner. There are 72 government programs that are available to directly benefit needy individuals with cash or in-kind benefits. If just the most popular seven of these programs were accessed by a single mother with two children, they would receive $38,004 in benefits in New York State. And, that figure is only the seventh-highest in the nation. Hawaii's benefit program is the most liberal, providing $60,590 to that same mother of two using the same programs. There are thirty-three states where the welfare benefits pay an equivalent of more than $8 per hour. The federal minimum wage is $7.25. In twelve states plus Washington D.C. the benefits package amounts to more than $15 per hour. It is no wonder that so many have stopped looking for work. They can't afford to take a job.

Charles Murray in his book, *Losing Ground*[642], dispelled the notion of poverty being related to racial prejudice. One of his findings was that poverty stopped[643] decreasing after President Johnson's War on Poverty got going.

See also Food Stamps; Unemployment rate.

Wright, Reverend Jeremiah: The pastor emeritus of Trinity United Church of Christ in Chicago, he retired in 2008 after being the senior pastor there for thirty-six years. Wright received a lot of notoriety during the 2008 presidential campaign because Barack Obama attended weekly services at Trinity United and because of the content of the reverend's sermons and remarks.

Wright's most famous quote[583], "No, no, no, not God bless America. God damn America," is not the only controversial thing he has said. He has made anti-Semitic and racist comments, is a believer and proponent of black liberation theology, and a supporter of Louis Farrakhan. Shortly after the attacks of September 11, 2001, he said[583], "America's chickens are coming home to roost." He has accused this country of terrorism, racism, lying, and not batting an eye over Hiroshima and Nagasaki. Hate speech such as this, even from a pastor, would probably have been ignored were it not for the fact that Obama listened to him for twenty years, was married by him, had his children baptized by him, and said[584] of him, "I can no more disown him than I can disown the black community. I can no more disown him than I can my white grandmother." Barack and wife Michelle contributed[585] $26,270 in 2007 to Wright's church.

The mission statement on the Trinity United website[586] mentioned a "commitment to Africa," but not to America, and lists the goal of working toward "economic parity." Part of their mission statement is to "...become agents of change for God who is not pleased with America's economic mal-distribution." That was on the website in 2012, it has since changed to a softer tone but the allegiance to Africa is still mentioned as is injustice.

This church which espoused black liberation theology, was preaching Marxist philosophy.

Obama eventually distanced himself from Wright during the 2008 presidential campaign and condemned[587] the reverend's comments but not the man.

See also Black liberation theology; Pfleger, Father Michael.

"You didn't build that" quote: See Business.

Zimmerman, George: See Trayvon Martin.

Issues and Decisions

with supporting evidence noted for cross reference

Issue 1: Is President Obama's governing philosophy pro-union/pro-socialist and conversely anti-free market capitalist?

Actions/inactions: Bondholders, secured; Delphi pensions; GM CEO fired; Obamacare exemptions; Solyndra; TARP.

Appointments: ACORN; Becker, Craig; Gaspard, Patrick; Jones, Van; NLRB; Solis, Hilda; Unions.

Associations: ACORN; Ayers, Bill; Davis, Frank Marshall; Drew, Dr. John C.; Pfleger, Father Michael; Socialist/Communist connections; Stanley Ann Dunham; Stern, Andy; Unions; Wright.

Incidents & reactions: BP oil spill; Drilling moratorium; NLRB; Occupy Wall Street; Right-to-work.

Philosophy: Alinsky, Saul; Ayers, Bill; Davis, Frank Marshall; Stanley Ann Dunham.

Policies: Card check; Climate change; Coal-fired power plants; Coal industry; Dodd-Frank; Fannie & Freddie; Green agenda; Obamacare; Obamacare exemptions; School vouchers; Too big to fail; Unions.

Quotes: Assault on unions; Bankrupt; Business; Fat-cat bankers; Fundamental transformation; I'll walk the picket line; Kick ass; Right-to-work; Rugged individualism; Single-payer; Private sector doing fine.

Decision, Issue 1: Evidence supports that President Obama governs from a pro-union/pro-socialist and anti-free market capitalist philosophy. See following section for Rationale.

Issue 2: Is President Obama weakening the United States by destroying individual wealth and by unprecedented spending?

Actions/Inactions: ACORN; Bondholders, secured; Credit rating; Delphi pensions; Keystone XL pipeline; Quantitative easing; Solyndra; Unions.

Appointments: Lew, Jack; Socialist/Communist connections.

Associations:

Incidents & Reactions: Drilling moratorium.

Philosophy: Alinsky, Saul; Collective salvation; Fair share; Redistribution.

Policies: Agenda 21; ANWR; Budget; Cap & Trade; Climate Change; Coal-fired power plants, Coal Industry; Debt; EPA's CO2 regulations; Fair share; Fannie & Freddie; Fiscal cliff; Food Stamps; GDP; Global Poverty Act; Green Agenda; Gross Debt as percentage of GDP; mpg; National Debt as percentage of GDP; Obamacare; Ocean Control by UN; Shovel-ready projects; Spending as percentage of GDP; Stimulus; TARP; Too big to fail; Unemployment rate; Welfare.

Quotes: Bankrupt; Constitution; Redistribution; Rugged individualism; Skyrocket.

Decision, Issue 2: Evidence supports a decision that Obama has weakened the United States by destroying individual wealth and by exorbitant spending. See following section for Rationale.

Issue 3: Does President Obama intentionally engage in race/class/cultural warfare?

Actions/Inactions: Arizona; Bondholders, secured; Voter ID.

Appointments: Jones, Van.

Associations: Pfleger, Father Michael; Stanley Ann Dunham; Wright, Reverend Jeremiah.

Incidents & reactions: Beer summit; New Black Panthers; Occupy Wall Street; Trayvon Martin.

Philosophy: Alinsky, Saul; Black liberation theology.

Policies: Agenda 21; Climate change; Fair share; Fannie & Freddie; Food stamps; Immigration; Kenya funding; New Black Panthers; Obamacare; Obamacare exemptions; Ocean control by UN; Unemployment rate; Welfare.

Quotes: Collective salvation; FOX News/Limbaugh; Guns or religion; Hard-wired; Punish our enemies; Redistribution.

Decision, Issue 3: Although the evidence does not prove Obama's intentional, explicit promotion of warfare between races, classes, or cultures, it does show him to be implicitly divisive. The rationale for this decision is in the next section.

Issue 4: Is President Obama's agenda pro-globalist and conversely anti-individual rights/anti-sovereign rights/anti-American?

Actions/Inactions: Apology Tour #2; Arizona; Kill list; National Counterterrorism Center; Libya's Arab spring.

Appointments: Bilderberg group.

Associations: Bilderberg group.

Incidents & Reactions: Arizona; Bow to Saudi king;

Philosophy: Collective salvation.

Policies: Agenda 21; Climate change; Debt; Disability treaty; Global Poverty Act; Ocean control by UN; Small Arms Treaty; START; Syria's Arab spring.

Quotes: Apology tour #3; Derisive; Exceptionalism; Fundamental transformation; Ideals; Rugged Individualism.

Decision, Issue 4: The evidence listed, particularly in the Policy section, argues that Obama is more in tune with ideologies fostered by the United Nations than with the Constitution of the United States. More reasoning will be presented in the Rationales section.

Issue 5: Is President Obama's alliance with Muslims a threat to the safety and security of Israelis and Americans?

Actions/inactions: Abbas, Mahmoud; Al Arabiya interview; Day of Prayer; Election campaign fraud; Global Counterterrorism Forum; Iran; Kenya funding; Missile defense shield; Mosque restoration; UN speech.

Appointments: Abedin, Huma; Alikhan, Arif; Elibiary, Mohamed; Hagel, Chuck; Hussain, Rashad; Ibrahim, Samira; Kimathi, Ayo; Magid, Mohamed; Mogahed, Dalia; Mustapha, Kifah; Parsi, Trita; Shora, Kareem.

Associations: Abbas, Mahmoud; al-Mansour, Dr. Khalid Abdullah Tariq; Arab-American Action Network; Mattson, Ingrid; Stanley Ann Dunham; Wright, Reverend Jeremiah.

Incidents & reactions: Apology tour; Boston marathon bombing; Bow to Saudi King; Fort Hood; Green movement; Israel; Times Square bomber; Underwear bomber.

Policies: Israel; NASA; Palestine; Rules of engagement.

Quotes: Israel; Muslim call to prayer; Muslim country; Stand with Muslims.

Decision, Issue 5: Circumstantial evidence and some of the president's inactions reveal a potentially dangerous favoritism toward Muslims and Arab states and antipathy towards Israel. See the Rationales section.

Issue 6: Has President Obama violated the Constitution and disregarded the rule of law in certain areas?

Area	Supporting evidence
Health care	Contraceptive mandate; Cornhusker kickback; IPAB; Kenya funding; Lawsuits against Obamacare; Obamacare; Obamacare exemptions.
Union support	Bondholders, secure; Czars, Delphi pensions; NLRB; TARP.
Green agenda	BP escrow; Cap-and-trade bill; Coal-fired power plants; Coal industry; Drilling moratorium; EPA's CO2 regulations; Ocean control by UN.
Anti-free market capitalism	BP escrow; Cap & Trade Bill; Coal-fired power plants; Coal industry; Consumer Financial Protection Bureau; Delphi pensions; Dodd-Frank; Drilling moratorium; Fannie & Freddie; GM's CEO fired; Obamacare; TARP; Too big to fail.
Group warfare	Arizona, Immigration, New Black Panthers, TARP, Voter ID.
Anti-individual /-sovereignty, pro-globalism	al-Awlaki, ANWR; AP leak investigation; Immigration; IRS; Libya's Arab spring; NSA; ocean control by UN; Small Arms treaty.
Pro-Muslim	Benghazi; Kenya funding; Mosque restoration.

Decision, Issue 6: It appears that there is sufficient evidence that President Obama has played fast and loose with the rule of law and interpretation of the Constitution. More on the subject will follow in the Rationales section.

Rationales

Rationale for Issue 1 decision: President Obama is pro-union, pro-socialism, and anti-free market capitalism.

From his words, actions, appointments, associations, policies, and reactions to incidents, it is clear that President Obama is pro-union.

Obama has said that he would walk the picket line if he thought collective bargaining rights were being challenged and that he thought Governor Scott Walker's fight to protect Wisconsin's state budget from excessive public union demands was an "assault on unions." Of course it was nothing of the sort. It was a fight for the reduction in the power of a public-sector union that had no management opposition, as appropriately occurs in the private sector, and it was breaking the state's budget.

The president has made unconventional and illegal appointments to the National Labor Relations Board. His choices were so pro-union that they rendered this body unlikely to make unbiased decisions that balance union and management demands.

Obama backed card check legislation and opposed right-to-work laws despite data showing that unionization is not advantageous to increasing employment, and opposed school vouchers despite data showing that students from nonpublic (non-unionized) schools outperform students from public schools in the same markets. These are examples of his blind support for unions, such as the NEA, regardless of their detriment to children and the country's belief in the basic values of right to work and a good education.

The favoritism Obama showed in the GM bailout to Delphi pensioners who were unionized (UAW) over those who were not is unconscionable and possibly illegal and unconstitutional as well.

Unions at first served a very beneficial purpose in this country, curtailing management's undue power advantage and ending the slavish working conditions that resulted. Later, the union movement fought to protect the working rights of women and minorities. These were all worthy causes successfully pursued. But along with the good came an increase in union power that skewed the balance in the system decisively in favor of the worker coalition. Of course union members overwhelmingly outnumbered management, giving them a huge political advantage. Their solidarity—each member concerned primarily with the good of the group—caused them to vote as a bloc in favor of liberal or socialist politicians who tended to believe in the sacrifice of the individual for the sake of the collective good of the group.

Union collectivism mirrors the goals of the socialist movement. There are many similarities. Profits in the union model (individual rights in the socialist model) are eschewed in favor of increased salaries and benefits for union members (entitlements for constituents of a socialist society); union contracts (entitlement guarantees in socialism) are more important than corporate profitability (local, state and national fiscal solvency). This is, no doubt, why union movements have long been associated with socialist movements.

So it is clear that Obama is pro-union and pro-socialism. However, the flip side of that is that he is also aggressively anti-free market capitalism. As with his pro-union quotes, some of his less well-coached or rehearsed utterances have given him away. Obama's threat that he would cause the owners of coal-fired power plants to go "bankrupt" if they wished to build new plants, his comment that he wanted to "know whose ass to kick" over the BP oil spill, his "you didn't build that" claim, and his disparaging remark about "fat-cat bankers" all reveal a mind-set that is virulently anti-capitalist.

Obama's policies are strangling the coal and oil industries, and his willingness to circumvent Congress to accomplish his goals reveals the intensity of his anti-capitalist ideology. Among these policies were the new CO2 regulations for coal-fired power plants, which were an unabashed, and probably illegal, end run around Congress after his cap-and-trade bill was defeated; the overly aggressive regulation of coal mining; his refusal to approve the whole Keystone XL pipeline after more than four years of favorable environmental analysis; his drilling moratorium after the BP oil spill; and his orders to the new EPA chief to proceed with a climate change plan without congressional approval. All these are job-killing, anti-business moves with the common thread of overzealous environmentalism and opposition to fossil fuel industries. Thus one might assume that his concern about climate change is the only driver. Climate change is, no doubt, one factor, but not the only one.

Obama has shown his anti-capitalist colors in non-energy areas as well. His bailout of Chrysler and GM essentially nationalized those car manufacturers—not exactly a free-market move. His firing of GM's CEO and closing down of car dealerships, some of which were profitable, were unprecedented and not consistent with free-market capitalism.

The Patient Protection and Affordable Care Act (Obamacare) is bound to bankrupt health care insurance companies in the long run because of the requirement that they cover those with pre-existing conditions and allow everyone to go without purchasing insurance until they need it. If individuals for whom insurance is not provided by their employer do not elect to buy their own policies, they may merely pay a fine which is much less than the cost of insurance premiums. Of course that is what most will do.

Under the new health care law, insurance companies are also told how much profit they are allowed to make and that they must refund "excess" profits to policyholders. Again, this is contrary to a free-market, capitalist society and will result in what Obama has wanted all along—a single-payer system, aka the government.

With its unprecedented interference in our financial industry, the Dodd-Frank Act has inadvertently picked winners and losers among banks. The law created the Consumer Finance Protection Bureau, which has unfettered power to seize financial institutions, tax banks, and subpoena their financial records. Under Obama, the financial industry no longer operates in a free-market environment.

So there is evidence that Obama is pro-union, pro-socialist, and anti-free market capitalism. If his policies were good for the country, he would face less criticism. However, his anti-capitalist stance has cost many jobs, and not just in the fossil fuel industry, and has not been good for our economy as evidenced by the anemic and protracted recovery from the recent recession. Socialist models around the world have not been as successful as the free-market capitalism model of the United States. Socialism is not something we should try to emulate.

Obama claims that "rugged individualism"—his mocking reference to free-market capitalism—doesn't work. He is wrong. America's past success and strength have proved it. Yes, our system leaves some in the dust, but there will always be a group of poor and disadvantaged. They should be strongly encouraged and given every opportunity to become successful, self-supporting members of society. If that is not possible, a safety net must be provided for them. The need for a safety net is, however, not sufficient rationale for taking the assets of those contributing to the economy and handing them over to so many who are anything but destitute and without options. Doing this will kill the goose that laid the golden egg and the recipients of such largess will merely be encouraged to demand more. It is already happening and the producers are going elsewhere or dropping out.

Rationale for Issue 2: President Obama has weakened the United States by destroying wealth and by unprecedented spending.

This country has always stepped up to meet a crisis. We were under tremendous strain during and after World War II, and our nation went into debt. But the cause was just, and we endured and came back even stronger.

However, spending has become a sport in Washington, and the rationale for much of it is vacuous if there is any at all. We have thrown billions at "green" companies that had practically no chance of succeeding, which was known before they were granted subsidies. We have spent billions saving jobs in the public sector (not creating them in the private sector) when it was clear that after federal subsidies ran out, state and local governments would be in the very same pickle they were in before the stimulus because the problem of bloated budgets, payrolls and employee benefits was not addressed. What a waste of taxpayers' money!

The one thing Obama has accomplished is redistribution of wealth from the earners and doers to the takers. And it did help buy President Obama his 2012 reelection. Apparently that was the aim, because it surely was not done for the good of the country.

Similarly wasteful and counterproductive are the incredible expansions of disability, food stamp, and Medicaid programs. These programs should not be growing, certainly not since 2009 when the recession ended, but they are growing. It is a disservice to able-bodied people to hand them a living without their earning it except as a temporary stop-gap. Too many on public assistance are able to work but do not. The cost to the taxpayer is tremendous and unwarranted. And, the cost should not be defined just in terms of dollars lost. There is a cost of lost productivity as more producers will have less incentive to produce when more and more of their earnings go to non-producers. Eventually, this could result in a noticeable difference in the character of our country. Of course the cost of entitlement programs is a useful argument of progressives for increased income taxes, which the Obama administration so cleverly calls revenues or investments.

Obama has promised billions (the exact number is not available) through the United Nations agreement signed in Copenhagen in 2009 (see Climate change) to reimburse developing nations for our grossly capitalistic contribution to the world's carbon footprint. This is global bureaucracy at its worst. There is little likelihood that any funds we contribute through the UN will reach the poor in those countries, and we can't afford this in any event. Beyond all this, there is no scientific justification for penalizing the United States.

Although it has the potential for covering those without health insurance, Obamacare will not increase the quality of health care, reduce the cost of medical care or medical insurance, and will cost individual taxpayers, and business owners money that will be funneled into the program's overwhelming bureaucracy and thus removed from the free market. This will be a drag on the creation of jobs and wealth in the private sector. Health care insurance companies are sure to begin crumbling and businesses will be greatly hindered under Obamacare regulations and constraints. The health care act is wealth-destroying.

The Obama administration has approved loans to Brazil for oil drilling in deep waters off its coast and to Mexico for drilling in our own waters while enforcing a moratorium on drilling by our own American companies. This is willful destruction of private US wealth and detrimental to our energy and financial security. It is not logical at all from a patriotic point of view.

Obama's reluctance to approve the whole Keystone XL pipeline is not justifiable. His inaction is particularly egregious in light of the tremendous boost the project would provide for good high-paying jobs. This is also true of the administration's, impediments to oil and gas drilling on land and off shore, and of its targeting of the coal mining and coal-fired power plant industries. There may be no greater wealth expander than cheap and plentiful energy. Conversely, the way to effectively and quickly reduce wealth would be to restrict energy production to the point where the cost to the public "necessarily skyrockets." It appears this is exactly what Obama is accomplishing.

Why is President Obama so seemingly intent on weakening the United States?

Rationale for Issue 3 decision: Obama's presidency has divided the country by class, culture, and race.

Barack Obama at the 2004 Democratic National Convention said, "... there's not a liberal America and a Conservative America; there's the United States of America. There's not a black America and Latino America and Asian America; there's the United States of America." At his victory speech in 2008, President elect Obama said, "Americans who sent a message to the world that we have never been just a collection of individuals or a collection of red states and blue states. We are, and always will be, the United States of America." It sounded too good to be true and it was.

Reading the literature, it is clear that Barack Obama was influenced by the writings of political activist Saul Alinsky, who organized Chicago's needy communities to fight what he saw as injustices perpetrated against the poor. Alinsky was very effective and instrumental in dramatically increasing the membership and power of the NEA union. His tactics were loud, crude, and in your face, and he relied on generating conflict to mobilize people for a cause. Obama followed in his footsteps, using many of the same organizing techniques and developing an alliance with ACORN, which also conducted their activities using principles from Alinsky's book, *Rules for Radicals*.

It is unlikely that Barack Obama was not influenced by the black liberation theology espoused for twenty years from the pulpit by the Reverend Jeremiah Wright as the future president sat in the congregation of Trinity United Church of Christ in

Chicago. It is a racist and divisive theology that is as much politics and social activism as it is religion. Wright himself appears to be a racist anti-Semite who supports wealth redistribution.

With this background, it is not surprising that Obama apparently jumped to conclusions in the Henry Louis Gates and Treyvon Martin incidents, deciding that racial prejudice was at work. The disposition of the New Black Panthers case and his stands on Arizona's S.B. 1070 and voter ID laws appear to be tainted with his own racial prejudice. These situations could have been managed without concern for any divisive effect. However, a true Alinsky acolyte would capitalize on such potential effects to whip up sentiment and use that to his advantage. Race relations are worse now than when Obama took office – this according to the opinions of both the white and black populations.

It is not just division based on race that has been exacerbated under the Obama administration. President Obama's statements regarding enough money, guns and religion, punishing his enemies and redistribution reveal a prejudice against those of strong Christian belief, gun owners, the wealthy, those who oppose illegal immigration, and those who oppose him politically. That is a lot of people in this country. These statements are extremely divisive and not appropriate for a man who is supposed to be president of all, not just the president of the disadvantaged, those who have been led to believe they are disadvantaged, illegal immigrants, and the rest who vote for him.

Many of the president's policies and actions—such as those on Agenda 21, climate change, fair share, Fannie & Freddie, food stamps, immigration, Kenya funding, Obamacare, Obamacare exemptions, ocean control by the UN, taxes, unemployment, and welfare—have strong wealth redistribution components. While not explicitly divisive along class, cultural, or racial lines, they are implicitly divisive, since they take from the haves and redistribute to those who have less — either in this country or to the poor of other countries. This strong prejudice against wealth accumulation and advocacy of wealth redistribution is clearly in keeping with Alinsky's philosophy and black liberation theology.

There is no doubt that Obama has stoked and exploited divisions in this country along class, racial, cultural, and partisan lines that already existed. However, early on there was an implied promise in his words to bring the country together—not just red states and blue states, but the United States. To impugn the intent of his actions, statements, and policies is not defensible. But, in light of Obama's background and actions, there is reasonable doubt that he is acting with the best intentions to bring all Americans together.

Rationale for Issue 4 decision: President Obama is more aligned with global governance and collectivism than with individual and sovereign rights.

The preamble of the United Nations Charter professes four main goals paraphrased here: to avoid war, to attain human rights in small and large countries, to promote justice through international law, and to make social progress by establishing better standards of life. The preamble says UN members will achieve these humanitarian goals by, again not word-for-word: practicing tolerance and living together in peace; uniting to maintain international peace and security; ensuring that armed forces shall not be used, except in the common interest, and employing international machinery to promote economic and social advancement of all peoples.

The UN's Millennium Summit in 2000 produced a Millennium Declaration, which set seven agenda items:

- peace, security, and disarmament
- development and an end to poverty
- protecting the common environment
- human rights, democracy, and good governance
- protecting the vulnerable
- the special needs of Africa
- strengthening UN institutions

Our Constitution's preamble is much more oriented to the needs of the United States, stating it's goal is "to form a more perfect Union, establish Justice, insure domestic Tranquility, provide for the common defense, promote the general Welfare and secure the Blessings of Liberty to ourselves and our Posterity."

President Obama took an oath of office to "preserve, protect, and defend the Constitution of the United States," not the UN's charter.

While the goals in the UN Charter and the US Constitution do not sound incompatible in general, they may be in specific situations. In addition, our Constitution was ratified by the people in conventions assembled for that purpose, while the UN Charter was approved by government agents and never ratified by the people or through legislatures or conventions. Our Constitution is very much concerned with the unalienable rights of individuals. The UN Charter is concerned with the rights of humanity in general—the collective, but not the individual—and does not consider those rights to be unalienable, but rather conferred by government, which, of course, can be taken away by government. The Constitution has a system of checks and balances. The UN Charter does not. The UN General Assembly includes despotic countries that are not our friends. Their votes are no less meaningful than ours in this body. Yet it appears Obama is more concerned about operating according to UN tenets than adhering to our Constitution and dealing with our Congress.

This policy is most egregious as it pertains to our recent military involvement in Libya. Our involvement was never approved by Congress, as required by the Constitution and the War Powers Act, and after another limit set by the act was exceeded, Obama still did not seek congressional approval. Yet, as soon as the UN Security Council authorized use of force in Libya, Obama committed our military to a "kinetic military action" led by NATO. In doing this, he relinquished our national sovereignty to the UN and NATO and exceeded his presidential powers.

In 2007, presidential candidate and then-Senator Obama said[588], "The president does not have power under the Constitution to unilaterally authorize a military attack in a situation that does not involve stopping an actual or imminent threat to the nation." He was right then, and the Libya situation did not qualify as such a threat.

In light of the way our president conducted policy toward Libya, it is possible that his reluctance to exert influence through military intervention in Syria and on the side of the Green Movement in Iran, where the justifications were much greater than in Libya, was due to lack of UN authorization. One could also ascribe a reluctance to fight to save our ambassador to Libya and three other Americans murdered in the Benghazi attack of September 11, 2012, to an administration fear of UN (global) criticism. That is pure speculation, of course.

There is a possibility that our ambassador to the UN, Susan Rice, took a lead role in explaining the Benghazi debacle not just because Secretary of State Hillary Clinton may have been reluctant to, but because Obama wanted to interject the UN into our conduct of affairs of state—just one more way to give the UN more prominence in our business. Again, this is speculation.

In addition to considerations of US military involvement, Obama has demonstrated a predilection for globalist thinking to the detriment of the rights of individual American citizens and US sovereign rights in other areas as well. His tacit endorsement of the UN's Agenda 21, which opposes individual property rights and supports government control of almost every aspect of our daily lives, is in line with the UN's globalist plan. He backed the 2009 UN Climate Change Conference accord, to which we are a signatory, and the 2012 UN Earth Summit's switch to "sustainable development." These moves are merely Agenda 21 repackaged and are antithetical to individual rights and national sovereignty.

Obama's claim[589] that "this country has not always been willing to make the sacrifices that are necessary to bring about a new day and a new age" implies that he wants not just the wealthy in this country to be more heavily taxed for the benefit of the poor, but that he thinks the whole country should sacrifice more for the sake of the rest of the world—a very globalist view.

Our escalating national debt, which makes us beholden to the countries holding that debt, is another threat to our sovereignty. That soaring debt does not seem to be a particular concern of the Obama administration.

The Disability Treaty, Small Arms Treaty, and Law of the Sea Treaty—all UN inventions not yet approved by the US Senate—are threats to our sovereignty and individual rights but are all supported by Obama. The Disability treaty was signed by Obama in 2009 but rejected by the Senate. It would have given the UN (not parents) authority to determine how children with disabilities are educated, may have interfered with abortion laws in this country, and even has been interpreted to prohibit the spanking of children.

Obama signed a draft of the Arms Trade Treaty (see Small Arms treaty) just hours after his reelection. The UN general assembly passed it in spring of 2013. If ratified by the US Senate it would require the tracking of conventional arms imported and exported and maintaining of those records for twenty years—more erosion of sovereignty and individual rights, particularly Second Amendment rights.

The Law of the Sea Treaty (see Ocean control by UN) is merely Agenda 21 under cover of a new name and would give the UN unprecedented powers to control our fisheries industry, our land use, our mineral and oil exploration industries, and our use of fossil fuels. It would impose an anti-growth tax on our energy use with the proceeds going to the UN.

The Global Poverty Act, cosponsored by Obama in 2008, resurrected by him in 2009, and submitted in modified form by Bill Gates to the 2011 G20 Summit, would force a gross international redistribution of American wealth if enacted. Directly tied to UN millennium goals, it would turn over 0.7 percent of our nation's gross national product to be redistributed by the UN.

Obama has also associated with and given appointments to Bilderberg group members; granted the National Counterterrorism Center and the NSA sweeping authority to gather data on innocent citizens and distribute the information worldwide; refused to enforce laws against aliens crossing our borders, and taken a weak position on START and the missile defense shield, stands that are in Russia's best interests, not ours. All of this is consistent with the globalist view usually reflected in the UN.

Obama's talk of collective salvation and his claims that we as a nation have been "dismissive, even derisive" and that Americans are no more exceptional than the British or the Greeks also reveal a submissive, back-seat attitude.

There is enough evidence to show that Obama is indeed much more attuned to pro-globalist policies and treaties pushed primarily by the United Nations than he is to the guiding principles of individual rights and national sovereignty enshrined in our Constitution.

Rationale for Issue 5 decision: President Obama's pro-Muslim stance may not always be in the best interest of the United States or of our ally, Israel.

There can be no doubt that President Obama has a special place in his heart for Muslims and Islam. There is nothing wrong with that, and it is understandable considering his heritage. It is also to his credit that he will not tolerate the persecution of the faith of so many around the world for the atrocities perpetrated by extremists. He has stated[590] that he thinks it is part of his responsibility as president of the United States to "fight against negative stereotypes of Islam." That too is okay—a bit one-dimensional, but okay.

However, changing NASA's mission from space exploration to reaching out to the Muslim world and engaging "more with dominantly Muslim nations to make them feel good," which the new NASA administrator, Charles Bolden, said was his foremost charge from Obama, is a highly unusual move and raises suspicions of a strong prejudice in favor of Muslims.

In a different time, this would probably not be a topic of conversation. However, since the explosion of a Pan-Am flight over Lockerbie, the World Trade Center bombing of 1993, the USS Cole bombing, the bombings of US embassies in Kenya and Tanzania and, most of all, 9/11 in 2001, it is imperative that we become more vigilant, not less vigilant, about protecting ourselves. We may not be at war with Islam, but some adherents of Islam are at war with us, and it is apparent that they don't plan to stop anytime soon. (See Benghazi; Boston marathon bombing; Fort Hood; Times Square bomber; Underwear bomber.)

Therefore, if there is any chance that appointment of Muslims or Muslim sympathizers to highly placed government positions could compromise our security or influence decisions that result in something less than our best interests or those of Israel, this is too great a risk to take.

This may have happened with the president's decision not to offer US help to the Green Movement in Iran; his strange vacillation in dealing with Syria; and his pro-Muslim Brotherhood bias in dealing with Egypt. It may also explain why Israel's deal to refuel its jets in Azerbaijan if needed for an attack on Iran was leaked. This revelation probably forestalled an attack by Israel on Iran if one had been imminent, but was a betrayal of our ally. Another possible betrayal is the publishing of the detailed construction plans of Israel's missile base. It was a "mistake."

Most recently, Chuck Hagel's past anti-Semitic words and actions and pro-Arab/Muslim activities cast doubts on our security and Israel's now that he has been confirmed as secretary of defense.

Israel is still not represented on the Global Counterterrorism Forum, which includes eleven Arab or Muslim countries. Obama established the group in September 2011. Hillary Clinton was the co-chair when she was secretary of state.

Why would we risk making Huma Abedin, a Muslim with reported ties to Wahhabism and the Muslim Brotherhood, a top aide to our secretary of state? Why is Obama advised by Dalia

Mogahed, a pro-sharia Muslim and Trita Parsi? Did advice received by Clinton and/or Obama from someone with radical Islamist allegiances have anything to do with the Benghazi debacle? Will we ever know? The risk is too great to take a chance on reaching out to Muslims in this way at this time.

Obama's decision to aid in the fall of Egypt's Hosni Mubarak and Libya's Moammar Gadhafi has resulted in the loss of secularized, although autocratic, governments in exchange for what will probably be Islamist-oriented regimes. Led by groups such as the Muslim Brotherhood, they will be governed by sharia law and remain autocratic—or possibly be theocratic. Was this the plan all along or merely a miscalculation? Either way, Obama's policy is not representative of strong leadership or the ideals of Americans.

The only member of the twenty-six-member Department of Homeland Security Advisory Council to have a "secret" clearance was a Muslim activist who abused the privilege, accessed sensitive data on his home computer, and reportedly tried to peddle it to a liberal website to smear Texas Governor Rick Perry, a candidate for the GOP presidential nomination at the time.

In fact, at least four Muslims have been appointed to Homeland Security positions under Obama. Arif Alikhan, described as a devout Muslim, is assistant secretary for policy development in Homeland Security. A position having to do with something like community outreach or religious understanding would be more reasonable, but appointing a Muslim to develop security policy was a move that should not even have even been considered. Even if Alikhan is as good as gold, why would we take the risk and why would he be singled out for a secret security clearance?

President Franklin D. Roosevelt ordered the draconian removal of more than 110,000 Japanese Americans from their homes and forced them to live in government relocation camps for more than two years during World War II. Nothing close to that need be or should be considered. Thankfully, as a country, we have moved past that kind of prejudice. However, the pendulum appears to have swung too far in the other direction. We are now being foolhardy.

Besides an affinity for Muslims and Islam, Obama appears to have an aversion to Israel. His associations with detractors of Israel such as Rashid Khalidi and the Reverend Jeremiah Wright, both believed to be anti-Semites, and his treatment of Israeli Prime Minister Benjamin Netanyahu lend credence to this possibility. Obama's statement about Israel's sitting on the sidelines, thereby damaging our credibility with Arabs and necessitating more light between Israel and the United States, was stinging. His decision to cancel the missile defense shield in the Czech Republic and Poland was not in Israel's best interest, nor is his weak reaction to Iran's aggressive nuclear weapons program or his comment to Russian President Dimitri Medvedev about "flexibility" regarding a new missile defense shield and caught by an open microphone. Obama's appointment of Hagel as secretary of defense should not please Israel, either.

The most notable example of Obama's poor treatment of Israel was probably his request that Israel return to borders approximating those that existed before the Six-Day War of 1967, which Israel won. This would make Israel "indefensible" against the Palestinians, as Netanyahu pointed out. Surely Obama knew that when he suggested it.

In light of all this, Obama's declaration that he would stand with Muslims if the winds shift the wrong way is absolutely chilling.

It appears that Obama's affection for Muslims and Islam, besides possibly fostering a more favorable worldview of Islam, is causing decisions that are dangerously naïve at best, are very likely detrimental to America's excellent reputation for representative democracy around the world, and are possibly damaging to our security and Israel's. If Obama is prejudiced against Israel, as appears to be the case, some very tense years lie ahead for the Jewish state.

Rationale for Issue 6 decision: President Obama has played fast and loose with the rule of law and interpretation of the Constitution.

It is difficult to know where to start on this subject. President George W. Bush was admonished for taking liberties with the Constitution, especially with regard to the Patriot Act. But his transgressions were mild compared with those of President Obama, who has a constitutional law background. Indeed, one wonders if Obama studied constitutional law just so he would know how best to get around constitutional constraints.

A couple of big hints are found in Obama's own words. In 2001, he bemoaned the fact that the Constitution limited what government could do instead of specifying what it must do for the people. Ten years later, in October 2011, Obama said[591], "We can't wait for an increasingly dysfunctional Congress to do its job. Where they won't act, I will." As outrageous as this is, the quote is posted at the top of the page on the whitehouse.gov website as if he were thumbing his nose at the Constitution.

Some may want the president to exceed his authority in crisis situations. At least one can understand that motivation. However, Obama has exceeded his constitutional authority or disregarded the law in so many situations that cannot be considered crises that we must ask why. He may be acting out of what he sees as pure altruism in providing health care insurance to the poor, backing union demands against greedy corporations, reducing the 'unfair' profitability of big companies and banks, supporting a globalist agenda even though it is contrary to our interest, and not worrying about exacerbating tensions between groups to achieve those ends. That might explain it all, but this is not a good enough excuse to trash the Constitution. Nothing is.

Obama may have violated finance law; racketeering law; the Religious Freedom Restoration Act; the Congressional Budget Act; the Administrative Procedures Act; the Immigration Act; the Siljander amendment; the War Powers Act; article I, section 8 (commerce clause); article I, section 9 (appropriations clause); article II, section 1 (natural-born citizen requirement) of the Constitution; article II, section 2 (congressional approval of appointments); article II, section 3 (faithful execution of laws); and articles I, II and III (the separation of powers); the Constitution's First Amendment (free exercise of religion), Second Amendment (right to bear arms), Fourth Amendment (unreasonable searches and seizures), Fifth Amendment (barring the unjust taking of life), and Fourteenth Amendment (due process, legal takings, equal protection). In some cases, it is not only possible but likely that he has broken these laws.

Obama has not only asserted powers not included in the Constitution and sometimes explicitly prohibited by it, but has also ignored responsibilities of the president dictated by the Constitution such as enforcement of immigration law on our southern border.

The problem with these alleged violations is not just their immediate impact on our freedoms, but the fact that if violations, known to Congress, are allowed to persist unchallenged, then, according to a 1952 Supreme Court decision[592] (The Steel Seizure case) they may be treated as vested powers in the president and can become a part of the Constitution. Then Congress can no longer do anything about it! Obama, the constitutional lawyer, may know very well the implications of the liberties he is taking with the law and the Constitution.

Analysis

The decisions on the six issues point to what President Obama has done and is doing to injure the republic. But the question of why he has acted this way remains. In writing this book, I have concluded that Obama is guilty of effectively and intentionally using divisive issues involving race, class, and unionized labor and creating national insolvency of the US as warfare tactics in pursuit of his major goals of global wealth redistribution and global governance. A belief in global wealth redistribution and global governance are the reasons why he has done what he has done.

The United States is the linchpin in his plan because of its wealth and power. I believe that, in his mind, its world standing must therefore be reduced; the nation's power and wealth must be diminished to ensure more even distribution of these things around the globe. He is working to assure that a new global order will benefit poor, underdeveloped nations, particularly Muslim countries, for which he has a soft spot. I believe that in Obama's mind, this requires a monumental redistribution of wealth—taking from the better off as opposed to encouraging success and wealth formation among the less well off. It is a socialist, not a capitalist approach.

To accomplish these goals or at least move significantly toward them, he has taken liberties with the rule of law and the Constitution. He probably feels justified in those actions because, in true Machiavellian style, he believes that his ends justify his means. That is dictatorial thinking and not in keeping with a constitutional republic. It is un-American.

Certainly there is some risk for the president in breaking the law. He could be sanctioned, impeached, or possibly even charged with treason. His legacy should be a concern. Why would he take such a risk? The answer may be that Obama, for all his cool exterior, is a driven man—driven not just by a passion to help the poor, but by an urge to reduce what he views as the excesses of capitalism, to curtail the power of what he may see as an imperialist nation, and to redistribute what he probably believes to be the ill-gotten gains of the wealthy to the poor not just in this country, but worldwide. His motivation appears to be a socialist/communist philosophy aimed more at reducing the power and wealth of the successful than at championing the underdog.

Saul Alinsky said that to take over the American economy and bring the people to heel, it was necessary to "destroy the middle class." The middle class was extremely important to Alinsky, because he saw this segment of society as "where the power is." He also cautioned that this must be done by "systematic deception, winning the trust of the naively idealistic middle class by using language of morality to conceal an agenda designed to destroy it." For all of Obama's championing of the middle class, he may have a hidden agenda to destroy it. The "fair share" argument is perceived as a moral one and is just the start.

Much of the evidence supporting the hypotheses that Obama is pro-socialist/anti-capitalist (Issue 1) and pro-globalist (Issue 4) also supports the thesis that he is a grand redistribu-tionist. Among the pieces of evidence are his push toward nationalized health care, his stance on Agenda 21 and his push for the Global Poverty Act. But in addition, Obama has already forced gross wealth redistribution with his policies on healthcare, welfare, unemployment, and food stamps, and most recently his successful effort to raise tax rates on the well off.

It is very telling that an offer by Republicans to provide the same amount of revenue by tightening tax deductions or closing loopholes was not acceptable to him. Instead, Obama required a marginal tax rate increase on the wealthy. This is punitive wealth redistribution and anti-capitalist at the same time. The House of Representatives, which had a Republican majority, is to blame for letting this happen.

Regarding the globalist theme, there may be indications that Obama has his eye on becoming the next secretary-general of the United Nations. His co-sponsorship of and push to pass the Global Poverty Act, his establishment of the Global Counterterrorism Forum, his backing of the Small Arms Treaty of the UN and his stance and actions on global climate change would suit the résumé of someone interested in that job. Those are all UN initiatives. His miss-handling of Syrian poison gas incidents and resultant tossing of the ball to the UN is also in line with a globalist approach.

Secretary Ban Ki-moon's second five-year term expires on December 31, 2016. While it is possible for him to be re-elected indefinitely, no secretary-general has served more than two terms. The timing would be perfect for Obama.

The UN General Assembly elects the new secretary-general, but the Security Council must propose the candidate.

Any of the five permanent members of the Security Council (the United States, Britain, Russia, China, and France) can veto a candidate. Could this be part of the reason Obama has appeased Russia (START, the missile defense shield) and why he has feted Chinese President Hu Jintao so disproportionately? China has also been the beneficiary of unbelievable deals between GM and the Chinese Communist Party to expand operations in China while diminishing them in the United States. China now owns a large GM plant in Saginaw, Michigan; it is the city's largest employer.

Could our inexplicably soft approach to Iran and Syria be part of a deal not to aggravate China and Russia with which they are allied? The US congress will never have to vote on a military strike on Syria and it will be with a wink and a nod that the international community recognizes that Obama never wanted to strike in the first place and expected Congress to turn down his request if it ever had gotten that far.

Obama also named British Prime Minister David Cameron as one of his five best friends among world leaders. It appears he may have four out of five Security Council votes on his side. French President Francois Hollande is a socialist, and maybe Obama could count on his country's vote as well.

If this supposition is correct, and if the Declaration of Independence and the Constitution are still our guiding documents, it is absolutely essential that the United States steel itself against an onslaught of socialist pressure from the United Nations that would severely compromise our republic—even destroy it.

If the Democrats hold the Senate and/or take the House in the 2014 mid-term elections our republic will be in crisis. Under the worst of 2016 election scenarios, should the Senate remain in Democrat control and the House be taken over by Democrats, and another Democrat elected president, we will have lost our Republic as founded for a long time. If in addition, Obama becomes UN secretary-general and with an overwhelmingly Democrat Congress, we would become just one more socialist country—no more exceptional than Greece.

The midterm elections are the key to getting a leg up on a firm defense against increasing global pressure to become just another cog in the global socialist movement. The presidential election of 2016 is critical to our Republic's survival.

The case for the prosecution has been presented. It is up to you, the jury, to vote the verdict and decide which way this country goes in November 2014 and again in November 2016.

Acronyms

ACLU	American Civil Liberties Union
ACORN	Association of Community Organizations for Reform Now
AFL-CIO	American Federation of Labor and Congress of Industrial Organizations
AIG	American International Group
AP	Associated Press
ATF	Bureau of Alcohol, Tobacco, Firearms, and Explosives
CBO	Congressional Budget Office
CEO	Chief Executive Officer
CIA	Central Intelligence Agency
CO2	Carbon dioxide
DHS	Department of Homeland Security
DOE	Department of Energy
DOI	Department of the Interior

DOJ	Department of Justice
EPA	Environmental Protection Agency
FBI	Federal Bureau of Investigation
FEC	Federal Election Commission
FHFA	Federal Housing Finance Agency
FISA	Foreign Intelligence Surveillance Act
FOIA	Freedom Of Information Act
GAO	Government Accountability Office
GDP	Gross Domestic Product
GED	General Educational Development
GM	General Motors
GSA	General Services Administration
GSE	Government-Sponsored Enterprise
HHS	Health and Human Services Administration
IAEA	International Atomic Energy Agency
ICE	Immigration and Customs Enforcement
IG	Inspector General
IPAB	Independent Payment Advisory Board

IRS	Internal Revenue Service
NAACP	National Association for the Advancement of Colored People
NASA	National Aeronautics and Space Administration
NATO	North Atlantic Treaty Organization
NEA	National Education Association
NIAC	National Iranian American Council
NLRB	National Labor Relations Board
NRA	National Rifle Association
NSA	National Security Agency
OIC	Organization of Islamic Cooperation
OMB	Office of Management and Budget
OPEC	Organization of Petroleum Exporting Countries
PLO	Palestine Liberation Organization
PPACA	Patient Protection and Affordable Care Act
SCOTUS	Supreme Court of the United States
SEIU	Service Employees International Union
SNAP	Supplemental Nutrition Assistance Program

START	STrategic Arms Reduction Treaty
TARP	Troubled Asset Relief Program
TSA	Transportation Security Administration
UAW	United Auto Workers
UK	United Kingdom
UN	United Nations
USAID	United States Agency for International Development
VRA	Voting Rights Act
WMD	Weapons of Mass Destruction

References

1. http://www.instituteforenergyresearch.org/2012/11/20/energy-department-keeps-spending-taxpayers-money-as-bankrupt-a123-gets-anotherpayment/

2. http://www.nytimes.com/2011/09/10/world/middleeast/10memo.html?pagewanted=all&_r=0

3. http://www.wnd.com/2012/08/humas-infiltration-into-state-department/

4. http://www.wnd.com/2012/08/another-huma-link-to-muslim-brotherhood/

5. http://www.nationalreview.com/articles/224610/inside-obamas-acorn/stanley-kurtz

6. http://www.eppc.org/publications/inside-obamas-acorn/

7. http://townhall.com/columnists/amandacarpenter/2008/10/13/obama_distorts_acorn_ties

8. http://www.canadafreepress.com/index.php/article/42119

9. Freedom Advocates, "Understanding Sustainable Development – Agenda 21, Freedom Advocates, PO Box 3330, Freedom, CA 95019, Fifth Printing 2012.

10. http://hotair.com/archives/2012/04/21/executive-order-13547-the-sleeping-power-grab/

11. http://www.canadafreepress.com/index.php/article/38394

12. http://www.freerepublic.com/focus/f-news/2860730/posts

13. http://www.forbes.com/sites/jimpowell/2012/04/29/obamas-plan-to-seize-control-of-our-economy-and-our-lives/

14. http://www.thenewamerican.com/tech/environment/item/14833-oklahoma-house-passes-bill-to-ban-un-agenda-21

15. http://www.pacificlegal.org/releases/PLF-statement-on-Koontz-property-rights-victory-at-the-Supreme-Court

16. http://www.huffingtonpost.com/2009/01/26/obama-al-arabiya-intervie_n_161127.html

17. https://en.wikipedia.org/wiki/People_linked_to_Anwar_al-Awlaki

18. http://articles.washingtonpost.com/2012-02-10/world/35445837_1_awlaki-cia-drone-strike-justice-department-memo

19. http://www.nytimes.com/2013/02/05/us/politics/us-memo-details-views-on-killing-citizens-in-al-qaeda.html?_r=0

20. http://en.wikipedia.org/wiki/Arif_Alikhan

21. http://www.nationalreview.com/corner/271019/obama-official-denies-calling-hezbollah-liberation-movement-says-it-terrorist-organiza

22. http://en.wikipedia.org/wiki/Saul_Alinsky

23. http://www.canadafreepress.com/index.php/article/50229

24. http://www.nationalreview.com/articles/294454/still-alinsky-playbook-john-fund

25. http://www.amazon.com/After-Alinsky-Community-Organizing-Illinois/dp/0962087335

26. http://www.americanthinker.com/2008/10/obamas_radical_revolutionits_a.html

27. http://www.clarionproject.org/analysis/all-dulles-area-muslim-society-center

28. http://www.discoverthenetworks.org/articles/katalm.html

29. http://www.newsmax.com/KenTimmerman/obama-sutton-saudi/2008/09/03/id/339914

30. http://www.dailyinterlake.com/opinion/columns/frank/article_79 24e4f0-0468-11e2-8da2-0019bb2963f4.html

31. http://blog.heritage.org/2008/06/29/the-truth-about-anwr/

32. http://www.anwr.org/Background/Making-the-Case-for-ANWR.php

33. http://www.anwr.org/Background/Drilling-in-Refuges.php

34. http://www.politifact.com/truth-o-meter/statements/2012/apr/02/american-energy-alliance/energy-group-says-obama-objects-energy-exploration/

35. http://www.motherjones.com/blue-marble/2011/08/anwr-wilderness-designation

36. http://www.washingtonpost.com/blogs/worldviews/wp/2013/05/13/heres-the-story-the-ap-suspects-led-to-sweeping-justice-dept-subpoena/

37. http://www.foxnews.com/politics/2013/05/17/plot-thickens-on-ap-records-scandal/

38. http://www.businessinsider.com/ap-phone-records-doj-justice-dept-eric-holder-2013-5

39. http://www.nytimes.com/2013/05/14/us/phone-records-of-journalists-of-the-associated-press-seized-by-us.html?pagewanted=all&_r=0

40. http://guardianlv.com/2013/05/eric-holder-has-committed-perjury-and-will-have-to-resign/

41. http://online.wsj.com/article/SB124044156269345357.html

42. http://michellemalkin.com/2013/05/04/obama-guns-mexico/

43. http://www.glennbeck.com/2013/07/01/who-says-that-obama-goes-off-the-rails-in-africa/

44. http://en.wikipedia.org/wiki/Arab_American_Action_Network

45. http://www.discoverthenetworks.org/viewSubCategory.asp?id=1521

46. http://www.discoverthenetworks.org/individualProfile.asp?indid=1511

47. https://en.wikipedia.org/wiki/Arizona_SB_1070

48. http://hotair.com/archives/2010/05/19/video-mexican-president-criticizes-arizona-law-at-white-house-presser/

49. http://www.heritage.org/research/reports/2012/06/obama-administration-s-response-to-the-supreme-court-ruling-on-arizona-s-immigration-law

50. http://michellemalkin.com/2010/09/01/arizona-vs-the-u-n-human-rights-police/

51. http://americanfreepress.net/?p=5432

52. http://www.dailymail.co.uk/news/article-2175183/Barack-Obama-Arpaio-probe-Obamas-birth-certificate-claims-document-definitely-fraudulent.html

53. http://freedomoutpost.com/2013/07/investigator-obama-eligibility-is-now-causing-congress-to-pay-attention/

54. http://www.washingtonpost.com/wp-dyn/content/article/2011/02/17/AR2011021705494.html

55. http://www.washingtonpost.com/blogs/erik-wemple/wp/2013/06/18/sharyl-attkisson-i-think-i-know-source-of-computer-breaches/

56. http://en.wikipedia.org/wiki/Bill_Ayers

57. http://www.nytimes.com/2001/09/11/books/no-regrets-for-love-explosives-memoir-sorts-war-protester-talks-life-with.html

58. http://townhall.com/tipsheet/guybenson/2011/11/30/confirmed_bill_ayers_hosted_a_fundraiser_for_obama

59. http://abcnews.go.com/GMA/Economy/story?id=6626721&page=1

60. http://sigtarp.gov/Audit%20Reports/Additional_Insight_on_Use_of_Troubled_Asset

61. http://money.cnn.com/news/storysupplement/economy/bailouttracker/

62. http://www.americanthinker.com/2010/07/race_played_role_in_
obama_car.html

63. http://www.usatoday.com/story/money/cars/2013/07/08/fiat-
exercises-option-to-buy-more-chrysler-stock/2498489/

64. http://www.reuters.com/article/2013/05/06/us-gm-treasury-
idUSBRE9450K020130506

65. http://www.westernjournalism.com/obama-administration-facing-
massive-federal-lawsuit/

66. http://spire-law.com/spire-law-group-announces-massive-
violations-of-national-bank-settlement/#more-180

67. http://www.foxnews.com/politics/2010/04/22/grassley-slams-gm-
administration-loans-repaid-bailout-money/

68. http://theweek.com/article/index/239307/the-180-degree-legal-
transformation-of-barack-obama

69. http://abcnews.go.com/blogs/politics/2011/10/obama-offers-
mortgage-relief-plan-we-cant-wait-for-congress/

70. http://www.whitehouse.gov/economy/jobsact

71. http://www.nytimes.com/2013/02/13/us/politics/obamas-2013-
state-of-the-union-address.html?pagewanted=all&_r=0

72. http://www.politico.com/news/stories/0412/74892.html

73. http://www.cnn.com/2009/US/07/22/harvard.gates.interview/

74. http://www.cnn.com/2012/10/24/us/libya-benghazi-e-mails

75. http://www.theblaze.com/stories/2012/09/25/obama-denounces-anti-islam-film-during-u-n-speech-an-insult-not-only-to-muslims-but-to-america-as-well/

76. http://www.weeklystandard.com/articles/benghazi-scandal-grows_722032.html?page=2

77. http://online.wsj.com/article/SB10001424127887324082604578485453453286058.html

78. http://www.theblaze.com/stories/2013/01/23/clinton-there-was-no-monitor-there-was-no-real-time-video-of-benghazi-attacks/

79. http://www.rushlimbaugh.com/daily/2012/12/19/benghazi_report_mistakes_were_made_but_nobody_made_them

80. http://www.thedailybeast.com/articles/2012/10/12/are-budget-cuts-to-blame-for-benghazi-attack-as-biden-suggested.html

81. http://townhall.com/tipsheet/guybenson/2013/04/24/benghazi-report-hillary-approved-reduced-security-measures-contradicting-her-testimony-n1576710

82. http://www.theblaze.com/stories/2012/10/26/explosive-benghazi-allegation-cia-told-to-stand-down-during-attack-3-urgent-requests-for-military-back-up-were-denied/

83. http://www.discoverthenetworks.org/viewSubCategory.asp?id=1755

84. http://www.westernjournalism.com/the-scandal-that-will-bring-obama-down/

85. http://www.freerepublic.com/focus/news/3013578/posts

86. http://mobile.wnd.com/2013/06/more-evidence-of-slain-u-s-ambassadors-secret-activities/

87. http://blog.foreignpolicy.com/posts/2013/06/04/obama_erdogan_turkey_protests_friends

88. http://news.investors.com/ibd-editorials/051613-656375-whitehouse-emails-implicate-brennan-in-benghazigate.htm

89. http://www.americanthinker.com/blog/2013/04/white_house_behind_alteration_of_benghazi_talking_points_report.html

90. http://abcnews.go.com/blogs/politics/2013/05/exclusive-benghazi-talking-points-underwent-12-revisions-scrubbed-of-terror-references/

91. http://www.weeklystandard.com/articles/benghazi-talking-points_720543.html?page=3

92. http://bigstory.ap.org/article/fbi-ids-benghazi-suspects-no-arrests-yet

93. http://www.globalresearch.ca/the-true-story-of-the-bilderberg-group-and-what-they-may-be-planning-now/13808

94. http://fellowshipofminds.wordpress.com/2012/05/31/bilderberg-meets-to-decide-us-presidential-election/

95. http://en.wikipedia.org/wiki/Black_liberation_theology

96. http://www.americanthinker.com/2008/03/the_real_agenda_of_black_liber.html

97. http://www.nationalaffairs.com/publications/detail/the-auto-bailout-and-the-rule-of-law

98. http://www.ijreview.com/2013/04/46970-left-wing-media-massacre-their-reputations-covering-boston-marathon-bombings/

99. http://www.examiner.com/article/boston-s-self-radicalized-bombing-conspiracy

100. http://usnews.nbcnews.com/_news/2013/05/16/18295633-dzhokhar-tsarnaev-scribbled-note-inside-boat-where-he-was-hiding-sources-say?lite

101. http://www.telegraph.co.uk/news/worldnews/barackobama/512 8171/Barack-Obama-criticised-for-bowing-to-King-Abdullah-of-Saudi-Arabia.html

102. http://en.wikipedia.org/wiki/National_Commission_on_Fiscal_Re sponsibility_and_Reform

103. http://www.nytimes.com/2012/02/27/us/politics/obamas-unacknowledged-debt-to-bowles-simpson-plan.html?pagewanted= all&_r=0

104. http://online.wsj.com/article/SB10001424052748704198004575 310571698602094.html

105. http://www.guardian.co.uk/commentisfree/2013/mar/01/bp-deepwater-horizone-oil-spill

106. http://www.sciencedaily.com/releases/2012/04/120417152648. htm

107. http://www.bbc.co.uk/news/science-environment-13123036

108. http://blog.al.com/press-register-commentary/2012/07/bp_says _microbes_study_is_inco.html

109. http://news.wgcu.org/post/researchers-say-gulf-seafood-safe-eat

110. http://en.wikipedia.org/wiki/2010_United_States_deepwater_dri lling_moratorium

111. http://www.westernjournalism.com/stunning-obamas-pick-for-cia-is-a-converted-muslim/

112. http://news.investors.com/ibd-editorials/051613-656375-whitehouse-emails-implicate-brennan-in-benghazigate.htm

113. http://articles.washingtonpost.com/2013-03-23/business/37959198_1_budget-plan-trillion-budget-senate-budget-cuts

114. http://budget.house.gov/news/documentsingle.aspx?DocumentI D=323365

115. http://www.heritage.org/research/reports/2008/12/fulfilling-your-budget-reform-promise-of-a-net-spending-cut-a-memo-to-president-elect-obama

116. http://townhall.com/tipsheet/guybenson/2012/07/17/if_youve_ got_a_business_you_didnt_build_that

117. http://blog.heritage.org/2009/08/06/heritage-foundation-releases-economic-study-of-waxman-markey-cap-and-trade-bill/

118. http://www.bloomberg.com/news/2010-11-04/obama-calls-cap-and-trade-just-one-way-northeast-carbon-market-falls.html

119. http://en.wikipedia.org/wiki/Employee_Free_Choice_Act

120. http://www.realclearpolitics.com/articles/2008/04/obamas_rem arks_to_the_aflcio.html

121. http://www.truth-out.org/archive/item/83457:us-president-leaves-uaw-behind-card-check-bill-could-resurrect-us-unionization-movement

122. http://www.quarles.com/rule_expediting_union_elections_2012/

123. http://wot.motortrend.com/detroits-cash-for-clunkers-sales-tally-less-than-us-market-share-5156.html#axzz2Zn0o3gsc

124. http://en.wikipedia.org/wiki/Car_Allowance_Rebate_System

125. http://www.breitbart.com/Big-Peace/2012/07/27/White-House-Now-Claims-It-Didnt-Remove-Churchill-Bust

126. http://en.wikipedia.org/wiki/Copenhagen_Accord

127. http://www.cbsnews.com/2100-205_162-5993825.html

128. http://www.reuters.com/article/2012/01/24/us-rio-idUSTRE80N1XB20120124

129. http://thehill.com/blogs/e2-wire/e2-wire/273737-obama-climate-change-one-of-top-three-priorities

130. http://www.climatecentral.org/news/text-of-president-obamas-speech-on-climate-action-plan-16158

131. http://www.forbes.com/sites/larrybell/2012/07/17/that-scientific-global-warming-consensus-not/2/

132. http://www.c2es.org/federal/courts/clean-air-act-cases

133. http://news.yahoo.com/supremem-court-justices-hear-epa-appeal-over-air-134238381.html

134. http://en.wikipedia.org/wiki/Coal_power_in_the_United_States

135. http://dailycaller.com/2013/05/03/report-epa-rules-to-shut-down-more-than-280-coal-fired-units/

136. http://www.instituteforenergyresearch.org/epa-powerplant-closures/

137. http://uk.reuters.com/article/2013/07/12/utilities-firstenergy-coal-idUKL1N0FI19L20130712

138. http://www.forbes.com/sites/patrickmichaels/2011/09/30/the-epas-endangerment-finding-is-very-endangered/

139. http://www.powerlineblog.com/archives/2011/09/the-vindication-of-alan-carlin.php

140. http://www.usnews.com/opinion/blogs/on-energy/2012/04/12/the-illogic-of-epa-carbon-regulatio

141. http://dailycaller.com/2013/04/23/federal-appeals-court-grants-epa-far-reaching-authority-to-revoke-pollution-permits/

142. http://epaabuse.com/2939/news/federal-judge-rules-against-epa-in-coal-mining-case/

143. http://jurist.org/paperchase/2012/08/federal-appeals-court-rules-against-epa-in-cross-state-pollution-case.php

144. http://www.discoverthenetworks.org/individualProfile.asp?indid=1511

145. http://departments.knox.edu/newsarchive/news_events/2005/obamaaddress.html

146. http://www.forbes.com/sites/paulroderickgregory/2012/09/23/why-the-fuss-obama-has-long-been-on-record-in-favor-of-redistribution/

147. http://www.nytimes.com/2012/01/05/us/politics/richard-cordray-named-consumer-chief-in-recess-appointment.html?page wanted=all&_r=0

148. http://www.foxnews.com/politics/2013/07/17/third-federal-appeals-court-invalidates-obama-nlrb-recess-appointments/

149. http://www.lexisnexis.com/legalnewsroom/banking/b/banking-finance/archive/2013/07/09/supreme-court-agrees-to-hear-recess-appointment-case-does-scotus-hold-cordray-s-fate-in-its-hands.aspx

150. http://www.civilrights.org/monitor/vol9_no2_3/art6.html

151. http://www.thedailybeast.com/articles/2012/05/23/court-could-thwart-obama-with-clinton-law-in-contraception-face-off-with-church-groups.html

152. http://www.becketfund.org/hhsinformationcentral/

153. http://en.wikipedia.org/wiki/United_States_debt-ceiling_crisis_of_2011

154. http://www.zerohedge.com/news/egan-jones-downgrades-us-aa-aa

155. http://en.wikipedia.org/wiki/List_of_U.S._executive_branch_czars

156. http://www.heraldextra.com/news/state-and-regional/obama-s-czars-bending-the-constitution/article_62145e68-216a-52eb-a450-eb202b5d2c98.html

157. http://www.judicialwatch.org/files/documents/2011/czar-report-09152011.pdf

158. http://www.americanthinker.com/2012/09/frank_marshall_davis_jr.html

159. http://www.theblaze.com/contributions/obama-and-that-bust-of-winston-churchill-dreams-from-frank-marshall-davis/

160. http://www.americanthinker.com/2012/10/obama_whos_your_daddy.html

161. http://dailycaller.com/2012/07/15/obamas-influential-communist-mentor/

162. http://www.wnd.com/2012/09/1979-article-ties-obamas-real-father-to-saudi-financier/

163. http://beforeitsnews.com/opinion-conservative/2013/06/obama-attacks-catholic-schools-2669274.html

164. http://blogs.wsj.com/developments/2012/08/14/fannie-and-freddie-the-loan-that-can%E2%80%99t-be-repaid/

165. http://useconomy.about.com/od/usdebtanddeficit/p/US-Debt-by-President.htm

166. http://www.treasurydirect.gov/NP/debt/current

167. http://www.nationalreview.com/articles/337299/when-big-deficits-became-good-victor-davis-hanson

168. http://abcnews.go.com/Politics/OTUS/fullpage/top-10-countries-holding-us-debt-17537074

169. http://grandfather-economic-report.com/debt-nat.htm

170. http://business.time.com/2012/05/23/which-advanced-economy-has-the-most-total-debt/#slide/more-lists/?&_suid=1374685825304098349240553558447

171. http://articles.latimes.com/2013/may/10/business/la-fi-mo-debt-limit-lew-fannie-mae-economy-20130510

172. http://townhall.com/columnists/michellemalkin/2010/09/22/the_delphi_disaster_an_economic_horror_story_obama_wont_tell/page/full

173. http://waysandmeans.house.gov/news/documentsingle.aspx?Do cumentID=310415

174. http://www.politifact.com/truth-o-meter/obama-quotes/

175. http://blog.heritage.org/2012/08/01/u-n-disabilities-treaty-leaves-door-open-for-abortion-advocates/

176. http://www.examiner.com/article/homeschoolers-urged-to-call-senators-regarding-dangerous-u-n-treaty

177. http://www.forbes.com/sites/realspin/2012/07/02/about-the-dodd-frank-act-george-washington-would-be-turning-over-in-his-grave/

178. http://www.bizjournals.com/albuquerque/print-edition/2013/02/01/dallas-fed-president-fisher-blasts-the.html?page=all

179. http://www.businessweek.com/magazine/content/10_37/b4194 026970590.htm

180. http://www.nationalreview.com/articles/343222/reining-consumer-financial-protection-bureau-paul-moreno

181. http://www.doi.gov/news/pressreleases/loader.cfm?csModule=s ecurity/getfile&PageID

182. http://www.instituteforenergyresearch.org/pdf/Our_Views_Are_Not_Appropriately_Represented

183. http://www.americanthinker.com/2011/02/meeting_young_oba ma.html

184. http://en.wikipedia.org/wiki/Timeline_of_the_Deepwater_Horizo n_oil_spill

185. http://blog.heritage.org/2010/10/13/morning-bell-the-oil-drilling-moratorium-doesnt-end-till-the-permits-begin/

186http://money.cnn.com/2011/02/28/news/economy/oil_drilling_d eepwater/index.htm

187http://blog.heritage.org/2010/12/01/seven-years-of-bad-policy-government-maintains-offshore-drilling-ban/

188. http://dailycaller.com/2011/02/15/first-gulf-of-mexico-drilling-company-seahawk-files-bankruptcy-because-of-offshore-drilling-moratorium/

189. http://forum.teambentoncounty.com/default.aspx?g=posts&t=2 093

190. http://naturalresources.house.gov/news/documentsingle.aspx?D ocumentID=267985

191. http://www.nola.com/business/index.ssf/2012/10/many_expect _gulf_oil_productio.html

192. http://www.225batonrouge.com/article/20121005/BUSINESSREP ORT0112/121009836

193. http://tucsoncitizen.com/wryheat/2013/03/18/the-hypocrisy-of-obamas-energy-boasts/

194. http://www.foxnews.com/politics/2010/09/11/backs-b-loan-mexico-oil-drilling-despite-obama-moratorium/

195. http://www.forbes.com/sites/kenrapoza/2011/03/17/dispelling-the-petrobras-loan-myth-as-obama-heads-to-rio/2/

196. http://www.instituteforenergyresearch.org/2013/02/28/oil-and-gas-production-decline-on-federal-lands-again/

197. http://naturalresources.house.gov/news/documentsingle.aspx?DocumentID=229180

198. http://www.nytimes.com/2012/11/15/world/middleeast/israeli-strike-in-gaza-kills-the-military-leader-of-hamas.html?pagewanted=all&_r=0

199. http://www.foxnews.com/world/2013/02/05/ahmadinejad-arrives-in-cairo-first-visit-by-iranian-leader-since-17/

200. http://content.usatoday.com/communities/theoval/post/2012/09/13/obama-puts-egypt-on-notice/70000288/1

201. http://www.nytimes.com/2012/11/23/world/middleeast/egypts-president-morsi-gives-himself-new-powers.html?_r=0

202. http://www.newsmax.com/Headline/Egypt-Morsi-decree-catastrophe/2012/12/08/id/466952

203. http://www.abc.net.au/news/2012-12-26/egypt-passes-new-constitution/4443588

204. http://online.wsj.com/article/SB10001424127887323899704578583191518313964.html

205. http://www.washingtontimes.com/news/2013/jul/3/obama-deeply-concerned-over-egypt-calls-civilian-r/

206. http://the-american-journal.com/obama-campaign-2012-voter-fraud/

207. http://www.breitbart.com/Big-Government/2012/10/08/Report-Illegal-Foreign-Campaign-Donations-Assault-on-American-Sovereignty

208. http://granitegrok.com/blog/2012/10/obama-com-made-in-china-part-2

209. http://freebeacon.com/report-foreign-nationals-donating-to-obama-campaign/

210. http://www.familysecuritymatters.org/publications/detail/the-deception-marathon-of-benghazigatebostongate-a-conspiracy

211. http://www.discoverthenetworks.org/individualProfile.asp?indid =2560

212. http://www.theamericanconservative.com/dreher/mohamed-elibiary-homeland-security/

213. http://www.epa.gov/epafoia1/docs/Endangerment_comments_v 7b.pdf

214. http://blog.heritage.org/2009/06/29/an-inconvenient-voice-dr-alan-carlin/

215. http://online.wsj.com/article/SB126020179812780059.html

216. http://online.wsj.com/article/SB10001424127887323320404578 216034024416590.html

217. http://www.reuters.com/article/2013/06/25/us-usa-climate-obama-plan-idUSBRE95O0G720130625

218. http://www.foxnews.com/politics/2012/04/30/top-epa-official-resigns-after-crucify-comment/

219. http://articles.washingtonpost.com/2012-04-27/politics/
35450879_1_epa-on-environmental-enforcement-first-five-guys-
epa-administrator

220. http://www.breitbart.com/Big-Government/2012/08/09/obama-
now-promotes-american-exceptionalism

221. http://www.heritage.org/federalbudget/top10-percent-income-
earners

222. http://www.foxbusiness.com/politics/2012/04/20/raise-taxes-
on-1-is-it-that-simple/

223. http://blog.heritage.org/2012/02/19/chart-of-the-week-nearly-
half-of-all-americans-dont-pay-income-taxes/

224. http://www.thenationalpatriot.com/2012/12/05/the-fiscal-cliff-
is-a-disguise-for/

225. http://www.guardian.co.uk/uk/2013/jan/06/falklands-uk-
argentina-fight-defence

226. http://blogs.telegraph.co.uk/news/nilegardiner/100130943/the-
obama-administration-knifes-britain-in-the-back-again-over-the-
falklands/

227. http://www.cato.org/sites/cato.org/files/pubs/pdf/bp120.pdf

228. http://georgewbush-whitehouse.archives.gov/news/releases/
2008/10/20081009-10.html

229. http://www.nationalreview.com/corner/284349/krauthammers-
take-nro-staff

230. http://online.wsj.com/article/SB122290574391296381.html

231. http://www.bloomberg.com/news/2012-10-23/demarco-shrinks-fannie-freddie-without-help-from-congress.html

232. http://www.forbes.com/sites/steveschaefer/2012/07/31/fannie-mae-freddie-mac-regulator-rejects-principal-forgiveness/

233. http://thehill.com/blogs/on-the-money/1091-housing/308237-watts-bid-to-head-housing-regulator-an-uphill-climb

234. http://www.thedailybeast.com/articles/2011/12/17/suit-against-fannie-and-freddie-execs-ignores-pols-also-to-blame.html

235. http://www.nationalreview.com/corner/285196/cbs-links-fast-and-furious-gun-control-robert-verbruggen

236. http://investigations.nbcnews.com/_news/2012/09/19/1396606 8-investigation-finds-no-evidence-ag-eric-holder-knew-of-fast-and-furious-gun-running-sting?lite

237. http://www.theblaze.com/stories/2012/06/26/the-5-biggest-differences-between-operation-fast-and-furious-and-operation-wide-receiver/

238. http://abcnews.go.com/blogs/politics/2012/06/holder-may-be-slapped-in-gunwalking-scandal/

239. http://blog.heritage.org/2012/09/21/morning-bell-5-ways-fast-furious-tarnishes-eric-holders-justice-department-2/

240. http://townhall.com/tipsheet/katiepavlich/2012/10/12/white_ho use_link_to_fast_and_furious_back_in_the_united_states

241. http://www.wnd.com/2013/04/author-documents-damning-for-holder/

242. http://www.cbsnews.com/video/watch/?id=5975092n

243. http://cagw.org/porker-of-the-month/cagw-names-fha-commissioner-galante-porker-month

244. http://www.reuters.com/article/2013/06/17/us-autos-fisker-specialreport-idUSBRE95G02L20130617

245. http://www.nbcnews.com/id/21138728/ns/politics-decision_08/t/obama-stops-wearing-american-flag-pin/

246. http://online.wsj.com/article/SB10001424127887323699704578 328601204933288.html

247. http://www.examiner.com/article/obama-hid-report-showing-surge-food-stamp-use-until-after-election

248. http://www.judicialwatch.org/press-room/press-releases/ judicial-watch-uncovers-usda-records-sponsoring-u-s-food-stamp-program-for-illegal-aliens/

249. http://www.nydailynews.com/news/national/gunman-fort-hood-shooting-maj-nidal-malik-hasan-shouted-allahu-akbar-deadly-attack-article-1.414268

250. http://godfatherpolitics.com/2503/fort-hood-massacre-was-workplace-violence/

251. http://hotair.com/archives/2011/02/03/new-report-on-ft-hood-says-fbi-missed-signs-of-radicalism/

252. http://www.youtube.com/watch?v=FW7PAhHKPyo

253. http://www.cbsnews.com/2100-201_162-5551286.html

254. http://www.washingtonpost.com/blogs/right-turn/wp/2013/ 05/28/holder-in-trouble-why-cant-they-just-tell-the-truth/

255. http://www.nytimes.com/2013/05/22/opinion/another-chilling-leak-investigation.html?_r=0

256. http://www.newrepublic.com/article/112190/obama-interview-2013-sit-down-president

257. http://www.heritage.org/research/reports/2012/08/hydraulic-fracturing-critical-for-energy-production-jobs-and-economic-growth

258. http://www.uwyo.edu/cee/_files/docs/201105_economic_oppor tunities_shale_energy_development

259. http://www.nationalreview.com/article/351819/epa-plants-story-jillian-kay-melchior

260. http://www.forbes.com/sites/halahtouryalai/2012/05/21/frackin g-is-midunderstood-its-the-key-to-energy-self-sufficiency/

261. http://www.bls.gov/web/laus/laumstrk.htm

262. http://pjmedia.com/tatler/2013/01/06/leaked-report-suppressed-by-cuomo-says-fracking-is-safe/

263. http://www.washingtontimes.com/news/2013/apr/29/pa-environment-agency-debunks-fracking-water-claim/?page=all

264. http://www.scientificamerican.com/article.cfm?id=can-fracking-be-done-without-impacting-water

265. http://patriotpost.us/commentary/16812

266. http://www.jsonline.com/blogs/news/31977114.html

267. http://wiki.answers.com/Q/Which_president_said_'I'm_in_this_r ace_not_just_to_hold_an_office_but_to_gather_with_you_to_transfo rm_a_nation'&view=classic

268. http://www.washingtontimes.com/blog/robbins-report/2012/oct/28/general-losing-his-job-over-benghazi/

269. http://online.wsj.com/article/SB1000142405311190389590457654
2942027859286.html

270. http://dailycaller.com/2013/05/26/paper-gibson-guitar-raids-may-be-another-case-of-obama-administration-targeting/

271. http://www.breitbart.com/Big-Peace/2012/07/10/Obama-admin-rejects-Israel-terror

272. http://cnsnews.com/news/article/administration-will-ask-partners-counter-terror-forum-involve-not-admit-israel

273. http://www.motherjones.com/mojo/2008/08/more-obama-and-africa-global-poverty-act

274. http://www.govtrack.us/congress/bills/111/hr2639

275. http://www.newswithviews.com/DeWeese/tom208.htm

276. http://online.wsj.com/article/SB123836090755767077.html

277. http://www.cnbc.com/id/29956752

278. http://www.cato.org/publications/congressional-testimony/ramifications-auto-industry-bankruptcies

279. http://www.gingrichproductions.com/2012/10/obamas-cascade-of-exotic-green-energy-scandals/

280. http://blog.heritage.org/2012/11/05/green-graveyard-19-taxpayer-funded-failures/

281. http://www.westernjournalism.com/media-keeping-americans-uninformed-

282. http://www.cnsnews.com/news/article/9-billion-stimulus-solar-wind-projects-made-910-final-jobs-98-million

283. http://www.foxnews.com/politics/2013/07/18/billions-spent-in-obama-climate-plan-may-be-virtually-useless-study-suggests/

284. http://www.washingtontimes.com/news/2012/oct/26/audit-green-jobs-stimulus-program-wastes-cash/

285. http://www.washingtonpost.com/blogs/wonkblog/wp/2013/07/21/why-its-hard-for-the-government-to-create-green-jobs/

286. http://iranprimer.usip.org/resource/green-movement

287. http://www.whitehouse.gov/blog/The-Presidents-Opening-Remarks-on-Iran-with-Persian-Translation

288. http://news.investors.com/ibd-editorials/022812-602609-obama-ignored-iran-freedom-fighters-in-2009.htm

289. http://www.americanthinker.com/2011/11/why_obama_betrayed_the_iranian_people.html

290. http://www.reuters.com/article/2013/06/28/fitch-affirms-united-states-at-aaa-outlo-idUSFit66136520130628

291. http://www.bloomberg.com/news/2011-07-14/too-much-debt-means-economy-can-t-grow-commentary-by-reinhart-and-rogoff.html

292. http://archives.republicans.transportation.house.gov/Media/file/112th/EDPBEM/GSA%20Timeline.pdf

293. http://freebeacon.com/admin-knew-of-gsa-vegas-scandal/

294. http://www.foxnews.com/politics/2012/04/17/lawmakers-slam-gsa-officials-for-south-pacific-trips-at-2nd-day-hearings/

295. http://www.cbsnews.com/8301-503544_162-57408365-503544/gsa-head-resigns-after-scathing-ig-report/

296. http://www.examiner.com/article/obama-s-condemnation-of-cheap-handguns-reeks-of-self-defense-poll-tax

297. http://www.examiner.com/article/obama-s-condemnation-of-cheap-handguns-reeks-of-self-defense-poll-tax

298. http://www.westernjournalism.com/hagel-endorsed-by-communist-party-usa/

299. http://www.wnd.com/2013/02/hagel-linked-to-iranian-lobby/

300. http://www.theatlanticwire.com/politics/2012/12/jewish-lobby-quote-could-ignite-chuck-hagel-confirmation/60130/

301. http://www.breitbart.com/Big-Peace/2012/12/14/It-s-Hard-To-Be-More-Anti-Israel-Than-Former-Sen-Hagel

302. http://www.politifact.com/truth-o-meter/statements/2013/jan/11/ileana-ros-lehtinen/ros-lehtinen-said-defense-secretary-nominee-hagel-/

303. http://www.nytimes.com/interactive/2013/01/07/us/politics/hagel-issue-quotes.html?_r=0

304. http://www.nytimes.com/interactive/2013/01/07/us/politics/hagel-issue-quotes.html?_r=0

305. http://www.foxnews.com/politics/2010/10/18/obama-voters-scared-thinking-clearly-election/

306. http://en.wikipedia.org/wiki/Rashad_Hussain#Deputy_Associate_Counsel

307. http://www.nytimes.com/2009/06/04/us/politics/04obama.text.html?pagewanted=all

308. http://thehill.com/blogs/blog-briefing-room/news/146091-obama-in-2007-ill-walk-on-that-picket-line-if-bargaining-rights-threatened

309. http://www.nytimes.com/2012/06/16/us/us-to-stop-deporting-some-illegal-immigrants.html?pagewanted=all

310. http://beforeitsnews.com/opinion-conservative/2012/08/ice-agents-sue-janet-napolitano-over-barack-obamas-dream-act-executive-order-2469324.html

311. http://commonconstitutionalist.com/tag/janet-napolitano/

312. http://www.breitbart.com/Big-Government/2013/05/10/Border-Agent-Rep-Explains-How-Administration-Inflates-Deportation-Numbers

313. http://standwitharizona.com/blog/2013/04/27/disgusted-ice-agent-faces-down-gang-of-eight-in-dramatic-senate-testimony/

314. http://www.statesman.com/news/news/new-rule-easing-immigration-hurdles-bypasses-congr/nTkpQ/

315. http://www.dickmorris.com/stop-obamacare-rationing-dick-morris-tv-lunch-alert/

316. http://en.wikipedia.org/wiki/Mahmoud_Ahmadinejad_and_Israel

317. http://www.youtube.com/watch?v=ew5qP2oPdtQ

318. http://www.haaretz.com/news/middle-east/un-watchdog-concerned-iran-secretly-developing-nuclear-weapons-despite-iaea-talks-1.513148

319. http://www.zerohedge.com/news/un-security-council-finds-iran-violating-nuclear-weapons-program-ban

320. http://www.reuters.com/article/2012/09/27/us-un-assembly-israel-iran-idUSBRE88Q0GI20120927

321. http://www.newparadigmsforum.com/NPFtestsite/?p=1182

322. http://www.usatoday.com/story/news/politics/2013/05/18/irs-scandal-planted-question/2216747/

323. http://www.usatoday.com/story/news/politics/2013/05/14/irs-tea-party-progressive-groups/2158831/

324. http://www.dailymail.co.uk/news/article-2329067/Congress-hosts-IRS-bloodbath-slamming-tax-authorities-partisan-targeting-conservatives-official-refuses-answer-questions.html

325. http://townhall.com/tipsheet/guybenson/2013/06/27/irs-inspector-general-liberal-groups-werent-targeted-like-conservatives-n1629048

326. http://www.cnsnews.com/news/article/irs-career-employee-deeply-offended-washington-officials-blamed-cincinnati-rogue-agents

327. http://washingtonexaminer.com/treasury-irs-targeted-292-tea-party-groups-just-6-progressive-groups/article/

328. http://washingtonexaminer.com/updated-irs-tax-exemptionobamacare-exec-got-103390-in-bonuses-did-obama-ok-them/article/2529899

329. http://dailycaller.com/2013/05/29/irss-shulman-had-more-public-white-house-visits-than-any-cabinet-member/

330. http://cnsnews.com/news/article/ex-irs-chief-i-certainly-believe-i-did-not-have-any-conversations-wh-about-tea-party

331. http://www.theblaze.com/stories/2013/05/16/obama-i-certainly-did-not-know-anything-about-irs-scandal/

332. http://www.nationalreview.com/corner/354238/was-irs-chief-counsel-william-wilkins-involved-scandal-eliana-johnson

333. http://www.washingtonpost.com/politics/obama-searches-for-middle-east-peace/2012/07/14/gJQAQQiKlW_story.html

334. http://www.foxnews.com/politics/2009/11/18/obama-warns-double-dip-recession/

335. http://spectator.org/archives/2010/03/17/blame-israel-first

336. http://www.foxnews.com/politics/2010/03/25/president-allegedly-dumps-israeli-prime-minister-dinner/

337. http://www.reuters.com/article/2010/03/15/us-israel-usa-palestinians-envoy-idUSTRE62E11O20100315

338. http://online.wsj.com/article/SB10001424052748704904604576 335071093979138.html

339. http://www.examiner.com/article/obama-makes-time-for-letterman-but-not-israeli-pm-netanyahu

340. http://finance.townhall.com/columnists/bobbeauprez/2012/09/1 3/obama_too_busy_campaigning_to_meet_with_netanyahu

341. http://en.wikipedia.org/wiki/Van_Jones

342. http://www.politifact.com/truth-o-meter/statements/2009/ sep/08/glenn-beck/glenn-beck-says-van-jones-avowed-communist/

343. http://www.youtube.com/watch?v=yt66eWnjoTo

344. http://www.youtube.com/watch?v=vO-D-ZeqN5U

345. http://dailycaller.com/2010/07/20/u-s-funding-of-groups-lobbying-for-pro-abortion-constitution-in-kenya-more-than-previously-thought/2/

346. http://www.lifenews.com/2011/11/16/probe-obama-admin-broke-law-to-push-abortion-in-kenya/

347. http://www.lifesitenews.com/news/archive//ldn/2010/jun/1006 2105

348. http://therightswriter.com/2011/11/guilty-obama-admin-illegally-used-u-s-funds-to-promote-abortion-in-kenya/

349. http://www.canadafreepress.com/index.php/article/4353

350. http://online.wsj.com/article/SB10001424052970204468004577 168892140746430.html

351. http://www.foxnews.com/politics/2012/03/22/obama-plans-to-fast-track-oklahoma-oil-pipeline-amid-criticism-over-keystone/

352. http://thinkprogress.org/climate/2013/06/25/2208941/obama-says-keystone-xl-should-be-rejected-if-it-will-increase-carbon-emissions/

353. http://www.realclearpolitics.com/video/2010/06/07/obama_see king_ass_to_kick_over_oil_spill.html

354. http://www.nytimes.com/2012/05/29/world/obamas-leadership-in-war-on-al-qaeda.html?pagewanted=all

355. http://news.investors.com/politics-andrew-malcolm/012612-599002-obama-white-house-staff-back-taxes.htm

356. http://www.nytimes.com/2013/02/02/us/politics/white-house-proposes-compromise-on-contraception-coverage.html?pagewanted=all

357. http://www.breitbart.com/Big-Government/2012/09/18/HHS-Mandate-Lawsuits-Obama-Admin-Argues-Government-Can-Make-a-Law-That-Violates-Religious-Beliefs

358. http://www.snopes.com/politics/obama/debtlimit.asp

359. http://larouchepac.com/node/25113

360. http://www.nationaljournal.com/whitehouse/sessions-sanders-say-lew-s-not-the-man-for-the-treasury-job-20130109

361. http://www.forbes.com/sites/merrillmatthews/2011/07/13/what-happened-to-the-2-6-trillion-social-security-trust-fund/

362. http://www.apostle1.com/daily-news-2013/january-2013/01-15-2013-lew_at_treasury_shows_obama_wants_confrontation.htm

363. http://en.wikipedia.org/wiki/2011_military_intervention_in_Libya

364. http://articles.washingtonpost.com/2011-06-15/politics/35234248_1_libya-operation-libya-campaign-libya-action

365. http://www.reuters.com/article/2011/03/30/us-libya-usa-order-idUSTRE72T6H220110330

366. http://www.nytimes.com/2012/12/06/world/africa/weapons-sent-to-libyan-rebels-with-us-approval-fell-into-islamist-hands.html?pagewanted=all&_r=0

367. http://www.nytimes.com/2011/06/16/us/politics/16powers.html?pagewanted=all&_r=0

368. http://www.breitbart.com/Big-Peace/2012/07/30/Muslim-Brotherhood-in-America

369. http://www.discoverthenetworks.org/individualProfile.asp?indid=2562

370. http://www.foxnews.com/politics/2009/01/17/feds-say-obama-prayer-leader-group-linked-hamas/

371. http://online.wsj.com/article/SB10001424052970204518504574418563346840666.html

372. http://www.foxnews.com/politics/2012/03/26/obama-tells-medvedev-hell-have-more-flexibility-after-election-during-missile/

373. http://www.investigativeproject.org/1904/dalia-mogahed-a-muslim-george-gallup-or-islamist

374. http://en.wikipedia.org/wiki/Dalia_Mogahed

375. http://wikiislam.net/wiki/Dalia_Mogahed#Muslim_Brotherhood

376. http://formermuslimsunited.org/the-pledge/pledge-recipients/

377. http://wikiislam.net/wiki/Dalia_Mogahed

378. http://www.wnd.com/2011/07/325625/

379. http://swordattheready.wordpress.com/2012/09/15/investigation-obama-funding-mosques-around-the-world-at-u-s-taxpayer-expense/

380. http://truthontarget.blogspot.com/2010/08/us-government-funds-mosque-renovation.html

381. http://counterjihadreport.com/tag/christian-persecution/

382. http://www.popularmechanics.com/cars/news/fuel-economy/obama-announces-54-6-mpg-cafe-standard-by-2025

383. http://jerusalemworldnews.com/2012/01/26/egypts-muslim-brotherhood-vows-no-talks-with-israel/

384. http://thespeechatimeforchoosing.wordpress.com/2010/08/18/fl ashback-barack-obama-says-muslim-call-to-prayer-%E2%80%9Cone-of-the-prettiest-sounds-on-earth-at-sunset-%E2%80%9D/

385. http://www.weeklystandard.com/weblogs/TWSFP/2009/06/oba ma_america_one_of_the_large_1.asp

386. http://www.weeklystandard.com/weblogs/TWSFP/2009/06/oba ma_america_one_of_the_large_1.asp

387. http://www.breitbart.com/Big-Peace/2010/10/19/FBI-Outreach-Partner-Kifah-Mustapha-Hosted-Hamas-Fundraiser-in-July-2009

388. http://counterjihadreport.com/tag/muslim-brotherhood-infiltration/

389. http://www.investigativeproject.org/documents/misc/735.pdf

390http://www.judicialwatch.org/blog/2010/02/nasa-focus-muslim-outreach/

391. http://abcnews.go.com/blogs/politics/2010/07/white-house-nasa-defend-comments-about-nasa-outreach-to-muslim-world-criticized-by-conservatives/

392. http://online.wsj.com/article/SB10001424127887324478304578 171623040640006.html

393. https://www.cia.gov/library/publications/the-world-factbook/rankorder/2186rank.html

394. https://www.cbo.gov/sites/default/files/cbofiles/attachments/43 907-BudgetOutlook.pdf

395. http://www.youtube.com/watch?v=neGbKHyGuHU

396. http://www.foxnews.com/politics/2010/06/30/justice-dept-lawyer-accuses-holder-dropping-new-black-panther-case-political/

397. http://online.wsj.com/article/SB1000142405297020355060457 4 361071968458430.html

398. http://bizblogger.blogspot.com/2010/07/doj-now-supporting-voter-fraud.html

399. http://www.mainjustice.com/2010/09/24/doj-prosecutor-blasts-handling-of-new-black-panthers-case/

400. http://www.breitbart.com/Big-Government/2012/08/06/Court-Rules-DOJ-Politicized-Black-Panther-Case-Awards-JW-Court-Fees

401. http://www.blackpanther.org/newsalert.htm

402. http://www.politico.com/blogs/joshgerstein/0311/Eric_Holder_B lack_Panther_case_focus_demeans_my_people.html

403. http://www.law360.com/articles/401768/house-panel-s-report-accuses-nlrb-of-pro-union-bias

404. http://online.wsj.com/article/SB1000142405297020351360457 7 141411919152318.html

405. http://www.biglaborbailout.com/2013/05/03/with-richard-griffin-the-nlrb-is-all-mobbed-up/

406. http://nrtwc.org/42-gop-senators-challenge-obamas-so-called-nlrb-recess-appointments/

407. http://www.politico.com/blogs/under-the-radar/2013/05/second-appeals-court-invalidates-obamas-nlrb-recess-164150.html

408. http://online.wsj.com/article/SB10001424127887324299104578529112289298922.html

409. http://en.wikipedia.org/wiki/Edward_Snowden

410. http://www.theguardian.com/world/2013/jun/20/fisa-court-nsa-without-warrant

411. http://www.wnd.com/2013/06/whistleblower-obama-used-nsa-for-politics/

412. http://www.dickmorris.com/nsa-wiretapping-repeal-of-4th-amendment-dick-morris-tv-lunch-alert/

413. http://www.theguardian.com/commentisfree/2013/may/03/fisa-court-rubber-stamp-drones

414. http://blog.sfgate.com/djsaunders/2012/10/11/nancy-pelosi-says-she-read-obamacare-bill/

415. https://wilsonncteaparty.wordpress.com/2012/05/11/obamacare-up-close-personal/

416. http://www.weeklystandard.com/blogs/obamacare-now-estimated-cost-26-trillion-first-decade_648413.html

417. http://www.whitehouse.gov/the_press_office/Remarks-by-the-President-to-a-Joint-Session-of-Congress-on-Health-Care

418. http://thehealthcareblog.com/blog/2013/05/28/california-rate-shock-and-awe/

419. http://taxfoundation.org/blog/obamacare-premiums-california-lower-expected-still-twice-cost-current-premiums

420. http://taxfoundation.org/blog/redistributional-effect-obamacare

421. http://uspolitics.about.com/od/healthcare/a/Are-Illegal-Immigrants-Covered-Under-Obamacare.htm

422. http://www.forbes.com/sites/theapothecary/2013/07/02/white-house-to-delay-obamacares-employer-mandate-until-2015-far-reaching-implications-for-the-private-health-insurance-market/

423. http://www.cleveland.com/healthfit/index.ssf/2012/06/affordabl e_care_acts_mandate_d.html

424. http://www.weeklystandard.com/articles/unions-vs-obamacare_707688.html

425. http://www.humanevents.com/2013/07/12/more-union-grumbles-about-obamacare/

426. http://www.politico.com/story/2013/04/obamacare-exemption-lawmakers-aides-90610.html

427. http://hotair.com/archives/2013/07/26/irony-irs-employees-union-wants-no-part-of-obamacare/

428. http://www.theblaze.com/stories/2013/08/01/obamacare-would-reportedly-increase-some-health-care-costs-by-198-in-this-state-and-officials-want-a-30-day-implementation-delay/

429. http://wearethe99percent.us/

430. http://www.verumserum.com/?p=33490

431. https://en.wikipedia.org/wiki/Occupy_Wall_Street

432. http://www.businessinsider.com/occupy-wall-street-brookfield-properties-zuccotti-park-loan-guarantee-2011-10

433. http://abcnews.go.com/Nightline/video/obama-compares-occupy-ws-tea-party-14763350

434. http://townhall.com/columnists/julieborowski/2012/05/31/the_uns_law_of_the_sea_treaty_threatens_our_national_sovereignty/page/full

435. http://www.freerepublic.com/focus/bloggers/2597023/posts

436. http://www.reuters.com/article/2012/11/29/us-palestinians-statehood-idUSBRE8AR0EG20121129

437. http://www.freerepublic.com/focus/news/2879179/posts

438. http://www.foxnews.com/politics/2012/09/05/democrats-restore-references-to-god-jerusalem-in-platform/

439. http://en.wikipedia.org/wiki/National_Iranian_American_Council

440. http://www.businessinsider.com/george-soros-taking-heat-over-ties-to-pro-iranian-group-2009-11

441http://www.politico.com/blogs/under-the-radar/2012/09/iranianamerican-group-leader-lose-libel-case-135502.html

442. http://freebeacon.com/niac-loses-defamation-suit/

443. http://www.washingtontimes.com/news/2009/nov/13/exclusive-did-iranian-advocacy-group-violate-laws/?page=all

444. http://atlasshrugs2000.typepad.com/atlas_shrugs/2011/12/court
-docs-iranian-american-lobbying-group-niac-defrauded-feds-lied-to-
congressmen-paid-for-congress.html

445. http://atlasshrugs2000.typepad.com/atlas_shrugs/2012/05/two-
jew-hating-terror-apologists-reza-aslan-and-hussein-ibish-to-duke-it-
out-at-ucla.html

446. http://iranian.com/main/blog/arash-irandoost/pdmi-open-letter-
secretary-state-hillary-rodham-clinton-decision-send-trita-par.html

447. http://www.westernjournalism.com/court-reveals-iranian-
operatives-in-charge-of-obamas-iran-policy-since-2009/

448. http://online.wsj.com/article/SB1000142412788732428100 4578
356581889324790.html

449. http://oversight.house.gov/release/grassley-goodlatte-and-issa-
release-report-how-assistant-attorney-general-thomas-perez-
manipulated-justice-and-ignored-the-rule-of-law/

450. http://www.foxnews.com/politics/2013/04/15/labor-secretary-
nominee-accused-quid-pro-quo-deal/

451. http://www.rpc.senate.gov/policy-papers/questions-for-labor-
secretary-nominee-perez

452. http://nation.foxnews.com/thomas-perez/2013/03/18/black-
panther-testimony-haunt-obama-labor-nominee

453. http://newsbusters.org/blogs/noel-sheppard/2010/06/24/
moveon-org-removes-general-betray-us-ad-website

454. http://online.wsj.com/article/SB1000142412788732407 3504578
109252422213868.html

455. http://www.dailymail.co.uk/news/article-2325230/Emails-David-Petraeus-objected-Obama-administrations-version-Benghazi-events.html

456. http://www.nytimes.com/1994/03/03/us/farrakhan-fiery-separatist-in-a-sober-suit.html?pagewanted=all&src=pm

457. http://michellemalkin.com/2008/05/29/hes-baaaack-obama-supporter-rev-michael-pfleger-flogs-hillarys-white-entitlement-on-the-pulpit/

458. http://www.huffingtonpost.com/2008/05/29/obama-pastor-michael-pfle_n_104224.html

459. http://www.realclearpolitics.com/video/2012/06/08/obama_the_private_sector_is_doing_fine.html

460. http://newsbusters.org/blogs/noel-sheppard/2012/06/11/paul-krugman-obama-screwed-private-sector-doing-fine-line

461. http://news.investors.com/ibd-editorials-viewpoint/032613-649412-data-link-more-government-spending-higher-unemployment.htm?p=full

462. http://hotair.com/archives/2010/10/25/obamas-turnout-pitch-to-latinos-get-out-there-and-punish-your-enemies/

463. http://www.nydailynews.com/news/politics/fed-hold-interest-rates-joblessness-dips-article-1.1218600

464. http://www.forbes.com/sites/paulroderickgregory/2012/09/23/why-the-fuss-obama-has-long-been-on-record-in-favor-of-redistribution/

465. http://www.newsmax.com/Newsfront/obama-redistribution-loyola-speech/2012/09/18/id/456677?s=al

466. http://cnsnews.com/news/article/spread-wealth-around-comment-comes-back-haunt-obama

467. http://hotair.com/archives/2010/04/29/obama-i-do-think-at-a-certain-point-youve-made-enough-money/

468. http://washingtonexaminer.com/how-the-uaw-made-michigan-a-right-to-work-state/article/2533498

469. http://object.cato.org/sites/cato.org/files/serials/files/regulation/2000/4/holmes/pdf

470. http://www.nrtw.org/es/blog/new-fact-sheet-shows-right-work-states-benefi-10262011

471. http://nrtwc.org/right-to-work-states-enjoy-growth-advantage/

472. http://cnsnews.com/blog/craig-bannister/right-work-states-have-lower-unemployment-higher-income-and-healthcare-coverage

473. http://www.mackinac.org/18216

474. http://online.wsj.com/article/SB10001424127887324339204578173701137303598.html

475. http://www.nrtw.org/en/blog/debunking-economic-case-against-right-work-la/12102012

476. http://www.washingtonpost.com/blogs/fact-checker/post/romneys-claim-that-right-to-work-states-get-more-good-jobs/2011/09/29/gIQAGsP17K_blog.html

477. http://wepartypatriots.com/wp/2012/05/03/obama-collective-bargaining/

478. http://thehill.com/homenews/administration/272017-obama-jumps-into-fight-over-michigan-labor-laws

479. http://thinkprogress.org/economy/2011/12/06/383348/trickle-down-economics-doesnt-work-obama-asserts-in-economic-speech/

480. http://www.wnd.com/2009/12/118941/

481. http://en.wikipedia.org/wiki/D.C._Opportunity_Scholarship_Program

482. http://www.forbes.com/2009/04/16/school-voucher-washington-dc-teacher-union-opinions-contributors-obama.html

483. http://reason.com/blog/2009/04/23/ignoring-facts-in-the-name-of

484. http://www.washingtontimes.com/news/2012/jun/18/white-house-relents-on-dc-school-voucher-bill/?page=all

485. http://www.aei.org/article/education/k-12/school-choice/school-choice-should-not-be-just-for-special-needs-students/

486. http://www.washingtonpost.com/blogs/fact-checker/post/obamas-fanciful-claim-that-congress-proposed-the-sequester/2012/10/25/8651dc6a-1eed-11e2-ba31-3083ca97c314_blog.html

487. http://www.forbes.com/sites/paulroderickgregory/2013/03/03/white-house-admits-third-time-president-obama-fibbed-on-sequester/

488. http://blog.al.com/wire/2013/02/one_day_to_go_president_obama.html

489. http://www.cbsnews.com/8301-250_162-57571396/sequester-impact-wont-be-overnight-but-will-be-real-obama-says/

490. http://blog.heritage.org/2013/02/28/organizing-for-action-uses-discredited-information-on-sequester/

491. http://www.foxnews.com/politics/2013/03/05/white-house-cancels-tours-citing-sequester/

492. http://wikiislam.net/wiki/Kareem_Shora

493. http://www.snopes.com/politics/religion/dhs.asp

494. http://www.discoverthenetworks.org/groupProfile.asp?grpid=61 73

495. http://en.wikipedia.org/wiki/Shovel_ready

496. http://hotair.com/greenroom/archives/2011/05/18/economic-study-stimulus-destroyedforestalled-1-million-private-sector-jobs/

497. http://nation.foxnews.com/president-obama/2011/06/13/obama-jokes-jobs-council-shovel-ready-was-not-shovel-ready-we-expected

498. http://mikesright.wordpress.com/2011/06/21/i-created-2-1-million-jobs-and-the-cow-jumped-over-the-moon/

499. http://cnsnews.com/news/article/19-million-fewer-americans-have-jobs-today-when-obama-signed-stimulus

500. http://cnsnews.com/news/article/19-million-fewer-americans-have-jobs-today-when-obama-signed-stimulus

501. http://www.pnhp.org/news/2008/june/barack_obama_on_sing.php

502. http://blog.heritage.org/2009/08/11/obama-in-2008-obamacare-will-eliminate-private-insurance-over-time/

503. http://www.reuters.com/article/2009/10/15/us-arms-usa-treaty-idUSTRE59E0Q920091015

504. http://www.thegatewaypundit.com/2012/11/hours-after-obama-victory-us-backs-un-arms-treaty/

505. http://joeforamerica.com/2013/06/john-kerry-says-obama-looks-forward-to-signing-un-gun-control-treaty/

506. http://www.wnd.com/2011/08/329449/

507. http://www.breitbart.com/Big-Government/2012/06/12/Democratic-Socialists-of-America-Endorsed-European-Social-Democrat-Obama-in-2000

508. https://en.wikipedia.org/wiki/Bernie_Sanders

509. http://www.washingtonpost.com/solyndra-politics-infused-obama-energy-programs/2011/12/14/gIQA4HllHP_story_2.html

510. http://www.bloomberg.com/news/2012-10-22/solyndra-wins-court-approval-of-bankruptcy-exit-plan.html

511. http://www.bloomberg.com/news/2012-11-02/solyndra-judge-s-approval-of-bankruptcy-plan-appealed.html

512. http://www.whitehouse.gov/omb/budget/historicals (Table 15.3)

513. http://www.factcheck.org/2012/06/obamas-spending-inferno-or-not/

514. http://www.forbes.com/sites/joshbarro/2012/04/16/lessons-from-the-decades-long-upward-march-of-government-spending/

515. http://wiki.answers.com/Q/Did_Obama_say_in_his_book_Audaci ty_of_hope_I_will_stand_with_the_Muslims

516. http://en.wikipedia.org/wiki/Ann_Dunham

517. http://www.americanthinker.com/2012/09/obama_love_him_ha te_him_you_havent_a_clue.html

518. http://en.wikipedia.org/wiki/START_I

519. http://www.nationalreview.com/node/253245/print

520. http://thehill.com/homenews/senate/134375-start-treaty-survives-threat-from-mccain-amendment-on-missile-defense

521. http://www.askheritage.org/what-are-the-problems-with-the-new-start-treaty/

522. http://www.washingtontimes.com/news/2010/jan/27/stimulus-price-tag-soars-as-jobless-rate-rises/?page=all

523. http://www.nydailynews.com/news/politics/president-obama-signs-26-billion-aid-bill-saves-jobs-thousands-new-yorkers-article-1.203182

524. http://www.businessinsider.com/sorry-america-stimulus-spending-on-road-construction-does-nothing-to-lower-unemployment-2010-1

525. http://www.cato.org/publications/commentary/stimulus-actually-raised-unemployment

526. http://www.breitbart.com/Breitbart-TV/2013/05/06/Obama-Admin-Warns-Syria-Days-Are-Numbered-For-600-Days

527. http://en.wikipedia.org/wiki/Kofi_Annan_peace_envoy_for_Syria

528. http://www.pbs.org/newshour/rundown/2013/06/administratio n-sharpens-focus-on-syria-with-chemical-weapons-report.html

529. http://globalpublicsquare.blogs.cnn.com/2013/04/25/obamas-empty-threats-on-syria/

530. http://blogs.the-american-interest.com/wrm/2013/05/05/syria-obamas-own-problem-from-hell/

531. http://frontpagemag.com/2010/stephenbrown/times-square-denial/

532. http://www.americanthinker.com/2010/11/airport_scanners_and_marxist_c_1.html

533. http://americaswatchtower.com/2010/05/04/times-square-terrorist-arrested/

534. http://en.wikipedia.org/wiki/Faisal_Shahzad

535. http://www.foxnews.com/us/2010/10/05/times-square-bomber-faces-sentencing-nyc/

536. http://en.wikipedia.org/wiki/2010_Times_Square_car_bombing_attempt

537. http://www.forbes.com/sites/realspin/2012/08/14/too-big-to-fail-has-become-a-permanent-bailout-program/

538. http://www.newyorkfed.org/newsevents/speeches/2012/dud12 1115.html

539. http://www.legislationandpolicy.com/425/dodd-frank-a-kiss-to-wall-street-or-the-watchdog-we-need-to-prevent-another-economic-collapse/

540. http://www.nytimes.com/2012/03/22/us/police-chief-draws-fire-in-trayvon-martin-shooting.html

541. http://www.theblaze.com/stories/2012/04/03/trayvon-martin-case-leads-to-multiple-embarrassments-for-nbc-msnbc/

542. http://www.humanevents.com/2012/03/28/allen-west-the-new-black-panther-bounty-on-zimmerman-is-a-hate-crime/

543. http://www.cbsnews.com/8301-503544_162-57403200-503544/obama-if-i-had-a-son-hed-look-like-trayvon/

544. http://www.judicialwatch.org/press-room/press-releases/documents-obtained-by-judicial-watch-detail-role-of-justice-department-in-organizing-trayvon-martin-protests/

545. http://www.prnewswire.com/news-releases/frequent-flyers-give-tsa-failing-grade-at-performing-security-screenings-169157096.html

546. http://usatoday30.usatoday.com/news/washington/2010-07-16-tsa16_ST_N.htm

547. http://reason.com/blog/2012/09/05/the-continued-mission-creep-of-the-tsa

548. http://www.canadafreepress.com/index.php/article/47844

549. http://www.weeklystandard.com/weblogs/TWSFP/2009/12/napolitano_says_system_that_di.asp

550. http://www.forbes.com/2009/12/31/airline-terrorism-al-qaida-opinions-columnists-claudia-rosett.html

551. http://data.bls.gov/timeseries/LNS11300000

552. http://www.bloomberg.com/news/2013-04-05/payrolls-in-u-s-rose-less-than-forecast-jobless-rate-falls.html

553. http://seekingalpha.com/article/1599422-recovery-less-recovery-unemployment-duration-july-2013?source=google_news

554. http://news.investors.com/politics-andrew-malcolm/121012-636426-americans-figure-out-public-employees-have-it-better-than-private-workers.htm?p=full

555. http://beforeitsnews.com/opinion-liberal/2013/01/senate-compromise-to-put-off-the-fiscal-cliff-to-continue-extended-unemployment-benefits-raises-taxes-on-working-people-2453006.html

556. http://www.brookings.edu/blogs/jobs/posts/2013/08/02-jobs-unemployment-rate-burtless

557. http://data.bls.gov/timeseries/LNS12300000

558. http://pjmedia.com/tatler/2013/07/05/june-jobs-report-part-time-jobs-up-full-time-jobs-down/

559. http://en.wikipedia.org/wiki/National_Education_Association

560. http://www.discoverthenetworks.org/viewSubCategory.asp?id=1 526

561. http://www.discoverthenetworks.org/individualProfile.asp?indid =2420

562. http://www.nrtwc.org/nl/nl200901p5.pdf

563. http://www.nytimes.com/2012/05/23/business/craig-becker-appointed-to-afl-cio-role.html?_r=0

564. http://www.washingtontimes.com/news/2012/aug/31/barack-obama-i-owe-those-unions/

565. http://www.youtube.com/watch?v=q6rslJl3Fl8

566. http://www.freep.com/article/20120905/NEWS15/120905105/Tr anscript-UAW-President-Bob-King-s-speech-Democratic-National-Convention

567. http://www.aflcio.org/Press-Room/Speeches/Remarks-by-AFL-CIO-President-Richard-L.-Trumka-2012-Democratic-National-Convention-Charlotte-North-Carolina

568. http://washingtonexaminer.com/obamas-top-funder-also-leads-the-nation-in-white-house-visits/article/141278

569. http://www.whitehouse.gov/the-press-office/president-obama-names-members-bipartisan-national-commission-fiscal-responsibility-

570. http://teachersunionexposed.com/dues.php

571. http://en.wikipedia.org/wiki/Andy_Stern

572. http://townhall.com/tipsheet/katiepavlich/2012/09/25/obama_t o_un_crude_and_disgusting_video_sparked_outrage

573. http://www.nytimes.com/2011/12/24/us/justice-department-rejects-voter-id-law-in-south-carolina.html?_r=0

574. http://www.projectonfairrepresentation.org/shelby-county-alabama-files-challenge-to-section-5-of-voting-rights-act/

575. http://www.scotusblog.com/case-files/cases/shelby-county-v-holder/

576. http://www.washingtontimes.com/news/2013/jun/25/obama-supreme-court-ruling-voting-rights-setback/

577. http://www.nytimes.com/2013/07/26/us/holder-wants-texas-to-clear-voting-changes-with-the-us.html?pagewanted=all&_r=0

578. http://godfatherpolitics.com/7374/why-is-photo-id-required-for-everything-except-to-vote/

579. http://www.ncsl.org/legislatures-elections/elections/voter-id.aspx

580. http://www.ajc.com/news/news/despite-voter-id-law-minority-turnout-up-in-georgi/nR2bx/

581. http://www.budget.senate.gov/republican/public/index.cfm/bud get-background?ID=3c687e99-a5c5-46f2-9f9d-0ea5a62c3183

582. http://www.aei-ideas.org/2012/07/julias-mother-why-a-single-mom-is-better-off-on-welfare-than-taking-a-69000-a-year-job/

583. http://en.wikipedia.org/wiki/Jeremiah_Wright_controversy

584. http://news.bbc.co.uk/2/hi/americas/7302938.stm

585. http://voices.washingtonpost.com/44/2008/04/16/obama_releas es_2007_tax_return.html

586. http://www.trinitychicago.org/index.php?option=com_content&t ask=view&id=114

587. http://www.huffingtonpost.com/barack-obama/on-my-faith-and-my-church_b_91623.html

588. http://www.cnsnews.com/news/article/obama-president-does-not-have-power-under-constitution-unilaterally-authorize-military

589. http://www.discoverthenetworks.org/individualProfile.asp?indid =1511

590. http://www.whitehouse.gov/the_press_office/Remarks-by-the-President-at-Cairo-University-6-04-09

591. http://www.whitehouse.gov/economy/jobs/we-cant-wait

592. https://ssl1.washingtonpost.com/opinions/obamas-kill-list-is-unchecked-presidential-power/2012/06/11/gJQAHw05WV_story_1.html

593. http://mercatus.org/publication/regulatory-burdens-impact-dodd-frank-community-banking

594. http://www.againstcronycapitalism.org/2013/02/why-do-us-taxpayers-give-the-big-banks-an-83-billionyear-subsidy/

595. http://actionamerica.org/guns/guns1.shtml

596. http://spectator.org/archives/2013/04/23/perez-abomination-grows

597. http://online.wsj.com/article/SB10001424127887324128504578346913994914472.html

598. http://www.theguardian.com/world/2013/may/08/benghazi-us-officials-blocked-congress-hearing

599. http://www.theblaze.com/stories/2013/05/08/white-house-spokesman-says-changes-in-benghazi-talking-points-were-stylistic-and-non-substantive/

600. http://www.foxnews.com/politics/2013/08/06/us-reportedly-files-charges-against-benghazi-attack-suspects/

601. http://dailycaller.com/2013/05/14/carney-white-house-notified-of-irs-targeting-tea-party-several-weeks-ago-obama-i-found-out-friday-video/

602. http://www.reuters.com/article/2013/05/14/usa-reid-ap-idUSL2N0DV38B20130514

603. http://www.breitbart.com/Big-Government/2013/05/14/Progressive-Group-Says-IRS-Gave-Them-Confidential-Docs-On-Conservative-Groups

604. http://www.foxnews.com/politics/2010/12/10/irs-scrutiny-pro-israel-group-cries-discrimination/

605. http://reason.com/blog/2012/09/20/fast-and-furious-report-exonerates-holde

606. http://www.breitbart.com/Big-Government/2013/05/19/Businessman-Frank-VanderSloot-I-was-audited-twice-by-IRS-once-by-DOL-investigated-by-Senate-staffer-after-giving-1-million-to-Romney-Super-PAC

607. http://en.wikipedia.org/wiki/ProPublica

608. http://www.weeklystandard.com/blogs/report-irs-deliberately-chose-not-fess-scandal-election_724711.html

609. http://news.investors.com/ibd-editorials/052413-657748-eric-holder-signed-james-rosen-warrant.htm?p=full

610. http://www.freerepublic.com/focus/news/3024822/posts

611. http://www.theblaze.com/stories/2013/05/21/why-were-dhs-agents-seemingly-monitoring-multiple-tea-party-irs-protests-across-the-country-on-tuesday/

612. http://online.wsj.com/article/SB10001424127887324682204578517563566848922.html

613. http://www.washingtontimes.com/news/2013/aug/2/cia-accused-pure-intimidation-silence-agents-bengh/

614. http://www.theblaze.com/stories/2013/06/04/report-u-s-government-publishes-details-of-israeli-missile-base-that-was-supposed-to-stay-secret/

615. http://www.independentsentinel.com/irs-scandal-moves-closer-to-barack-obama/

616. http://www.redstate.com/2013/08/07/david-vitter-fights-back-against-obamacare/

617. http://www.freedomworks.org/blog/andrewmontgomery39/elitist-washington-congress-gets-pass-from-obamaca

618. http://www.washingtonpost.com/blogs/wonkblog/wp/2013/04/25/no-congress-isnt-trying-to-exempt-itself-from-obamacare/

619. http://news.heartland.org/newspaper-article/2013/06/16/california-assembly-rejects-fracking-ban

620. http://www.washingtonpost.com/blogs/fact-checker/post/james-clappers-least-untruthful-statement-to-the-senate/2013/06/11/e50677a8-d2d8-11e2-a73e-826d299ff459_blog.html

621. http://www.nytimes.com/2013/06/12/us/aclu-files-suit-over-phone-surveillance-program.html?pagewanted=all&_r=0

622. http://www.foxnews.com/politics/2013/06/14/assad-use-chemical-weapons-confirmed-us-officials-say/

623. http://www.forbes.com/sites/theapothecary/2013/08/06/labor-unions-latest-problem-obamacares-cadillac-tax-harms-their-gold-plated-health-insurance-plans/

624. http://www.thepoliticalguide.com/Profiles/President/US/Barack_Obama/Views/TARP/

625. http://hotair.com/archives/2010/07/19/tarp-audit-claims-obama-admin-destroyed-tens-of-thousands-of-jobs-in-dealer-closures/

626. http://www.americanthinker.com/2010/07/race_played_role_in_obama_car.html

627. http://wot.motortrend.com/official-fiat-now-owns-majority-stake-in-chrysler-99687.html#axzz2bVkPZcDr

628. http://hotair.com/archives/2011/05/27/the-fake-chrysler-loan-payoff/

629. http://www.forbes.com/sites/halahtouryalai/2013/07/30/the-goods-on-general-motors-and-why-its-still-so-cheap/

630. http://projects.propublica.org/bailout/list

631. http://www.dsnews.com/articles/report-26-of-hamp-borrowers-have-redefaulted-rate-continues-to-worsen-2013-07-24

632. http://business.time.com/2013/05/02/new-hope-for-underwater-homeowners/

633. http://www.whitehouse.gov/blog/2013/07/26/president-obama-hosts-iftar-dinner-white-house

634. http://online.wsj.com/article/SB10001424127887324110404578628542498014414.html

635. http://www.foxnews.com/politics/2013/07/31/republican-report-concludes-holder-misled-congress-on-reporter-targeting/

636. http://www.ctmirror.org/story/2013/08/05/aetna-withdraws-states-health-insurance-exchange

637. http://www.stltoday.com/business/local/large-insurers-opt-out-of-health-exchange-in-missouri/article_33ff7e3c-2ae7-56df-b258-7b775b5ef1c7.html

638. http://articles.latimes.com/2013/may/22/business/la-fi-health-insure-20130523

639. http://waysandmeans.house.gov/news/documentsingle.aspx?Do cumentID=345279

640. http://www.politifact.com/truth-o-meter/statements/2013/jul/19/tom-cole/rep-tom-cole-says-food-stamp-spending-doubled-unde/

641. http://www.thenewamerican.com/usnews/politics/item/12944-obama-rule-doubled-number-of-able-bodied-on-food-stamps

642. http://www.conservativemonitor.com/top-ten/losing-ground.shtml

643. http://www.renewamerica.com/columns/popp/100206

644. http://www.anwr.org/Background/Making-the-Case-for-ANWR.php

645. http://www.wnd.com/2012/03/sheriff-joe-tons-more-shocking-obama-info/

646. http://www.breitbart.com/Big-Government/2013/08/12/Obama-DHS-Publishes-Instructions-For-Asylum-Loophole-On-Internet

647. http://www.forbes.com/sites/theapothecary/2013/08/13/yet-another-white-house-obamacare-delay-out-of-pocket-caps-waived-until-2015/

648. http://www.reuters.com/article/2013/08/12/us-usa-voting-northcarolina-idUSBRE97B0UI20130812

649. http://en.wikipedia.org/wiki/Samira_Ibrahim

650. http://www.weeklystandard.com/blogs/michelle-obama-and-john-kerry-honor-anti-semite-and-911-fan_706547.html

651. http://www.washingtonpost.com/world/national-security/nsa-broke-privacy-rules-thousands-of-times-per-year-audit-finds/2013/08/15/3310e554-05ca-11e3-a07f-49ddc7417125_story_3.html

652. http://dailycaller.com/2012/07/03/usda-combats-mountain-pride-self-reliance-to-boost-food-stamp-rolls/

653. http://www.examiner.com/article/voting-away-your-gun-rights

654. http://nationalreview.com/corner/355816/muslim-brotherhood-reprisals-enemies-islam-andrew-c-mccarthy

655. http://www.theguardian.com/world/video/2013/aug/16/barack-obama-egypt-statement-video

656. http://www.gopusa.com/news/2013/08/15/obama-epa-plan-climate-change-action-without-congress/

657. http://frontpagemag.com/2013/arnold-ahlert/exposed-obamas-years-of-collaboration-with-terror-supporters/

658. http://news.investors.com/ibd-editorials/081213-667243-obamacare-first-step-to-single-payer.htm

659. http://www.cato.org/publications/commentary/when-welfare-pays-better-work

660. http://www.cnn.com/2013/08/20/world/africa/libya-state-department-employees/

661. http://video.foxnews.com/v/2619303749001/ex-acorn-top-lobbyist-tapped-by-wh-to-run-obamacare-contest/

662. http://www.ipsnews.net/2013/08/as-egypt-smoulders-churches-burn/

663. http://www.foxnews.com/politics/2013/08/21/3-members-172-dolphins-decline-invite-to-white-house-over-political-differences/

664. http://www.nationalreview.com/campaign-spot/355666/benghazi-whistleblowers-lawyer-warns-stolen-missiles-jim-geraghty

665. http://www.standard.net/stories/2013/08/21/state-dept-officials-placed-leave-after-benghazi-reinstated

666. http://www.reuters.com/article/2013/08/21/us-syria-crisis-gas-idUSBRE97K07O20130821

667. http://www.foxnews.com/opinion/2013/08/22/where-was-samantha-power/

668. http://www.freep.com/article/20130328/BUSINESS06/13032808 5/After-sale-to-Chinese-firm-Michigan-battery-maker-A123-gets-a-new-name-B456

669. http://frontpagemag.com/2013/colonel-phil-handley/betrayal-in-benghazi/

670. http://www.theblaze.com/stories/2013/08/22/homeland-security-employees-hate-filled-website-to-prepare-blacks-for-the-inevitable-clash-with-the-white-race/

671. http://www.theatlanticwire.com/national/2013/08/homeland-security-employee-moonlights-race-warrior/68600/

672. http://www.foxnews.com/politics/2013/06/05/house-votes-to-curb-dhs-stockpiles-ammo/

673. http://www.foxnews.com/politics/2013/08/22/obama-administration-considers-new-plan-to-bolster-mexicos-southern-border/?test=latestnews

674. http://www.westernjournalism.com/obama-bankrolled-attack-on-the-benghazi-consulate/

675. http://www.cnbc.com/id/49343911

676. http://www.washingtontimes.com/news/2013/aug/21/nsa-collected-56000-us-emails-over-3-years-no-terr/?page=all

677. http://www.bibliotecapleyades.net/ciencia/ciencia_globalwarmi ngpseudo97.htm

678. http://www.tradingeconomics.com/united-states/gdp-growth

679. http://www.washingtonpost.com/blogs/wonkblog/wp/2013/07/31/we-should-be-horrified-at-1-7-percent-gdp-growth/

680. http://hotair.com/archives/2013/08/27/justice-sues-louisiana-to-stop-school-voucher-program-irony-overwhelming/

681. http://www.examiner.com/article/syrian-chemical-weapons-may-shed-light-on-saddam-s-missing-wmds

682. http://www.washingtonpost.com/blogs/govbeat/wp/2013/08/22/local-governments-cutting-hours-over-obamacare-costs/

683. http://dcclothesline.com/2013/08/22/americans-in-shock-as-businesses-cut-work-hours-and-health-benefits-because-of-obamacare/

684. http://www.cnbc.com/id/100962203

685. http://blogs.wsj.com/washwire/2013/08/23/nsa-officers-sometimes-spy-on-love-interests/

686. http://data.bls.gov/timeseries/LNS14000000

687. http://www.nytimes.com/2013/08/30/business/economy/second-quarter-gdp-revised-sharply-higher.html?_r=0

688. http://www.nypost.com/p/news/international/assad_gassed_syria_times_oVrvUseCzROsKoRCPlp20H

689. http://www.nypost.com/p/news/international/syria_horror_toll_dead_AmnBj8OB7V9SjPWjJXi2yM

690. http://www.foxnews.com/politics/2013/08/27/kerry-evidence-chemical-weapons-strike-in-syria-undeniable/

691. http://www.washingtonpost.com/world/middle_east/hollande-france-ready-to-act-against-syria/2013/08/30/8a439b2a-1167-11e3-b4cb-fd7ce041d814_story.html

692. http://www.nytimes.com/2013/08/30/us/politics/obama-syria.html?_r=0

693. http://www.bloomberg.com/news/2013-08-31/un-team-quits-syria-after-kerry-sets-stage-for-u-s-action.html

694. http://michellemalkin.com/2013/09/02/backfire-obamacare-fallout-continues-as-40000-longshoremen-quit-afl-cio/

695. http://abcnews.go.com/blogs/politics/2013/09/obama-on-syria-my-credibility-is-not-on-the-line/

696. http://www.judicialwatch.org/blog/2013/08/dhs-rebrands-illegal-alien-advocate-to-avoid-congressional-ax/

697. http://video.foxnews.com/v/2652316710001/obama-admin-rebrands-job-outsmarts-congress/?playlist_id=2114913880001

698. http://www.foxnews.com/politics/2013/09/05/nra-joins-aclu-spying-lawsuit-over-gun-registry-fears/

699. http://news.investors.com/politics/090413-669682-obamacare-employer-mandate-spurs-work-hours-job-cuts.htm

700. http://www.businessweek.com/articles/2013-09-06/not-looking-for-work-labor-force-participation-hits-35-year-low

701. http://online.wsj.com/article/SB10001424127887324549004579063170451763800.html

702. http://www.theguardian.com/world/2013/aug/09/nsa-loophole-warrantless-searches-email-calls

703. http://www.usatoday.com/story/news/world/2013/09/09/russia-syria/2785703/

704. http://www.washingtonpost.com/world/middle_east/kerry-says-saudi-arabia-has-agreed-to-support-military-strike-against-syria/2013/09/08/e966e0b8-188c-11e3-8685-5021e0c41964_story_1.html

705. http://www.foxnews.com/science/2013/09/09/arctic-sea-ice-up-60-percent-in-2013/

706. http://www.denverpost.com/breakingnews/ci_24066168/colora do-senate-president-john-morse-recalled-angela-giron

707. http://www.theblaze.com/stories/2013/08/28/report-u-s-official-says-white-house-wants-syria-strike-just-muscular-enough-not-to-get-mocked/

708. http://en.wikipedia.org/wiki/Syrian_civil_war

709. http://www.nytimes.com/2013/09/10/world/middleeast/kerry-says-syria-should-hand-over-all-chemical-arms.html?pagewanted=all&_r=0

710. http://thehill.com/blogs/defcon-hill/operations/321103-white-house-insists-it-may-strike-syria-without-congressional-approval

711. http://firstread.nbcnews.com/_news/2013/09/09/20409207-nearly-sixty-percent-of-americans-want-congress-to-vote-no-on-syria?lite

712. http://www.breitbart.com/Big-Government/2013/08/31/Obama-Hits-Golf-Course-After-Announcing-National-Emergency

713. http://www.foxnews.com/politics/2013/08/22/newly-confirmed-un-ambassador-absent-from-syria-emergency-meeting/

714. http://worldnews.nbcnews.com/_news/2013/09/10/20416189-syrias-foreign-minister-well-declare-chemical-weapons-sign-arms-ban?lite

715. http://www.foxnews.com/politics/2013/09/10/president-obama-to-address-nation-on-syria/

716. http://www.breitbart.com/Big-Peace/2013/09/08/House-Intel-Chair-Obama-Would-Not-Get-Authorization-if-Vote-Held-Today

717. http://www.nytimes.com/2013/09/15/world/middleeast/syria-talks.html?emc=edit_na_20130914&_r=0

718. http://www.washingtontimes.com/news/2013/sep/12/house-approves-bill-requiring-new-income-verificat/?page=all

719. http://www.foxnews.com/politics/2013/09/10/infamous-47-percent-not-paying-federal-taxes-now-43-percent/

Made in the USA
Monee, IL
07 July 2026

56551287R00184